100 THINGS
TENNESSEE FANS
SHOULD KNOW & DO
BEFORE THEY DIE

Craig T. Smith

TRIUMPH
BOOKS

This book is available in quantity at special discounts for your group or organization. For further information, contact:
    Triumph Books LLC
    814 North Franklin Street
    Chicago, Illinois 60610
    (312) 337-0747
    www.triumphbooks.com

Printed in U.S.A.
ISBN: 978-1-62937-106-1
Design by Patricia Frey
Photos courtesy of AP Images unless otherwise indicated

For Tennessee fans

Contents

Foreword

Craig T. Smith has written a must-read book, if you enjoy college football, SEC football, and especially Tennessee football. The Tennessee football program has a long and distinguished history. From the accomplishments of the great General Neyland, who set a standard of excellence in college football and whose maxims are still used in Knoxville today, to the team raising the crystal football on a cool Tempe evening in January 1999, the University of Tennessee has set a standard of excellence that has stretched longer than a century and has captured the passion of an entire state.

I grew up in Winchester, Tennessee, and played my college ball for the Orange and White, and I understood early on what it meant to don the *T* on the side of my helmet. I wasn't just playing for my school; I was representing the state of Tennessee. Later, as head coach, I traveled all over the country for recruiting, and it became even more evident to me how widespread the enthusiasm for the Tennessee football program is. The Vol Nation is a proud group, and that pride comes from generations of great and exciting moments that unfolded between the chalk lines on Shields-Watkins Field.

100 Things Tennessee Fans Should Know & Do Before They Die covers many of those important moments. It brings to life historical events and legendary players, coaches, games, and plays. You can feel the pulse of the book as the pressure rises and events unfold. Craig takes you to the highs of Johnny Butler's great run against Alabama; Tennessee's thrilling comebacks against Notre Dame, LSU, and Virginia (to name a few); and Peyton announcing "I'm staying." He covers the real-life stories and struggles of memorable Volunteers who traveled interesting and varied roads to their places in the athletic history at the University of Tennessee. Go Vols!

—Coach Phillip Fulmer

Acknowledgments

After imploring editor Tom Bast multiple times to consider including the rich history of the University of Tennessee football program in his company's highly successful *100 Things* book series, Mr. Bast agreed to the project and let me be the one to author it.

I want to first thank Mr. Bast and the excellent people at Triumph Books for believing in this proposal when I made it to them in 2013. The University of Tennessee football program has a unique, longstanding, and successful history, and Tom Bast and Triumph recognized that. The Triumph staff has been patient and professional through every minute of this process.

My wife, Jennifer, more than patiently put up with several long nights with me hidden away in my man cave doing research for this book and putting fingers to keyboard. My stepdaughter, Morgan, also let "Daddy Craig" get this done, which is pretty impressive for a three-year-old. Thank you, ladies. I love you. You are my life.

My parents, Tom and Linda Smith, always encouraged me and told me that, with hard work and dedication, anything is possible in life. I couldn't have asked for better parents and better role models in life. Thanks, Mom and Dad.

A big thank-you to Coach Fulmer for agreeing to pen the foreword to this book. I wrote Coach Fulmer a letter explaining the book series, my connections to the university as an alumnus, my background in sports media, and my passion for this project. Days later, I received a call from an 865 area code, and it was Coach Fulmer. Aside from agreeing to be involved in the project, he shared his thoughts on great moments from the past, as well as personal reflections on the program since his dismissal that will remain between his mouth and my ear. Thank you, Coach.

Finally, a big thank-you to the men who, over decades of dedication to the University of Tennessee, made the Big Orange the second-most-successful program in the history of the Southeastern

Conference in almost every single statistical team category that matters. There are so many more moments and men that made the Vols special than I can name here. That's what the list of 100 is for, even though I could have easily doubled it. To all the men and women I've named herein, and to all the others who have made their mark on the University of Tennessee football program, thank you for representing our alma mater with heart and hustle...and for helping shape a program and develop traditions that all of us who love and support the University of Tennessee can be proud of.

Introduction

When I sat down to write this book, I already had a working list of 100 things Tennessee fans should know and do before they die. At least I thought I did.

As I researched and wrote each chapter, I often found another gem of a story that was intriguing to me, a Tennessee graduate and college football history junkie. Granted, there are some things that are ingrained in Tennessee lore so deeply that they will make *any* list of 100 things. Or 50 things. Or 10 things. The 1998 national championship. General Robert Neyland. Peyton Manning. The Third Saturday in October. The history of Neyland Stadium. Whether you are a Tennessee student now, or watched General Neyland coach from a knee on Shields-Watkins Field during Tennessee's dominant single-wing era, there are things that define the program, and these are certainly accounted for in this book.

But that current student and that old-timer have unique, temporally specific memories that set their generations apart as well; I paid special attention to this issue of fans' ages as I wrote. For instance, while I remember charging onto the field at Neyland Stadium after Collins Cooper's kick sailed wide left, there are current students who either barely remember it or don't at all. For some the magical 1998 season is as clear as yesterday, and is as special as any year in Tennessee football history. Others were in New Orleans and remember the Orange Crush defense harassing Vinny Testaverde and shutting down a potent Miami offense on the way to a 35–7 win in one of the most special years in the Johnny Majors era. Some readers may even have weathered the rainy New Year's Day in Dallas in 1951, when Tennessee came back to stun Texas 20–14 with a fourth-quarter rally that made General Neyland downright giddy in the locker room afterward.

And how do you rank a comeback? Well, I don't know if you really can. It depends on whom you ask, and who was there. The win against LSU in 2005 was the shining moment in an otherwise abysmally underwhelming campaign. The Miracle in South Bend was an all-timer, as was the 28–24 thriller over Arkansas in what turned out to be Tennessee's toughest test of the 1998 season.

Don't take the rankings on this list too literally. The accomplishments and courage of Condredge Holloway and Lester McClain during a major transition in college football in the early 1970s are unmistakable. Those who were there will forever cherish the upset of Heisman Trophy winner Billy Cannon and No. 1 LSU in one of the most exciting games in the history of Neyland Stadium. It was one of the shining moments of the entire Bowden Wyatt coaching era following General Neyland's retirement. Reggie White was a true Tennessee treasure, both during and after his time on the field in Knoxville.

They're all here…somewhere.

You'll probably disagree with some of the rankings, or perhaps omissions. I was asked to list 100 things. In my mind, that meant a combination of the hallmarks and foundations of the program, great and/or memorable games and players, school traditions—especially those tied with game weekends and the UT campus—championship seasons, and little-known stories or facts about a player or team. This book is meant to combine all of these elements, and isn't intended to literally rank the most important moments from 1 through 100. They are all important, and have a well-deserved place in the program's history.

I hope you enjoy the book, learn a thing or two along the way, and cherish the terrific history of excellence and sustained success that Tennessee football has enjoyed during the last 100 years. Enjoy the ride.

The 1998 National Championship

Team of destiny? Lucky? Call them what you will. The 1998 Tennessee Volunteers did what elite programs do—find ways to win games. And they managed to find a way to win every single week. Because of that, for one cool night in the Arizona desert, the color orange shone the brightest, and any hater or doubter of the program could say nothing.

"The Doubters are silenced, finally," wrote Mike Strange of the *Knoxville News Sentinel.* "Tennessee came to the desert...certain there would be a national championship for the taking.... They were right. It was no mirage.... A few minutes after midnight back in Knoxville, four months to the day after they began their unlikely quest with an unlikely win at Syracuse—the No. 1 ranked Vols completed their perfect season of destiny."

Sometimes great things spring up from unexpected places. After all, stars Peyton Manning, Marcus Nash, and Leonard Little were gone from a team that had been manhandled months earlier by Nebraska 42–17 in the Orange Bowl. The Vols were predicted by the SEC media to finish second behind the Gators in the SEC East. Oh, and the Vols would be breaking in a new quarterback, always a concern for a team looking to make national waves.

But *destiny* was a hard word to escape for this football team, even from the start of the season. Against 17th-ranked Syracuse, the No. 10 Vols drove 72 yards and capitalized on a questionable fourth-down pass-interference penalty on Syracuse, with Jeff Hall booting through a 27-yard field goal as time expired for a 34–33 thriller in the Carrier Dome.

Peerless Price led Tennessee in the Fiesta Bowl with four catches for 199 yards and a touchdown.

Two weeks later, the Vols hosted the Florida Gators in a Neyland Stadium night game, looking to snap a five-game losing streak to Steve Spurrier. Behind a swarming and opportunistic defense that forced five turnovers and an offense that garnered just enough production, Coach Fulmer shed the Florida monkey off his back in a 20–17 overtime victory, the first overtime game in UT history. A key goal-line stand and victory at Auburn masked the season-ending injury of star tailback Jamal Lewis. But the Vols rode the legs of Travis Henry and Travis Stephens to blowout wins against Georgia and Alabama.

When their times were called in Lewis' absence, Stephens and Henry rose to the challenge. Henry carried the Vols to victory in the waning moments against Arkansas after a fumble recovery. With formerly undefeated UCLA and Kansas State having lost in the season's final week, and the Vols against the ropes in the second half against Mississippi State, quarterback Tee Martin came to life in the fourth quarter, finding both Peerless Price and Cedrick Wilson for touchdowns within minutes to clinch a trip to Tempe and the Fiesta Bowl.

It had been a season of making plays: Billy Ratliff's fumble recovery against Arkansas, Deon Grant's leaping interception late versus Florida, and Shaun Ellis' rumbling interception for a touchdown against Auburn. The Lewis run that set up Hall's winning kick at Syracuse. Price's kickoff return for a touchdown to put away the Tide. Key contributions and impact plays came from everywhere.

"This team has consistently found ways to win," Coach Fulmer said. "It's not one or two guys. It's a whole football team believing they can get it done and working hard to get it done."

And in the Fiesta Bowl vs. Florida State, it was no different. After Shawn Bryson's catch in the corner of the end zone to open the scoring, Dwayne Goodrich picked off a Marcus Outzen pass and raced 54 yards for a 14–0 lead. The Noles fought back and drew within five, at 14–9. The Vols held Peter Warrick to one catch for seven yards, but his long punt return set up a Sebastian Janikowski field goal before the half. After an idling third quarter, the final paint stroke on the Big Orange masterpiece came from Price. He hauled in a 79-yard TD pass, a Fiesta Bowl record, for a 20–9 lead with just more than nine minutes remaining. A late desperation pass from Outzen was intercepted, and the Big Orange ran out the last 76 seconds on the clock for a historic 23–16 victory.

The stadium was mainly hued orange-and-white, and for those who attended, they got to see Tennessee history 47 years in the making.

"I want to say an unbelievable thank-you to the crowd of loyal Tennessee Volunteers," said Coach Fulmer, clutching the national championship trophy.

"It's been 47 years since Tennessee football has brought one of these home. We've got a special place for it."

2 General Robert R. Neyland

General Robert R. Neyland is the first name in coaching at the University of Tennessee and, with all due respect to the other coaches of his generation, one of the most influential and imitated coaches of his time. Behind Neyland's single-wing offenses, consistent and disciplined blocking schemes, fierce defenses, and efficient special teams, Coach Neyland was consistently on the winning side of the ledger, even in his early coaching years.

Neyland arrived in Knoxville in 1925 as an assistant defensive coach. He made his presence felt that first season when he filled in one game for head coach M.B. Banks, who was sick. Neyland led the Vols to a 12–7 home win over Georgia. Newspapers proclaimed it the biggest upset of the year in the South. Banks left that December for the head coaching job at Knoxville Central High School, and Neyland was promoted as his successor. In his first seven seasons, his teams lost only twice in 68 games. For his career, he only lost 31 times in 216 games.

One of his biggest accomplishments was emerging victorious against the University of Alabama, perhaps most notably in 1928. The Tide had not regularly been on the Vols' schedule (they hadn't played in 14 years), and Alabama coach Wallace Wade was willing to take on Neyland's boys. He most likely wished he hadn't that day. Gene McEver stunned the Tide with a 98-yard opening kickoff return for a score, and the Vols won 15–13 in Tuscaloosa. McEver later said, "Not that that was the greatest game, but that's the game that put Tennessee on the map."

Neyland quickly earned the respect of Wade that day. "First, [Neyland]'s a very brilliant man, and had a lot of character, and could influence young people," Wade said. "Inspire them. His teams were always well trained, well-conditioned, and played with spirit."

Wade continued, "One of the things I used to misjudge: I used to think he was lucky. I began to realize after time that luck turns sometimes, but it never did with him, because he trained his players to take advantage of opportunities."

In whatever endeavors Neyland took on, he seemed to find success. In 1912 Neyland attended the United States Military Academy, where he was a successful student and became the heavyweight boxing champion at the academy. After college, he was offered a baseball contract by the New York Giants, which he turned down to join World War I.

Neyland went on to a lengthy and decorated military career. He took his first military leave from coaching to serve a year in Panama in 1935. In 1941 Major Neyland returned to active duty as a soldier in the army, in the midst of World War II. In 1944

Neyland was promoted to brigadier general and sent to the Far East. He was then sent to Calcutta, India, where he helped to move supplies and war materials to British, American, and Chinese forces.

He returned to Knoxville in 1946 and immediately picked up where he left off. His team went 9–2, tied for first place in the SEC, and earned a trip to the Orange Bowl. However, the 1947 and 1948 seasons were a bit more troubling, and saw Tennessee go .500 in each. The temporary letdowns were enough to turn some of the fan base against the much-loved and revered Neyland.

Said former tackle Denver Crawford, "When [he wasn't] winning them all or going to a bowl game, then, they were saying, 'Get rid of General Neyland. He's too old, using the single-wing, outmoded, outdated.'"

But the offense, defense, and special teams employed by Neyland hadn't been passed by. In 1950 his team went 10–1 and beat the No. 5 Texas Longhorns 20–14 in the Cotton Bowl on a late touchdown that paved the way for a magical 1951 national championship season.

Neyland's coaching style was simple but effective: interior containment on defense, fundamental blocking on offense, and winning the net punting battle in the special teams game.

"The punting game was so vital," said former tailback Hank Lauricella. "He would add up the yardage in exchange of punts. To him, if you could gain 50 yards in a game in exchanging punts, it was as good as a guy breaking loose for 50 yards because that was net yardage."

Ben Jones, formerly of the *Knoxville Journal*, said about Neyland, "He said, 'The only reason I went to the single-wing with a balanced line is that it gave me a little quicker power between tackle and end,' which he felt was the most vulnerable place on a defensive football team." Jones added, "He said, 'I never worried about offense at all.' He said, 'I would have gone to the *T* if it had offered me anything that I didn't already have.' But he said defense was football as far as he was concerned, defense and the kicking game."

"Neyland always felt that no one was going to beat him at the end," said Tom Siler, formerly of the *Knoxville News Sentinel.* "You were not going to beat Tennessee running wide. And they didn't. Of course, that sounds so simple. Certainly, if you turn the plays in, a lot of people are going to get a shot at the runner. If he gets outside, and he's fast, then nobody may touch him."

General Neyland retired from coaching in 1952 after 21 seasons of coaching the Vols. He was inducted into the College Football Hall of Fame in 1956. His 1939 team was the last team in college football history to be unscored-upon in the regular season.

But all of Neyland's accomplishments did not come on the field. Among other highly notable contributions Neyland made to the University are the architectural plan for Neyland Stadium and the creation of the Vol Network.

How he came to be able to draw up building plans is an interesting story. By the age of 27 Neyland was one of the youngest regimental commanders in the US Army. But when the *New York Times* reported that fact, Neyland almost immediately was demoted to captain. Brigadier General Douglas MacArthur faced a similar situation but accepted the superintendency at West Point to avoid being demoted to major. When Neyland protested his demotion, his successor rewarded him with a below-satisfactory rating and had him shipped off to MIT for one year of postgraduate studies in civil engineering.

This led to the future of Neyland Stadium and its design. Neyland arrived in Knoxville when the UT football site, Shields-Watkins Field, seated only 3,200. By the time of his death in 1962, the stadium seated more than 52,000 and Neyland had developed architectural plans for its eventual growth to more than 100,000.

Those dreams became reality in 1996, when the upper bowl was completed.

Neyland also was credited by Hall of Fame broadcaster Lindsey Nelson with the creation of UT's first radio network. Nelson thought it should be called the Volunteer Network and approached Neyland with his idea. Neyland had the ultimate veto power and said, "Let's call it the Vol Network." Nelson immediately replied, "Yes, sir. Let's call it the Vol Network."

Perhaps the greatest mark of the respect that Neyland had carved out among the college football coaching elite came from Bear Bryant. The College Football Hall of Famer never defeated a Neyland-coached team, and was said to have muttered at Neyland's retirement banquet, "Thank God the old guy finally quit."

The General's Seven Maxims of Football

Over the course of his splendid coaching career, General Neyland developed a set of principles for playing the game of football at the highest level. Neyland actually came up with 38 maxims, but he repeated his seven favorites to his team on each game day. To this day, before the team takes the field on game day, players read these seven maxims proffered by Neyland together in the locker room. And for the average fan slipping some Jack Daniel's into his plastic cup of Coke in Neyland Stadium, waiting for the kickoff after hours of tailgating, these maxims might not mean that much. But try saying them out loud minutes before the Vols take the field. Think about their importance, and imagine Neyland, Johnny Majors, Phil Fulmer, and now Butch Jones saying them with each of their teams before bolting from the locker room to do battle in

South Bend against Notre Dame, at Legion Field against the Tide, or at home against Florida.

These football maxims have been handed down for decades, and have become words for Tennessee players, past and present, to live by and play by:

1. The team that makes the fewest mistakes will win.
2. Play for and make the breaks, and when one comes your way—SCORE.
3. If at first the game—or the breaks—go against you, don't let up….put on more steam.
4. Protect our kickers, our QB, our lead, and our ballgame.
5. Ball, oskie, cover, block, cut and slice, pursue and gang tackle…for this is the winning edge.
6. Press the kicking game. Here is where the breaks are made.
7. Carry the fight to our opponent, and keep it there for 60 minutes.

In looking at Neyland's career record over 21 seasons—173 wins, 31 losses, and 12 ties—it's not hard to see that he believed in these values, and that his players bought in as well. Of his 173 wins, 106 were shutouts. From the opening kickoff to the final gun, Neyland's players fought for 60 minutes, whether the score was tight or the game was in hand. The 1951 come-from-behind 20–14 victory in the Cotton Bowl, which merits its own chapter in this book, is proof of the value of these maxims. The 1947 12–7 comeback victory against Vanderbilt behind the legendary three-man block by tackle Denver Crawford, which Neyland called the best he'd ever seen, is further evidence of his staunch belief in and reliance on blocking and fundamentals.

And these virtues, especially the will to keep the fight for 60 minutes and "put on more steam" when facing adversity, were evident in later Vols teams. They were evident both in victory—such as when the team came back from a 31–7 deficit in 1991's

Miracle in South Bend, or the furious rally in 2006 in Athens to win going away—and in defeat, for example when a furious rally against Florida in 1996 came up short.

Next time you watch the Vols kick off, recite Neyland's seven maxims, and see if the boys in the orange-and-white carry the fight for 60 minutes like Neyland would want.

4 Neyland Stadium

Nestled along the Tennessee River separating UT's campus from the edge of downtown Knoxville, Neyland Stadium stands as one of the largest, loudest, and most scenic college football venues in the country. The school currently states maximum seating capacity at 102,455, making it the largest venue in the Southeastern Conference and the third-largest venue in the entire country. On game days, a filled Neyland Stadium equates size-wise to the fifth-largest city in the state of Tennessee.

The facility has seen its share of impressive streaks and successes. From 1928 until 1933, UT won 30 consecutive games at home. They also managed a 55-game unbeaten streak from 1925 to 1933. Both streaks ended with a 12–6 loss to Alabama. During UT's championship runs in the late 1990s, the Vols won 23 straight home games from 1996 until 2000, ended by a 27–23 loss to Florida on September 16.

Rome wasn't built in a day, and certainly neither was Neyland Stadium. Including the original construction of the field, the facility has undergone 18 renovations, growing from a capacity of 3,200 fans in the West Stands in 1921 to as high as 104,079 in 2000 after completion of the East Executive Suites opposite the main

Neyland Stadium by the Numbers

Neyland Stadium has always maintained a place at the top of the list of capacity crowds in college football. With the completion of the north end zone upper deck in 1996, Neyland Stadium became a double-decked house of horrors, capturing the sound of the crowd on field level as much as any stadium possibly could. In the 1990s and 2000s, the stadium set school and SEC football records with capacity crowds in several memorable contests for Tennessee fans, some with more memorable outcomes than others. Here is a look at some key historical numbers for Neyland Stadium:

- 109,061: largest crowd in stadium history. September 18, 2004. Tennessee 30, Florida 28. In one of the most exciting finishes in Tennessee history, James Wilhoit booted home the game-winning 50-yard field goal after shanking an extra point only minutes earlier.
- 27–0: the score of the first game at Shields-Watkins Field on September 14, 1921, a Tennessee victory over Emory & Henry.
- 55: the number of consecutive home games without a loss, stretching from October 3, 1925, a 51–0 home win over Emory & Henry, until a 12–6 loss to Alabama on October 21, 1933.
- 30: longest home winning streak in school history. Starting on December 8, 1928 with a 13–12 home win against Florida and ending on October 21, 1933 with a 12–6 loss to Alabama.
- 35: the number of undefeated seasons at home. The last team to go undefeated at home was the 1999 team that went 7–0 at Neyland Stadium, with key wins over Auburn, Notre Dame, and Georgia.
- .799: Tennessee's all-time winning percentage at Neyland Stadium / Shields-Watkins Field

press box and West Suites. The total number dropped to 102,037 when some seats were taken out to put in a Club Level Section, then jumped to its current total with the addition of the Tennessee Terrace.

The present-day Neyland Stadium, Shields-Watkins Field, had its beginning in 1919. Colonel W.S. Shields, president of

Knoxville's City National Bank and a UT trustee, provided the initial funding for the project. Thus, when it opened its gates in March 1921 it was dedicated Shields-Watkins Field in honor of the donor and his wife, Alice Watkins-Shields. Today it is known as Shields-Watkins Field at Neyland Stadium. The stadium was dedicated as Neyland Stadium in 1962 following the death of General Neyland.

By 1929, the West Stands had increased by more than 11,000 seats and the East Stands were set up, moving the total seating to more than 17,000. By 1948, as the Vols prepared a historic run that culminated in a national title, more than 12,000 seats had been added to the East Stands and a 15,000-seat South Stands was installed, putting the total at more than 46,000. A press box and additional 5,837 seats were added in 1962. The vastly improved press boxes were also a product of Neyland, according to former sports information director Gus Manning.

"I worked for General Neyland, and he was an engineer," said Manning. "Back in those early days I was sitting in the old press boxes, and they were awful. The general sent me one time to go around and visit a bunch of press boxes [at other schools] and see which [was] the best one," said Manning. "I remember visiting Michigan and some other schools. We eventually came up with guidelines for building press boxes."

Today, the stadium has exploded beyond seating expectations that even the general could imagine. A stadium-record crowd of 109,061 saw Tennessee beat Florida 30–28 on September 28, 2004. The now-two-level bowl setting has created a deafening and intimidating atmosphere for visitors over the years. In 82 seasons, 509 home games, UT has amassed a record of 398–94–17 at home, which comes to a winning percentage of .799. That means, roughly, the Vols have won four out of every five home games in the house that Neyland built.

5 Third Saturday in October

Although it no longer falls on the weekend for which it is named, thanks in large part to the expansion of the SEC schedule, fans in the states of Alabama and Tennessee know the significance and history of the Third Saturday in October. For decades, the game was ingrained into the third Saturday of the month as much as the Nathan's hot-dog-eating contest and fireworks are a part of the Fourth of July.

The series wasn't always held on the third Saturday of October, and wasn't held every year. It began in 1901, when the Tide and Vols played to a 6–6 tie in Birmingham. From there, it was pure dominance by the Crimson Tide, as they won eight of the next nine matchups until 1913, with all but the 1909 matchup taking place in the state of Alabama, and all taking place at the end of November. The Tide won all eight games by shutout. UT's lone victory was a 5–0 win in Birmingham in 1904.

After Tennessee's 17–7 win in Knoxville in 1914, the series took a 14-year hiatus, until General Neyland called on the Tide to play again on October 20, 1928, the first year the game was held on the third Saturday in October, where it would remain for decades.

Wallace Wade arrived at Alabama in 1923 as head coach and quickly began building a program that won its first national title in 1925 with a Rose Bowl victory over Washington. Neyland, who had played at Army, was promoted to head coach at Tennessee the next season.

"Wallace Wade and Neyland were responsible for the series between Tennessee and Alabama," said Bob Gilbert, author of the book *Neyland: The Gridiron General* and a retired Associated Press reporter. "Neyland was obviously aware of the success Wade had at Alabama in the 1920s. Neyland respected him and they had become friends and decided to play.... They started playing in 1928, and it has survived every year since, except the one year in World War II [1943] that neither school fielded a team."

Following the shocking 15–13 win in 1928, Neyland carried on the success against the Crimson Tide, going 12–5–2 against the Tide before retiring after the 1952 season. With the Vols having see-sawed the edge in the series throughout the past two-plus

Alabama-Tennessee: A Series of Streaks

The Crimson Tide vs. the Volunteers remains a staple of Southern football rivalries, outdating the hallowed Iron Bowl. Part of that rivalry has been the presence of some of the greatest coaches in college football history. General Neyland, Bear Bryant, Phillip Fulmer, and Nick Saban, all college football royalty in their own rights, have led their respective teams during different parts of the last 85-plus years of the rivalry. Between the two sides, there have been nine streaks of four straight wins or more since the series first started back in 1901. The longest for each team:

11: Alabama 1971–81. In snapping a four-game losing streak to Tennessee with a 32–15 win on October 16, 1971, Alabama went on a run of success against Tennessee never before seen in the rivalry, and not seen since. The Crimson Tide won three national championships (1973, 1978, and 1979), while Tennessee slipped into a period when they won seven or fewer games per season from 1974 to 1980. Tennessee only stayed within one score of the Crimson Tide twice (1972: Alabama 17, Tennessee 10; 1976: Alabama 20, Tennessee 13).

7: Tennessee 1995–2001. In 1995 Tennessee blistered Alabama 41–14, tying its biggest margin of victory in the series ever. As Phillip Fulmer continued to raise Tennessee to national prominence, Alabama continued to slide further away from its more recent success under Bill Curry and Gene Stallings. By the time the Tide snapped the series in 2002, Alabama's third head coach in that span, Dennis Franchione, was on the sideline.

decades, the Crimson Tide were poised to regain control in the series behind a man named Paul "Bear" Bryant.

Bear Bryant knew General Neyland well, both as a player and as a coach, though Bryant found much more success as the former than the latter. Bryant was a defensive end for the Tide from 1933 to 1935, and Alabama swept the Vols in the three meetings, although Neyland was called back to active duty and did not coach the 1935 matchup. Playing with a broken leg, Bryant helped lead the Tide defense to a 25–0 shutout victory in Knoxville that season.

However, as coach of the Kentucky Wildcats from 1946 to 1953, Bryant squared off with the general each year before Neyland retired after the 1952 season. Neyland was undefeated against Bear from the sideline, going 5–0–2. During the 1953 season—Bryant's last in Lexington and Neyland's first in retirement—Kentucky beat Tennessee 27–21 in Lexington, the Wildcats' first win against the Volunteers since 1935.

Having never beaten the general was about the only thing Bryant lacked on his résumé. He led his 1950 Wildcats squad to its first Southeastern Conference title in 1950 and took Texas A&M to the No. 5 ranking in the final polls of 1956 with a 9–0–1 record.

But more important, he morphed into a legend in a houndstooth hat, winning three national championships in five seasons from 1961 to 1965 and reestablishing Alabama as an undisputed national power. In that span he went 4–0–1 against Tennessee.

From there, the Volunteers and Crimson Tide series has been defined by extended winning streaks by one team over the other, in a fashion rarely seen in college football. Tennessee bounced back to win four straight under coach Doug Dickey from 1967 to 1970. Bear Bryant led the Crimson Tide to an 11-game winning streak over the Vols from 1971 to 1981. The Tide claimed three national championships and one undefeated season (1979) in that stretch.

Johnny Majors defeated Bear Bryant in his final matchup against Tennessee—35–28 in Neyland Stadium in 1982. Tennessee's ensuing four-game winning streak against Alabama spawned an 8–0–1 response from the Tide through the 1994 season. Suddenly, under the poise of rising star quarterback Peyton Manning and guidance of head coach Phillip Fulmer, the Vols put their stamp on the rivalry, winning 10 of the next 12 matchups, including the schools' first clash in Tuscaloosa since 1921, on October 23, 1999.

Recently Nick Saban, in reestablishing the Crimson Tide as arguably college football's elite program, has flipped the series with Tennessee in the Tide's favor. In perhaps the most dominating run in the series to date, Saban's teams have beaten Tennessee by 20 or more points in every matchup since 2007 except for two—a 12–10 Orange and White heartbreaker in 2009 on a blocked field-goal attempt by Crimson Tide defensive tackle Terrence Cody at the gun, and a 34–20 defeat in 2014.

6 Peyton Manning

The most celebrated player in the history of Tennessee football, Manning shattered NCAA, SEC, and Tennessee records during his time in Knoxville. After appearing in three Super Bowls and winning an NFL-record five league MVP awards, there isn't much that Manning hasn't accomplished in what is sure to become a first-ballot Pro Football Hall of Fame career.

As the son of former Ole Miss Rebel and New Orleans Saints quarterback Archie Manning, Peyton's arrival in Knoxville was somewhat of a surprise, given his father's history and legacy in Oxford. Before Peyton carefully chose Tennessee in 1994, he strongly considered other schools, especially the University of Michigan.

Peyton Manning led Tennessee to an SEC championship in the 1997 season.

"I'll tell you what—at one time I thought he was going to Michigan," Archie Manning recalled to MassLive.com. "I thought the Ole Miss thing was weighing really heavy on him, and he's thinking, 'All right, if I don't go to Ole Miss, I don't want to play against Ole Miss. I'm getting away from the whole thing.' And I really think [Michigan] was his getaway."

Archie continued, "At some point, the [Tennessee] coaches convinced him or he convinced himself that by going to the other side of the conference, he wouldn't have to play [Ole Miss] every year."

Peyton's brother Cooper echoed the sentiment: "It's funny—for a while there, I really thought he was going to go to Michigan. It was just kind of outside the box...I think he kind of liked that scene."

According to Archie, Peyton was strongly taken by the coaching staff of both Tennessee and Michigan, specifically David Cutcliffe of Tennessee and then–Michigan quarterbacks coach Cam Cameron.

Peyton visited Ann Arbor with Archie in December 1993. They saw the campus and met Bo Schembechler. Like at Tennessee, the starting job would be open and up for grabs relatively soon, with senior Todd Collins penciled in to start for the Wolverines in 1994.

But ultimately, Fulmer and Cutcliffe won the recruiting battle. After thinking it over for a few weeks, Peyton called Fulmer on the morning of January 26, 1994, and told the coach he was going to become a Volunteer.

And what a decision it was. The impact that Manning made on the program cannot be overstated. The forward pass took a big step forward when Dewey Warren became the first Tennessee quarterback to throw for more than 1,000 yards in a season back in the late 1960s. It moved forward light years with the precision, accuracy, and intelligence Peyton Manning brought to the position.

After season-ending injuries to Jerry Colquitt and Todd Helton in 1994, the door opened for Peyton Manning and fellow freshman Branndon Stewart to fight for the starting job. When the smoke cleared and the 1994 season was over, Manning had earned the job, and Stewart was transferring back to his native Texas to play for R.C. Slocum's Aggies.

While some fans at the time actually felt that Stewart's athleticism might have made him the better option, those thoughts were quickly dispelled by an 11–1 season in which Manning and the Vols crushed Alabama 41–14 at Legion Field to snap a nine-year winless streak at the hands of the Crimson Tide. Peyton Manning went on to finish 3–1 for his career against Tennessee's chief rival, sparking a run of seven consecutive Volunteers wins over the Tide.

It was the struggles against Florida that kept Manning from taking the Vols all the way to the top of the mountain. Manning's ignominious 0–4 record (0–3 as a starter) against Spurrier and the Gators kept the Vols on the outside looking in at SEC and national championship pictures.

But on November 29, 1997, after his final game at Neyland Stadium, Manning stood on the director's podium in front of the Pride of the Southland Marching Band, directing them as they played "Rocky Top" after Tennessee's 17–10 SEC East–clinching win over Vanderbilt.

He had passed up the NFL Draft in 1997 for a chance at a championship. In the SEC Championship Game, Manning threw for 373 yards in Tennessee's frantic 30–29 comeback victory against Auburn. Manning's 73-yard strike to Marcus Nash in the fourth quarter sealed the Tennessee victory, and Manning took home MVP honors while Fulmer raised Tennessee's first SEC championship trophy since the 1990 season.

But the season ended on a sour note for Peyton Manning and the Vols. Though Manning was thought to be the front-runner for the Heisman Trophy for much of the season, Michigan's Charles Woodson beat him out for the award, becoming the first primarily defensive player to win it. Tennessee's outside chances at a national championship were derailed in Miami, as Nebraska bludgeoned Tennessee on both sides of the ball in a 42–17 romp.

However, Manning's career accomplishments remain unmatched in Knoxville. His passing attempts (1,381), completions (863), yards (11,201), and touchdown passes (89) stand as the school's best to this day, and very well could take up permanent residence in the record books. His dedication to the University of Tennessee, through his financial support and time spent in and around university events, is solid.

And his success at the next level of the game has made him one of those generational players who fans can brag about watching play and media can brag about covering. Over his 16 NFL seasons, Manning has passed for an incredible 69,691 yards and set NFL records for career touchdowns (530), passing yards in a single season (5,477), and touchdown passes in a single season (55).

His No. 16 jersey number at Tennessee is one of only eight that have been retired by the university.

7 The 1999 Fiesta Bowl

The 1999 Fiesta Bowl was supposed to be college football's answer to determining the "mythical" national champion. After split titles in 1990, 1991, and 1997, and an undefeated Penn State team getting left out in the cold in 1994, the BCS had been created to solve just that conundrum and crown a single champion. If only the teams would cooperate.

As would be the case in future years, there would be one clear-cut No. 1 team in 1998 going into the final poll—the undefeated Tennessee Volunteers. Their opponent would result from a series of late-season upsets that would shake up the college football landscape. No. 1 Ohio State, typically susceptible to having its season wrecked by a school from Michigan, had that happen again. This time it was a 4–4 Michigan State team that knocked out the Buckeyes. Trailing by 15 points in the second half, Nick Saban's Spartans ripped off 19 straight points in Ohio Stadium, ending with an interception of Buckeyes quarterback Joe Germaine in the end zone with 1:12 left.

Then came December 5, 1998. With three undefeated teams in the running on conference championship Saturday, would the new system already create an unjust result?

Bob Toledo's No. 3 UCLA Bruins had stormed through the Pac-10 and had to get past an unranked, three-loss Miami Hurricanes team to complete a perfect season and have a shot at making it to Tempe for the national championship game. In a game that was rescheduled from September due to Hurricane Georges, it was Miami—who had been thrashed 66–13 a week earlier at Syracuse—who tore through the Bruins defense, with running back Edgerrin James setting the school rushing record with 299 rushing yards. Cade McNown's last-second desperation pass sailed out of the end zone, and Miami, Kansas State, and Tennessee fans celebrated a 49–45 Miami win that eliminated the Bruins.

No. 2 Kansas State kicked off next in the Big 12 Championship Game against Texas A&M, with a victory guaranteeing a spot in the Fiesta Bowl / national championship. Three hours (and some free overtime football) later, Wildcats hearts broke as the Aggies rallied from a 27–12 deficit, tying the game with 1:05 left in regulation on a Sirr Parker touchdown catch and ensuing two-point reception. Parker delivered the dagger in double overtime, beating the Kansas State defender to the pylon from 32 yards to end the game and the Wildcats' title hopes.

Top-ranked Tennessee kicked off last, in the SEC Championship Game, knowing a win would send Big Orange to the Fiesta Bowl to play for the school's first national championship in nearly half a century. Clinging to a 10–7 fourth-quarter lead, UT fans felt their hearts shoot up into their collective throat as Mississippi State punt returner Kevin Prentiss scampered for an 83-yard touchdown to give the Bulldogs a late lead.

Two and a half minutes later, Vols fans started to relax after Tee Martin hit game MVP Peerless Price for a 41-yard touchdown to give the Vols the lead for good. Martin found Cedrick Wilson minutes later for the clinching score, and the Vols had claimed back-to-back SEC titles and booked their trip to Tempe, Arizona.

The Vols' opponent in the Fiesta Bowl would be a team on no one's radar as of December 5—the Florida State Seminoles. An afterthought for much of the season, the Noles had slowly climbed back up near the top of the rankings after losing 24–7 at NC State in their second game of the season. A 23–12 season-ending win over fourth-ranked Florida represented the closest margin of victory any team could muster against an FSU squad that beat four other ranked teams on the way to an 11–1 season.

And it was the man who had engineered the victory over the Gators who created the biggest question mark going into the BCS National Championship Game between the Noles and Vols: an unheralded third-string quarterback named Marcus Outzen. A knee injury to Dan Kendra in the spring paved the way for 26-year-old Chris Weinke to start, and he led FSU to an 8–1 mark before succumbing to a herniated disc in his back against Virginia. Outzen, nicknamed "the Rooster," carried the Noles the rest of the way—to a state championship with a win over Florida and all the way to play for the national title.

"[N]othing against Tennessee, but down where we are in Florida, playing the Gators is a championship in itself," Outzen said. "I went into it with the goal of staying calm, and I did." Nothing against Outzen, but the Tennessee team that had also beaten Florida would prove to be a bigger challenge than perhaps the quarterback could have imagined. Tennessee jumped out to a 7–0 lead in the second quarter after Martin rolled left and found future Buffalo Bill Shawn Bryson for a four-yard strike.

Tennessee's defense made the play of the half—and at the expense of Outzen—on the ensuing drive. On first down from their own 49-yard line, Outzen fired for Peter Warrick, but cornerback Dwayne Goodrich broke in front of the pass and sprinted 54 yards untouched for a 14–0 lead.

Aided by an interception return inside the 5-yard line, Florida State cut the lead to 14–9 by halftime. Had it not been for an incredible open-field tackle by punter David Leaverton on Peter Warrick shortly before the half, FSU would likely have hit the locker room with the lead.

The teams battled through a scoreless third quarter before a fourth quarter that equated to the fifteenth round between two championship prizefighters. Price and the Vols delivered the decisive blow.

With 9:30 to play from their own 21-yard line and facing third-and-8, Price took off on a go route down the sideline. Thirteen seconds later, amongst a booming version of "Down the Field" from the Pride of the Southland Marching Band and a sea of orange-and-white shakers, the scoreboard read: Vols 20, Seminoles 9. Price outleaped FSU cornerback Mario Edwards and came down with the football in stride, coasting into the end zone across the Florida State logo.

Although the Noles cut the final margin to 23–16, the story had been written: Tennessee had just put the final touches on an orange-hued masterpiece of a season and claimed the first-ever BCS national championship.

As legendary ABC announcer Keith Jackson said, "We should have understood the symbols. Remember I told you this at Chiricahua country. When that moon came up from behind that mountain a little while ago, it was orange, wasn't it?" Color commentator Bob Griese responded, "It was orange. Yes it was."

8 Understand the History of "Rocky Top"

There have been many important numbers in the history of Tennessee football. Peyton Manning's No. 16. Championship seasons in 1951 and 1998. And the numbers of points allowed in the regular season by the 1939 squad: zero. But few, if any, fans would relate the number 388 with a Tennessee football tradition.

On August 28, 1967, songwriters Felice and Boudleaux Bryant checked into Room 388 of the Gatlinburg Inn. The couple, known for writing such hits as "Wake Up, Little Susie," "Bye Bye, Love," and "Love Hurts," were frequent guests of the inn and friends of its owners, Rel and Wilma Maples.

The Bryants came to Gatlinburg in 1967 to work on an album for Archie Campbell and wound up authoring one of the most recognized songs in the country—one that would be celebrated by an entire state for decades to come.

The Osborne Brothers were one night away from going into the recording studio. They planned to cut a ballad, "My Favorite Memory," as the A-side of a record. They needed a B-side, and Bobby Osborne paid the Bryants a visit.

After only ten minutes of thought, the famous words to the song were on paper, although it would take some time for it to catch on across the state.

The song was recorded first by the Osborne Brothers and released in late 1967. But it was Nashville disc jockey Ralph Emery who first understood the song's potential. On Christmas Day 1967, he flipped the Osbornes' record and played the "Rocky Top" B-side on his radio program.

"It just took off," Osborne told Kentucky.com. "Nobody ever requested 'My Favorite Memory' after that. It was always 'Rocky Top.'"

The song was first performed as part of a halftime country music show at the 1972 Tennessee-Alabama game, and it attracted immediate attention and has become so beloved that longtime UT band director W.J. Julian said that not playing it would cause a mutiny among Vols fans.

Over the years, the song has become a staple of Tennessee athletics and has been played at all football and men's and women's basketball games since the 1970s. It has been described as "simplistic and clever" by fans wearing orange-and-white, and by those who simply enjoy the song's five basic chords and its title being repeated 19 times.

Yet opposing coaches have mentioned the influence and impact of "Rocky Top" on their teams and their game preparation. It also drives a nail through the nerves of all opponents and their supporters who either visit Neyland Stadium or hear the Pride of the Southland Marching Band boom out the song several times per game on the road.

There have been more than 100 renditions of "Rocky Top" recorded by individuals, country groups, bluegrass bands, and even East Tennessee rock groups. Country music legends Dolly Parton, John Denver, and Conway Twitty have all performed the song, as have more contemporary country artists such as Rascal Flatts, Keith Urban, and Brad Paisley.

"Rocky Top" was adopted as an official state song of Tennessee by Chapter 545 of the Public Acts of 1982.

Although the exact location of "Rocky Top" as envisioned by the Bryants has long been speculated about, Rocky Top became a tangible place in 2014. On June 26, 2014, Lake City, Tennessee, located approximately 24 miles northwest of Knoxville, changed the name of the town to Rocky Top, Tennessee. Although the descendants of the Bryants attempted to block the name change on the grounds that it could cause damage to its brand, a federal judge denied the request and the name change went through.

As a tribute to the Bryants and their work, the Gatlinburg Inn has left Room 388 virtually untouched, with just a few modern updates.

"I suspect you will in the future see a historical marker in front of this inn, which will indicate that this is the birthplace of 'Rocky Top,'" David Cross, nephew of the Maples and member of the Gatlinburg Inn Board of Directors, told WBIR.com.

9 Phillip Fulmer

With the sounds of "Rocky Top" piercing the thick, damp November evening, Phillip Fulmer raised his hand to the orange pockets of cheering fans remaining in Neyland Stadium on November 29, 2008. He turned and walked off the field, up through the tunnel.

These would be his final moments as the head coach of the Tennessee Volunteers.

Fans shuffled from the concourses into the night, and the scoreboard operator turned out the lights that read TENNESSEE 28, KENTUCKY 10. The season was over with a win against Kentucky, and with it ended a beloved era in Tennessee football history.

What a difference a year can make. In the 2007 season finale, Fulmer's squad battled in Lexington against a game group of Wildcats (that had already toppled No. 1 LSU), with a coveted berth in the SEC Championship Game on the line for the Big Orange. After several tense overtime periods, Kentucky faced a two-point attempt, needing a conversion to extend the game. Antonio Reynolds tackled quarterback Andre' Woodson, leading to an Orange and White celebration on the field and in the stands, as Fulmer claimed his sixth Eastern Division title and a trip to Atlanta to play LSU.

Tennessee fought but fell short 21–14 in Atlanta. Still, it seemed that after a couple forgettable seasons, Tennessee football was moving back in the right direction.

On November 2, 2008, then–athletic director Mike Hamilton informed Fulmer that he would be dismissed at the end of the season. A 3–6 start had, in the minds of Hamilton and those championing his decision, erased the goodwill from a divisional championship a season prior.

Ask a group of UT fans about the decision to fire Fulmer, and invariably you'll get differing opinions. The firing of Fulmer was lauded by some, and to the chagrin of others.

What cannot be denied are the heart, soul, and passion that Phillip Fulmer poured into the University of Tennessee for almost 40 years.

As head coach, he led the Volunteers faithful on one of the greatest rides in school history. Fulmer compiled an overall record of 152–52, making him the second-winningest coach in school history, trailing only the namesake of the stadium he helped fill each Saturday in the fall.

Where previous coaches struggled, Fulmer found great success—most notably against Tennessee's primary rival, Alabama. After taking over for Johnny Majors following the 1992 season, Fulmer dominated his Southern counterpart, going 10–5–1 over his career (later, the 1993 tie was changed to a Tennessee win due to Alabama sanctions).

Perhaps one of Fulmer's most memorable wins was in 1995 against the Tide. On the strength of the arm of sophomore quarterback Peyton Manning and the sure hands and speed of wideout Joey Kent, Tennessee jumped to a 7–0 lead on the first play from scrimmage. After Manning slowly trotted into the end zone on a bootleg and running back Jay Graham scampered 75 yards for a third-quarter lead, it was all over but the celebrating for the Big Orange. After nine winless and painful years for UT fans, Fulmer had scratched their collective 10-year itch with a 41–14 win, one of the Big Orange's most lopsided—and satisfying—wins in school history.

Fulmer had knocked off the school's unofficial-official crimson-colored fly in the ointment and would help make the Third Saturday in October a memorable one for UT fans for years to come.

The 1995 freshman class experienced unprecedented success starting in Fulmer's third full season. From 1995 to 1998, Tennessee rolled up a record of 45–5. Of the five losses, three came to Florida, one to Nebraska in the 1998 Orange Bowl, and one at Memphis in 1996. By the time they finished their collegiate careers in the Fiesta Bowl, those teams had rolled up four AP Top 10 finishes (two in the Top 5), two SEC championships, and the school's first national championship since 1951.

Fulmer was a rising star. The program's success was undeniable, and the spoils could even have been greater, if not for Fulmer's struggles against Steve Spurrier and the University of Florida. Almost as strongly as Fulmer had a vise grip on

Tennessee's border rivals Alabama, Georgia, and Kentucky, and in-state rival Vanderbilt, Spurrier and his Fun 'n' Gun offense blew holes in the Vols' hopes of a national championship in multiple seasons. Losses to Florida in 1995 and 1996 ultimately kept the Vols just out of the national championship picture. Falling 33–20 in 1997 in Gainesville, Manning finished his career 0–4 against Florida. The loss also kept the Vols' title chances on life support entering the 1998 Orange Bowl, with a Michigan loss to Washington State needed for hope at a national championship. Michigan and Nebraska went on to win the Rose and Orange Bowls, respectively, by comfortable margins and split the national title.

Fulmer finished with a 5–12 record against Florida.

Yet Fulmer should not, and cannot, be judged solely on his résumé as head coach, albeit a strong and respected one.

Starting in 1968, Fulmer entered the University of Tennessee as a student. Hailing from Winchester, Tennessee, he earned a football scholarship and played guard for the Vols from 1969 to 1971 under the tutelage of head coaches Doug Dickey and Bill Battle.

Fulmer was a successful and smart football player, earning All-Conference honors at guard and helping lead the Vols to an SEC championship in 1969, an 11–1 record and Sugar Bowl victory in 1970, and a 10–2 record with a win over Joe Paterno's fifth-ranked Nittany Lions in 1971. The Vols' win in Gainesville in 1971—20–13—would also serve as their last win in Ben Hill Griffin Stadium until Fulmer returned as Tennessee head coach and won 34–32 in 2001.

Fulmer used his superior knowledge of offensive line play and blocking schemes to serve under Johnny Majors as offensive line coach from 1980 to 1988, and as offensive coordinator and line coach from 1989 to 1992. It should be no surprise that he helped mold a number of offensive linemen who went on to extended

NFL careers, including two-time Super Bowl champion Raleigh McKenzie, Bruce Wilkerson, Harry Galbreath (an All-American in 1987), Charles McRae, and Antone Davis (unanimous All-American in 1990).

Fulmer presently serves as a founding partner at BPV Capital Management in Knoxville. He also serves as a consultant to the reboot of the East Tennessee State University football program, which is returning after 12 years of dormancy. Despite the opportunity to go into an assistant coaching role at the professional level, Fulmer has focused on his opportunity with BPV Capital Management and his children and six grandchildren.

"When I had this opportunity to be partner here at BPV, it kind of made me think, *You know, I've played with everybody else's children and grandchildren but mine.* At my age, and place in life, if I were ever going to do that, this is where I need to do it so that I could live a different quality of life with my family," Fulmer told the *Tennessean*. "You just re-gear into a different thing and go about your business."

10 The 1951 National Championship

The 1947 and 1948 Tennessee Volunteers did not live up to the normal standards of Tennessee football. With records of 5–5 and 4–4–2, Tennessee was shut out of a bowl game, and the natives began to get restless in Knoxville. Denver Crawford, a tackle and team captain on Neyland's 1947 team, came back and talked with the general about coaching, and the criticism Neyland was receiving from the media.

Portrait of a Champion

Many Tennessee fans remember where they were or what they were doing when Jeff Hall booted through the game-winning field goal in Syracuse. Or when Collins Cooper's kick sailed wide left in Tennessee's thrilling overtime victory against Florida. Or who called them to turn the television back on after Clint Stoerner's fumble in the Vols' 1998 matchup against Arkansas.

That's what championship seasons, and games that built them, become: unforgettable moments fans proudly carry with them forever.

For the 1951 Tennessee Volunteers, the dramatic finishes weren't there like they would be in 1998. However, the dominance from Week 1 through the end of the regular season was the hallmark of a championship football team. This 1951 Tennessee team did not have the luxury of any bye weeks, as they played 10 straight games from September 29 through December 1. They didn't get the public exposure and glory of traditional national powers, either; their October 20 game against Alabama was the first-ever televised SEC game.

But the Volunteers whitewashed the competition using General Neyland's single-wing offense. Led in the backfield by College Football Hall of Famer Hank Lauricella, the 1951 team rewrote the Tennessee record books with marks that still stand, including single-game records for the most net yards rushing (513 versus Washington & Lee), highest rushing average per play (10.7 against Washington & Lee), most touchdowns rushing (6 versus Washington & Lee), and single-game punt-return yardage (192 against Chattanooga).

The 1951 Schedule:
- September 29: Tennessee 14, Mississippi State 0 (Knoxville)
- October 6: Tennessee 26, Duke 0 (Knoxville)
- October 13: Tennessee 42, Chattanooga 13 (Knoxville)
- October 20: Tennessee 27, Alabama 13 (Birmingham)
- October 27: Tennessee 68, Tennessee Tech 0 (Knoxville)
- November 3: Tennessee 27, North Carolina 0 (Chapel Hill)
- November 10: Tennessee 60, Washington & Lee 14 (Knoxville)
- November 17: Tennessee 46, Ole Miss 21 (Oxford)
- November 24: Tennessee 28, Kentucky 0 (Lexington)
- December 1: Tennessee 35, Vanderbilt 27 (Knoxville)

Crawford later recounted:

I had always planned to go into coaching, and I wanted to thank him for the scholarship and everything he'd done for me. But that year we'd gone 5–5, and you know that's not good for Tennessee football. And they were after the general like they do when you're not winning them all or going to a bowl game. Then I talked to him. They were saying, "Get rid of General Neyland. He's too old, using the single wing. Outmoded, outdated." All this stuff I was hearing. I talked to him about that. I said, "Coach, I wanted to go into this game of football, but you've been here 20 years, and the way they're after you now, I don't know if I want to go into that kind of game."

He grinned and said, "Let me tell you, Crawford. I don't care what field you go into. You can't live on your clippings. You've got to produce."

General Neyland's grin communicated something that nobody else in Knoxville knew: that good times were straight ahead for Tennessee football.

The Vols took a step forward in 1949, improving to 7–2–1. Finishing on a three-game winning streak, including a win at No. 11 Kentucky, the team finished ranked No. 17 in the 1949 AP poll.

The revival of the Tennessee program was in mid-swing for Neyland's men. In 1950 the fourth-ranked Vols started off with a second-week loss at unranked Mississippi State that knocked the Vols out of the rankings. UT responded with nine straight wins, including five shutouts. A 7–0 win over No. 3 Kentucky in late November helped push UT into the Cotton Bowl against No. 3 Texas. In one of Neyland's most remembered games, Tennessee scored 13 points in the fourth quarter to upset the heavily favored Longhorns 20–14 and finish the season at No. 4 in the AP poll.

Robert Neyland led Tennessee to greatness with his innovative coaching techniques. The 1951 national championship was one of four for Neyland's Volunteers teams.

The scene was set for a championship run in 1951, and the team had the discipline instilled by General Neyland, and the players to do it. Led by a backfield trio of Hank Lauricella, Andy Kozar, and Herky Payne, who combined for more than 2,000 yards rushing, Tennessee rolled through the competition, starting by avenging its only 1950 loss with a 14–0 win over Mississippi State at Shields-Watkins Field.

Tennessee had shut out five opponents entering the season's final week, against Vanderbilt's Commodores. No team had come within single digits of the top-ranked Vols all season. The Commodores, however, gave the Vols a run for their money, ultimately falling 35–27 to Neyland's squad. Vandy's 27 points were the most points allowed by the Vols all season, and the most by Tennessee since a 30–13 loss to Georgia Tech on November 5, 1949.

Before their matchup with Maryland in the Sugar Bowl, the final polls were announced. Tennessee was listed atop the AP and UPI polls, ahead of Michigan State and Maryland. The third-ranked Terrapins took out some of their frustration on Tennessee in the Sugar Bowl, winning 28–13 in what amounted to a meaningless game in the rankings that had already crowned Tennessee as its national champion.

The national championship marked a great turnaround that a calm General Neyland had predicted and planned for in the late 1940s. It also was amidst a finishing stretch in the general's career that most coaches today would drool over. The Vols ran off a 29–4–1 record in Neyland's final three years as UT's head coach, from 1950 to 1952.

11 The SEC Championships

The Tennessee Volunteers are one of the 10 remaining founding members of the Southeastern Conference, beginning conference play in 1933. Since that time, the Volunteers have won outright or shared 13 conference championships, second to Alabama's 24. Tennessee's 811 career wins and .680 winning percentage are also second-most in SEC history, to Alabama's 850 and .716, respectively.

As such, while the years have been lean since Phillip Fulmer's last SEC Championship Game appearance in 2007, the strength of Tennessee's historical success is rock solid. As the SEC's second-most-successful program going back to its inception, Tennessee has given its fans plenty to cheer about over the years, and many championships to celebrate.

From 1938 to 1940, Tennessee rolled the opposition, claiming two national championships (1938 and 1940) and compiling a record of 31–2 and a perfect 18–0 mark in SEC play. In all 18 games, only Auburn came within seven points of Tennessee, losing 7–0 in 1938 and 1939. In fact, only 2 of 18 SEC opponents even *scored* against the Vols during the stretch, with LSU falling 14–6 in 1938 and Alabama losing 27–12 in 1940.

General Neyland's next SEC crown came in 1946, when his Vols tied eventual national champion Georgia with matching 5–0 SEC records, as Tennessee avoided the Bulldogs on their slate. It was a bittersweet season for the Vols, as a home loss to heavy under-dog Wake Forest knocked the then-fourth-ranked Vols out of the national championship picture; Tennessee ultimately lost to Rice in the Orange Bowl to finish 9–2.

The years were lean in Knoxville in the late 1940s, with .500 records in 1947 and 1948 generating buzz that the game had passed General Neyland by. His 1950 and 1951 squads showed that even the greats can have down seasons. The Vols stormed back to finish in the Top 5 of both major polls in 1950 with an 11–1 record. Although they beat recognized conference champion Kentucky 7–0, they finished with a 4–1 SEC record to UK's 5–1, losing out on the SEC title, in part, due to scheduling.

The 1951 season was the last of General Neyland's SEC titles before he retired following the 1952 season. The general won five SEC titles and four national championships.

Head coach Bowden Wyatt produced the school's sixth con-ference title in 1956, as Tennessee finished the regular season at a perfect 10–0. Unfortunately, so did Oklahoma, and the Sooners were voted No. 1 in the final AP and UPI polls following the regular season. Tennessee was No. 2. It was also a year of snubs in Knoxville, as Notre Dame's Paul Hornung was awarded the Heisman Trophy over a host of other candidates, including very deserving running back Johnny Majors, who ultimately finished second to Hornung.

Tennessee's futility continued for more than a decade, until Doug Dickey's 1967 and 1969 teams won conference titles. The 1967 team turned around a season-opening 20–16 loss by ripping off nine straight wins to end the regular season, including a 24–13 win over No. 6 Alabama at Legion Field that ultimately gave UT the SEC's top spot. They were recognized by the Litkenhous poll as national champions, before losing to 26–24 to Oklahoma in the Orange Bowl.

The 1969 team started the year winning seven games by double-digit margins. With a defense anchored by future L.A. Rams and San Francisco 49ers linebacker Jack Reynolds and nine-year NFL veteran Steve Kiner, Tennessee rolled up ranked Auburn, Alabama, and Georgia teams before traveling to Ole Miss. The Rebels gave the Vols their only loss in the regular season, a 38–0 trip behind the proverbial woodshed. The Vols finished a game ahead of LSU and Auburn for the SEC title, losing to Florida 14–13 in the Gator Bowl.

The longest wait in Tennessee history, 16 years, ended in 1985, thanks to a defense called the Orange Crush, a clutch performance by Daryl Dickey and the Tennessee defense in a 16–14 win at Alabama, and a Florida team made ineligible due to NCAA sanctions. The Gators beat Tennessee 17–10, but UT's 5–1 record was a win better than both Alabama and LSU, sending Tennessee to New Orleans for the Sugar Bowl. The Sugar Vols manhandled No. 2 Miami 35–7.

Coach Majors helped guide the Vols to a pair of SEC championships in 1989 and 1990. Alabama beat UT head-to-head in 1989 to earn the trip to the Sugar Bowl against No. 2 Miami, but Tennessee benefitted from Florida's ineligibility yet again in 1990, to earn a trip to New Orleans against Virginia, a thrilling 23–22 comeback victory for UT.

With the advent of the SEC Championship Game in 1992, Florida and Alabama dominated the game...until Peyton Manning guided Tennessee to a 10–1 1997 campaign and the SEC East championship, edging Vanderbilt 17–10 on Senior Day at Neyland Stadium to earn the Vols' first trip to Atlanta. Trailing 20–7 to Auburn, Tennessee, which turned the ball over six times and had an extra point blocked and returned for a two-point conversion, rallied behind the tough running of Jamal Lewis (31 carries for 127 yards) and one of Peyton Manning's finest performances in his UT career (25 of 43 for 373 yards and 4 touchdowns).

In 1998 No. 1 Tennessee made it back-to-back come-from-behind SEC Championship Game victories. After Mississippi State's Kevin Prentiss returned a punt 83 yards for a go-ahead touchdown midway through the fourth quarter, Tee Martin dug deep and carried the Vols to victory, finding Peerless Price to give the Vols the lead back, and then Cedrick Wilson to ice the game after Mississippi State fumbled away the ball.

Although the 16 years between 1998 and the end of the 2014 season matches the longest period of time Tennessee has gone without an SEC title, Tennessee's rock-solid history and success throughout the decades has made it a revered program, and one that no doubt has many more SEC championships in its future!

12 "No Sirree. Final Score: Tennessee 20, Florida 17. Pandemonium Reigns!"

The chain-link fences around Neyland Stadium buckled and gave way. Just like the Florida offensive line in overtime, they didn't stand much of a chance from the onrushing, orange-clad mob streaking ahead.

Tennessee play-by-play announcer John Ward was ecstatic, proclaiming "pandemonium." Indeed, as the scoreboard flashed the final score—Tennessee 20, Florida 17—fans flooded onto Shields-Watkins Field, screaming wildly, arms raised high. Between the thousands who scurried to celebrate a program-defining win with their heroes, lines of white-jerseyed, orange-helmeted Florida players made their way through the chaos toward the visitors' locker room.

Among them, head hanging low, was Florida kicker Collins Cooper.

It was Cooper's fateful kick from 32 yards out that sailed wide to the left and set off the ensuing jubilation among the partisan, sellout, then-record crowd of 107,653.

The joy amongst hugging fans was palpable. For five straight matchups, Florida had spoiled Tennessee's season before the fall temperatures began to appear. Three terrific Tennessee teams from 1995 to 1997, who won every regular-season game except for four in that span, fell at the hands of Florida. The Vols became fodder for the sharp-tongued Steve Spurrier, who quipped publicly, "You can't spell *Citrus* without *UT*," a dig at Tennessee being relegated to what was considered at the time an inferior bowl game.

However, on September 19, 1998, at half past 11:00 PM, Spurrier had nothing to say. His familiar confident smirk was hidden because his hands were on his knees and his head was down.

His Fun 'n' Gun offense had failed him, thanks in large part to a Tennessee defense that bent but didn't break and made the big play when needed, all evening long. For a few tense moments, it didn't look like that terrific defensive effort would matter.

Tied at 17 entering overtime, Florida won the toss and elected to defend, hoping to maintain the same success against Tennessee's offense they had enjoyed for the majority of the game. Tennessee ended regulation with only 235 yards of total offense, and 57 of them came on a first-quarter Shawn Bryson touchdown run to give Tennessee—who never trailed the rest of the day—a 7–3 lead.

The decision to defend appeared to pay off for Florida. Tee Martin misfired deep toward Peerless Price out of the back of the end zone on first down. Florida cornerback Dock Pollard tipped away a pass in the corner of the end zone intended for Price on second down. A holding penalty on third down set the Vols back to third-and-23 from the 38-yard line, seemingly out of field-goal range. Martin, who had struggled throwing the football for most of the day, made a potential game-saving play with his legs, scrambling up the middle to the Florida 24-yard line and setting up kicker Jeff Hall with a manageable kick from 41 yards out. Hall had beaten Syracuse on the final play in the Vols' previous game and had made his only attempt against Florida from 39 yards out in the second quarter to extend the Vols' lead to 10–3 at the time.

As he was for much of his career, Hall was true, and the kick sailed through the middle of the uprights.

On Florida's first series, Doug Johnson, who alternated plays with sophomore Jesse Palmer, found Terry Jackson for four yards. Wide receiver Travis Taylor took an end around for six yards and a first down.

On first down from the 15, a corner route—and a victory for Florida—trickled off the fingertips of Taylor in the end zone. On second down, middle linebacker Al Wilson came on a blitz and drilled Palmer, sending the ball fluttering harmlessly to the turf.

Facing third-and-10, an aggressive defense, and the deafening sound of 100,000-plus screaming antagonists, Tennessee brought the blitz again, forcing an errant throw behind Taylor near the goal line.

Spurrier picked the senior Cooper for the game-tying kick over sophomore Jeff Chandler, the latter who would go on to have a sterling career for the Gators. The kick sailed wide left, Cooper's name was etched in Gators infamy for years, and the Vols, beaten in the stat column, had finally won the most important battle of all—the scoreboard.

It wasn't always pretty. Palmer and Johnson combined to throw for more than 400 yards on the day. Conversely, Tennessee didn't have much of an offensive presence after Martin connected with Price between two Gators defenders for a 29-yard score and a 17–10 lead early in the third quarter. Against a defensive front seven led by Jevon Kearse and Johnny Rutledge, featured back Jamal Lewis carried 21 times for 82 yards for the game.

But it was enough. Just barely enough. To any Tennessee fan, that's all that mattered.

When asked by Mike Mayock during the postgame interview if it was the biggest win in the history of Tennessee football, Coach Fulmer responded, "I don't know. We've got such a storied tradition, but it's the biggest win in a long time. I am so proud of our kids. They came to fight. You've got to give Florida a lot of credit. They fought their guts out. Our kids wanted this one tonight."

And it was the Tennessee defense, and particularly Wilson, who wanted it most. Aside from Wilson's pressure on Palmer in overtime, he and safety Deon Grant forced a fumble by running back Terry Jackson as the big back stretched toward the end zone on the Gators' first drive, thwarting a seemingly inevitable Florida touchdown. Grant also made a leaping interception of a deep pass from Palmer intended for Naris Karim with six minutes and change left in a tie game deep in Tennessee territory. For the game, the Tennessee defense forced five turnovers.

The teams' fates had been settled by midnight. Tennessee would defeat all comers through the remainder of its schedule, finishing 13–0 and winning its first national championship since 1951. Florida would cut a swath through the rest of the SEC competition, topping No. 11 LSU 22–10 in Gainesville and No. 11 Georgia 38–7 in Jacksonville. Although Florida climbed as high as No. 4 in the AP poll, a season-ending 23–12 loss to Florida State in Tallahassee dropped the Gators to 9–2 and sent them to the FedEx Orange Bowl for a tilt with the Donovan McNabb–led Syracuse Orangemen. Florida won 31–10.

Although Spurrier and the Gators continued to pose a roadblock that Coach Fulmer struggled to overcome throughout his career, for one night, he showed the Volunteer Nation and the college football world that Tennessee was a national contender and a top-tier program under his guidance.

Asked by Mayock whether the Florida monkey was finally off his back, Coach Fulmer responded, "That monkey's gone."

13 Al Wilson: A Natural Leader

The hits he put on the opposition were fierce. The intensity that he brought on the field and in the locker room was irreplaceable.

It's safe to say that no player like Al Wilson has come through the University of Tennessee in its storied history. While Peyton Manning, Joey Kent, Jamal Lewis, Jay Graham, Cosey Coleman, and many other contributors helped instill a level of excellence on the offensive side of the football, exciting crowds and lighting up scoreboards, Wilson and a nucleus of All-American defenders helped ultimately bring the 1998 Tennessee Volunteers to the top of the college football world.

Aldra Kauwa Wilson was born and raised in Jackson, Tennessee. At Jackson Central-Merry High School, Wilson played football and basketball, and was a member of the track team. His aptitude and ability on the football field was evident, as he played quarterback, running back, and linebacker. He rushed for 1,000 or more yards in three of his four seasons, and scored 15 touchdowns in his senior season.

However, Wilson was a natural defender, able to channel his aggression and intensity into becoming arguably the best linebacker ever to play at the University of Tennessee. After playing sparingly as a freshman in 1995, Wilson held his own personal coming-out party in 1996, accumulating 87 tackles—eight of them for a loss. By the time he graduated in 1998, Wilson had 272 tackles, 8 fumble recoveries, 11 sacks, 23 tackles for a loss, 10 passes broken up, and 2 interceptions.

The Volunteers defense was close in 1997, but not quite up to the challenge of a Nebraska team that rolled up 409 rushing yards in a 42–17 Orange Bowl romp. With the departure of seniors Leonard Little, Bill Duff, Shaun Ellis, Terry Fair, and Jonathan Brown on defense, and with the loss of Manning under center, the 1998 squad would need a new face to take the reins and lead a team left full of talent but suddenly without significant veteran leadership.

Yet Phillip Fulmer needed to look no further than the halftime locker room of the 1997 SEC Championship Game to know he had the heart and soul of his 1998 defense and the ultimate leader in soon-to-be-senior Wilson.

Trailing 20–10 to Auburn at the half, Wilson exploded in the locker room. With tears in his eyes, he implored his teammates and

Linebacker Al Wilson is one of the all-time greatest Volunteers.

coaches to come together to win what would be the school's first conference title in seven years.

"I'll tell my kids about how he cried about never winning a championship in his life and how I felt it," Peerless Price said. "I wanted to win for him, and the team wanted to win for him. He broke down in tears and said we had to dig deep, that nobody believed we could come back and win. He convinced me. I think he convinced the coaching staff. I think he convinced everyone in the locker room."

"I told them to remember how hard they'd played all season," Wilson said. "We didn't come down here to lose, we came to be victorious. We came down here to bring the championship back to Knoxville.

"If the guys took it to heart, then that means so much to me. I was pretty emotional. I told them I had never won a championship. I told them I'd do anything in this world to win this game. I shed a few tears. I knew we had to play a better game than we did in the first half."

The team rallied around Wilson's fiery comments and edged Auburn 30–29 in the biggest comeback victory in SEC Championship Game history to date.

But Wilson had his sights set higher for his senior season. His goal was simple: a national championship, nothing less. Wilson certainly played the 1998 season like a man possessed to win his first championship at any level. He came up with big play after big play when close games were on the line.

On September 19, 1998, against Florida, Wilson was all over the field, making a game-high 12 tackles and forcing a school-record three fumbles. His hit on Jesse Palmer in overtime forced an incompletion and led to Collins Cooper's 32-yard wide-left attempt to end the game.

Throughout the season, Wilson's hair-on-fire style of play was contagious among his teammates, but it also resulted in groin and shoulder injuries that caused him to miss three games. However, his fellow linebacker Raynoch Thompson referred to him as the Energizer Bunny because he just kept on going and going and going.

Coach Fulmer even compared Wilson's impact on the Tennessee defense to what Peyton Manning had on the UT offense in his time.

Wilson's inspiring play paid off, as Tennessee's swarming defense held the opposition to fewer than 20 points in 10 of 13 games. While the SEC championship was special in 1997 as his first major championship victory, Wilson fulfilled his destiny in 1998 by leading Tennessee to its first-ever BCS national championship.

Wilson was drafted by the Denver Broncos with the 31st overall pick. He enjoyed an eight-year career with Denver, in which he was selected to five Pro Bowls and was named AP first-team All-Pro in 2005.

Wilson announced his retirement from professional football on September 10, 2008.

14 The Checkerboard End Zones

A Tennessee trademark from the mid-1960s was reinstated in 1989 with the installation of the orange-and-white checkerboard end zones on Shields-Watkins Field; the atavism continued in 1994 with the return of grass.

Former Tennessee coach and athletic director Doug Dickey first envisioned the checkerboard end zones. When Dickey took over as coach in 1964, he had the end zones painted with the checkerboards.

"I got the idea to use checkerboard when I saw it in a magazine, maybe in an ad," Dickey told espn.com. "The design caught my eye and I thought we needed to dress up the stadium. It was drab and we needed some color.... People liked the checkerboard end zones, and it's nice to have an identifying product that's lasted over the years."

Johnny Payne: Big Orange Virtuoso

As the Vols take the field through the Pride of the Southland Marching Band's *T*, or whenever John Ward and now Bob Kesling calls a player running "into the checkerboard" for six points, most folks don't think who's responsible for painting the end zones that serve as the backdrop for these exciting moments.

Enter Johnny Payne.

Since Tennessee returned to natural grass in 1994, Payne, who was employed by the University of Tennessee from 1978 to 2015, was responsible for putting the orange-and-white checkerboard in each end zone the week of a home football game.

After two decades, Payne had the process down to a science. Payne employed a square sheet-metal template he place down on the grass, and he put two coats of paint in each square. There are 120 5'x5' squares in each zone. After carefully putting down two coats of paint on 240 squares, the checkerboards are set for action.

Over his career, Payne has put paint to grass on an incredible number of squares: more than 30,000. The result has been so impressive that schools from around the country have contacted Payne about ideas for improving their football fields.

"I've had people call from all over the country who want to paint their end zones like us to find out how we paint them," Payne told espn.com. "I'll just draw it up on a piece of paper and fax it to 'em. It's easier than trying to explain it to them."

Although Payne is no longer with the University, his Picasso-esque work on the canvases that are the end zones of Shields-Watkins Field are unmistakably a part of Tennessee's football lore and continue to provide a colorful backdrop for exciting and unforgettable moments in Tennessee football history.

The colorful and popular end zones were a part of Tennessee football until 1968, when the natural sod was dug out and artificial turf was put in its place. New artificial turf was placed down in 1989, and the checkerboards returned, albeit slightly different. The orange-and-white checkerboard stretched to the chalk of each of the four lines of the end zone, making an orange-and-white checkerboard on a large orange background that encompassed every inch of the end zone.

In 1994, when the Vols switched the field covering to natural grass, they altered the checkerboard design such that it would not stretch from pylon to pylon. Instead of facing the potential of confusing the officials with the white checkerboards touching the goal line, Bob Campbell, UT's director of sports surface management, decided to put a five-foot grass buffer between the checkerboard and the boundary lines. The current version has remained proudly in place for the past 21 years.

It costs $800 worth of paint per home game—20 gallons at $40 per gallon—to paint the checkerboards. The end zones are normally painted on Wednesdays and Thursdays each week before a home game. The process for the grounds crew takes three to four hours each day during the two days, because the white squares are painted one day and the orange squares are painted the next. The logic being that you can't stand in a square that's drying as you paint the one next to it.

The great popularity of the checkerboard end zones, and their widely recognized association with the University of Tennessee, has carried over to the hardwood, where the pattern appears on the baselines of the basketball court at Thompson-Boling Arena.

15 Smokey

They hooted and hollered back and forth at each other. Indeed, the selection of Smokey as the Tennessee mascot was as much a love affair between the student body roaring in approval and a dog that howled back in apparent appreciation.

The UT pep club held a contest in 1953 to select a coonhound, a native breed of the state, as the school's live mascot. Announcements of the contest in local newspapers read, "This can't be an ordinary hound. He must be a 'Houn' Dog' in the best sense of the word."

Reverend Bill Brooks made the decision to enter his award-winning bluetick hound in the contest. At home against Mississippi State in their season opener on September 29, the dogs were brought out and introduced to the crowd for voting at Shields-Watkins Field. The PA announcer announced each of the animals, the crowd would cheer for the animal they wanted to win the competition. When Brooks' hound, named Brooks' Blue Smokey, was introduced, the crowd roared, especially when Blue Smokey howled.

The legend of Smokey the bluetick hound was officially born.

Rev. Brooks supplied UT with the line of canines until his death in 1986 when his wife, Mildred, took over taking care of the revered pets. She did so until 1994, when her brother and sister-in-law, Earl and Martha Hudson, assumed responsibility for Smokey VII through Smokey IX.

Charles and Cindy Hudson then took over the bloodline, and they were charged with the suddenly challenging task of keeping the legend of Smokey alive. With the Smokey bloodline ending and Smokey IX battling an ACL injury, finding Smokey X was no easy task.

"So here we were stuck with a situation of where are we going," Cindy told WBIR.com.

They were determined, anywhere but out of state.

"Charles and I really wanted it to be a Tennessee bluetick born and raised. And we immediately began the search to find one."

Fortunately in Shelbyville, Tennessee, Smokey X was found, and the tradition of the bluetick hound lives on in its 62nd year.

Smokey X continues the great tradition of bluetick hounds with a celebratory romp through the checkerboard end zone.

One of the most beloved figures in the state, Smokey is famous for leading the Vols out of the giant *T* prior to each home game.

Smokey the bluetick hound is more than just a sideline bystander. He and his descendants have been through adversity (rivalry pranks and heat exhaustion) and have witnessed some of Tennessee's best moments in the program's history.

The Tennessee players aren't the only orange-clad creatures to suffer injury and mishap on the football field. Smokey II was abducted by students from Tennessee's northern rival, Kentucky, in 1955. Smokey even crossed paths with the Baylor Bear mascot in 1957 and lived to tell the tale. Smokey VI was sidelined by scalding 140 degree temperatures in 1991 in the Vols' tilt against the UCLA Bruins. Out of all the Smokey bluetick hounds to come through Knoxville, it was Smokey VIII who saw the most success, with the Vols compiling a 91–22 record with two SEC titles and a national championship in his time.

In the past 60-plus years, Smokey has become as synonymous with the University of Tennessee as the colors orange and white, Davy Crockett, checkerboards, "Rocky Top," and the Power T.

16 Running Through the *T*

"Ladies and gentlemen, wherever you may be listening from...*it's football time in Tennessee!*"

These famous words, spoken by John Ward and carried on by current play-by-play commentator Bob Kesling, are the final precursor to the Volunteers taking the field at Neyland Stadium. The Pride of the Southland Marching Band, playing the school's official fight song, "Down the Field," marches down to the goal line in front of the Vols' locker room in the north end zone tunnel. The players congregate in the tunnel, jumping and ready to rush onto the field. The band, which stretches from the goal line to near the 50-yard line, spreads apart, forming a pathway up the field and to the sideline. The State of Tennessee flag and orange Power T flags are raised, and Smokey—with the cheerleaders in tow—leads the Big Orange onto the field for battle below the explosion of fireworks that glisten over the Tennessee River running alongside Neyland Stadium.

Without question, it's one of the most incredible entrances in all of sports. Few visiting fans who make the trip to Neyland Stadium will honestly say that the band's parting of the orange sea and the players flooding onto the field through the roar of 100,000 fans and the boom of orange-hued, mortar-shell fireworks didn't give them goose bumps.

It is so electric, in fact, that one wealthy Tennessean paid the school a million dollars to run through the *T* with the team. John "Thunder" Thornton, who previously served as a member of the university's board of trustees, donated $1 million to the school's Thornton Athletics Student Life Center. In return, Thornton was allowed to run through the *T* prior to the Vols' 1995 homecoming game against Southern Miss.

For less fortunate (and less financially able) fans wanting a first-hand experience of the trek out of the tunnel and through the *T*, Clay Travis, lifelong UT fan and author of the book *On Rocky Top*, got the chance to live out one of his childhood fantasies in 2008 and run through the *T* with his favorite football team. He wrote:

One moment you're unable to move in a low-ceilinged enclosure just off the field and the next you're in the middle of an undulating sea of orange and the skies are clear as far as you can see, the fresh air a pleasant shock to your skin and lungs. Running onto the football fist at night, as the T splits open before you, it seems possible that you could jump into the air and take flight on the roaring yells of the Tennessee faithful. This is as close to the gladiatorial experience as exists in modern American society.

Historically, the run through the *T* developed and changed significantly from the time General Neyland's teams took the field. From Neyland's teams in the 1950s through the 1963 season, the Vols had their team bench on the east side of the field, close to their dressing room, which entered the field on the 50-yard line.

In 1965 Doug Dickey changed all that as the Vols opened the season against Army. He moved his team's bench to the west side, allowing the Vols to enter the field just before the opening kickoff through a giant *T* formed by the Pride of the Southland Marching Band.

When the Vols moved to the new dressing room quarters under the north stands in 1983, the *T* remained, forming from north to south instead of east to west.

The show has been taken on the road more than once. The *T* has occasionally been formed for road games and bowl games, most notably at Liberty Bowl Memorial Stadium in Memphis, at Vanderbilt Stadium in Nashville, and at the 1986 and 1991 Sugar Bowls in New Orleans.

17 Stoerner Stumbles and Fumbles

Ask a group of Vols fans about the greatest game they ever witnessed at Neyland Stadium, and chances are one of them will respond with the 1998 Arkansas-Tennessee game. Unlike the Florida overtime thriller, there may have actually been more at stake going into the game with the Hogs, and certainly more obstacles to overcome within the game. The week prior, during a ho-hum 37–13 homecoming cakewalk against an overmatched UAB squad, Neyland Stadium received perhaps its biggest cheer when an announcement came down at the end of the game from the booming voice of Bobby Denton, longtime Neyland Stadium public-address announcer: "Final Score: Michigan State 28, No. 1 Ohio State 24!"

And with that, the Vols were poised to take over the nation's top spot in the rankings in the home stretch of the season. With home matchups against No. 10 Arkansas and Kentucky before a season-ending road trip to Vandy, it appeared for the orange-hued Vols fans that everything was setting up for the Vols to head to Atlanta in position for a spot in the Fiesta Bowl for all the marbles. Kansas State and UCLA were also in the race and nipping at Tennessee's heels.

Arkansas came into the game undefeated but relatively untested, having faced (and bested) only one opponent ranked in the AP Top 25—a 42–6 win over No. 22 Alabama in September. In his first season as the Razorbacks' head coach, Houston Nutt had done yeoman's work with a team coming off back-to-back 4–7 seasons. After dispatching the Tide, the Hogs survived Tim Couch and the Wildcats and won road games at South Carolina and Auburn. But all that had earned them was a No. 10 ranking in the polls, and it gave Nutt perhaps the greatest trump card a coach can play to motivate a team: the disrespect card.

As if on cue, the Razorbacks looked like the team who wanted it more. In a drizzle that developed into a steady and driving rain-storm over the next three-plus hours, Arkansas proved early on to be the more physical and aggressive team, on both sides of the ball. And WR Anthony Lucas proved to be a major thorn in the Vols' side.

Following a Travis Stephens fumble, QB Clint Stoerner found WR Emanuel Smith, who trampled a small army of defenders and ran into the end zone for a 7–0 Hogs lead. After a jailbreak sack of Tee Martin and a punt, Stoerner and the Hogs faced a first-and-34 after a comedy of errors. The play resulted in a 38-yard pass to Lucas. Stoerner found Lucas again, deep for 62 yards, and he beat the UT corner and raced to the end zone for a 14–0 lead.

Meanwhile, Tennessee continued to try to ride the Travis Henry and Travis Stephens combo, but a promising drive sputtered out, resulting in a 41-yard FG. On the ensuing drive, the Hogs turned to their ground game, with long runs by Chris Chukwuma and Madre Hill quickly moving Arkansas down the field. And with three minutes left, the Hogs moved ahead on a red-zone strike to a seemingly uncoverable Lucas.

Arkansas 21, No. 1 Tennessee 3.

The Vols were put on the ropes by a faster, tougher, and by all appearances hungrier undefeated team in their own house. Behind a defense that had allowed 17 points to Florida, 7 to Houston, 9 to Auburn, 3 to Georgia, 18 to Alabama, 14 to South Carolina, and 13 to UAB, Tennessee had surpassed those numbers in the first 27 minutes of the game against Arkansas. Lucas, who would finish the game with eight catches for 172 yards and two TDs, was simply uncoverable by Dwayne Goodrich and the UT secondary.

"I don't think Tennessee is a good come-from-behind-type team this particular year," said CBS color commentator Terry Donahue. "Doesn't mean they can't. But that's not their forte. Their forte is their running game, ball control, field position, and no turnovers. And that hasn't gone that way for them this half yet."

Tennessee was able to finally break into the end zone in the final three minutes of the half, on a 36-yard strike from Martin to Peerless Price in the back of the end zone. It was a bright spot in an otherwise dismal day for Martin, who finished 10 of 27 for 155 yards. At halftime, Tennessee trailed 21–10, and their dreams of perfection were very much in doubt.

In the second half, Lucas and Stoerner picked up where the left off, which ended with a 33-yard field goal and a 24–10 advantage. With Martin struggling, offensive coordinator David Cutcliffe turned to the sure legs of Travis Henry, who powered the Vols down a sloppy field and into the red zone. Martin ran it in from four yards out, and suddenly the Vols were within a touchdown. In fact, on the following drive, Martin's legs took the Vols to the Arkansas 5-yard line.

And that's where the Vols hit a wall offensively. They settled for a 21-yard Jeff Hall field goal to trail 24–20. Meanwhile, Stoerner, Lucas, and the Arkansas offense were just good enough to stay on the field in the early part of the fourth quarter and keep Martin, Henry, and Peerless Price on the sideline. After a time-consuming drive down to the UT 21-yard line, Todd Latourrette's field goal attempt was blocked, scooped up by Al Wilson, and returned to the Arkansas 36-yard line.

However, even with Neyland Stadium in the throes of ecstasy, the Vols moved backward and were forced to punt with five and a half minutes to play. Punter David Leaverton pinned the Hogs inside their own 1, which resulted in a Hogs punt. In a controversial call, Arkansas punter Chris Akin kicked the ball out of the back of his own end zone after the snap flew over his head. A later announcement from the SEC would say the officials erred in not giving the Vols the ball at the Hogs' 4-yard line following an illegal kicking penalty, rather than awarding the safety.

Down 24–22, the Vols had what seemed to be one final drive to get in range for Jeff Hall to kick another dramatic field goal and keep their magical season alive. Hall had already booted the game winner at Syracuse and the winning points in overtime against Florida. As it turned out, he wouldn't get the chance to decide the outcome.

Starting at their own 49-yard line, Martin and the Vols moved the ball one yard in three plays, setting up a fourth-and-9 from midfield. Martin's pass sailed over the middle in the direction of Price, but was broken up by Hogs CB David Barrett. The Arkansas bench exploded, the Vols' undefeated season appeared at an end, and waterlogged fans began looking for their belongings so they could leave the stadium.

Then the unthinkable happened.

On second-and-12, Stoerner pulled out from center and tripped over the leg of his guard Brandon Burlsworth. Rather than falling to the ground and taking the short loss with the clock running, he put the ball down to brace himself, and it slipped out of his grasp and into the arms of Vols DT Billy Ratliff. Neyland Stadium erupted with the same fever pitch of two months prior against Florida. The Hogs were shell-shocked.

Four Henry runs gashed the Razorback defense and had the Vols at the 1-yard line, where Henry dove over the top with seconds remaining to give the Vols something they hadn't had the entire day—a lead. Tennessee players hugged and tackled each other to the ground. The fans who stuck around did the same thing. Tennessee had escaped devastation through a solid second-half defensive effort, Henry's bullish running, and a huge helping hand from Lady Luck.

Final Score: Tennessee 28, Arkansas 24. Coach Fulmer lauded the guts of his players; Stoerner was devastated.

"I don't think I'll ever forget about it, or even allow myself to forget about it," Stoerner said. "It's a tough thing to swallow, but it's all part of the game."

When asked if he believed in miracles, Fulmer pointed to something else. "I believe in determination," he said. "We got some help from them late, but we gave them some help in the first half. Those kinds of things tend to even out over the course of a game."

Call them determined, call them lucky, but one thing had been cemented: Tennessee was that proverbial team of destiny in 1998. The Vols rode the momentum of the win to hammer Kentucky and Vanderbilt before claiming the SEC title against Mississippi State 24–14 en route to the school's first national title in 47 years. Arkansas's chances of an SEC title game rematch with the Vols fell by the wayside the next week, as the Razorbacks came out flat and lost in Starkville, Mississippi, in heartbreaking fashion yet again—on a last-second field goal by the Bulldogs. The Hogs finished the season 9–3 after a Citrus Bowl loss to Michigan.

Two undefeated teams, two destinies changed by one stumble.

18 The Evolution of the UT Uniform

It seems as often as the leaves have changed color to beautiful shades of orange in the fall, so have the Tennessee Volunteers donned the Orange and White on football Saturdays. In reality, the Volunteers football team has yet to hit the 100-year mark in wearing orange uniforms on game days.

The school colors of orange and white were originally selected by Mr. Charles Moore, associate athletics president and member of the first UT football team in 1891. He spotted a cluster of orange-and-white daisies on the Hill and was inspired to nominate the colors to be recognized officially as the school's colors. The student body later voted on and ratified the colors.

From 1891 to 1921, Tennessee wore black jerseys. However, starting with the season opener in 1922, under the direction of head coach M.B. Banks, General Neyland's predecessor, the Volunteers football team began wearing orange-colored jerseys. Inspired or not by the change in gear, Tennessee ran roughshod over Emory & Henry College 50–0 at Shields-Watkins Field on their way to an 8–2 season.

The 1931 season brought an orange-painted leather helmet. In 1935 the team changed things up, wearing white jerseys with white-painted leather helmets.

In 1936 the team switched back to orange jerseys, and for the first time ever, wore white numbers on the chests and backs of the jerseys. The size of the numbers increased slightly in 1947, and the Vols wore white pants for the first time that year as well.

In 1949 white plastic helmets with an orange stripe going down the middle became the standard for the Vols. Orange pants stripes were also added to their standard white pants that year. In 1956 gray face masks were added to the helmets for the first time.

In 1962 then-coach Bowden Wyatt added numbers to players' helmets, which was short-lived. In 1964, under new coach Doug Dickey, new white helmets with an orange *T* were introduced, the numbers were removed, and said design has remained the standard for the Tennessee helmet through today.

Tennessee wore its standard orange jersey with white pants and white helmets through Dickey's tenure and the start of Bill Battle's time as head coach. Then UT put a new twist on its uniforms in the early 1970s—white road jerseys with orange stretching from shoulder to shoulder. This style of jersey, although disposed of in 1975, gained almost a cult popularity with fans decades later, as former Tennessee great Condredge Holloway starred in them from 1972 to 1974. The style's first usage accompanied a 20–13 victory over Florida in Gainesville on October 2, 1971.

Tennessee moved to an all-white road jersey with orange numerals in 1975, but the big change came in 1977. Tennessee debuted orange pants on October 15, 1977, against Alabama at Legion Field, a Tennessee loss. The Vols dropped the next two orange-pantsed contests—at Florida and Kentucky—before ending the season with a 42–7 victory over Vanderbilt.

Moving forward, Tennessee wore white jerseys and orange pants on the road. Some memorable road victories in the white jerseys and orange pants include a 42–0 whipping of Auburn in 1980, Johnnie Jones' game winner at Legion Field to beat the Tide 41–34 in 1983, a 16–14 win at Legion Field on the way to winning the 1985 SEC title in a one-loss season, wins over No. 6 UCLA and No. 10 Arkansas in an 11–1 campaign in 1989, and the unforgettable 35–34 comeback victory over Notre Dame in South Bend in 1991.

Then–interim head coach Phillip Fulmer changed the road uniforms to the "storm trooper" look—white top, white pants—in 1992 at Georgia, a 34–31 win. It became the official road uniform in 1993. The orange stripes were removed from the pants in 1995, setting up an unforgettable run in one of the most successful and popular uniforms in school history—the all-whites with orange numerals outlined in black.

The orange jersey and white pants appeared to be the permanent staple, until Tennessee broke out the all-orange uniform in 1999, a narrow homecoming victory over cross-state foe Memphis. Tennessee has gone all-orange one more time since—a 21–14 loss to LSU in the 2007 SEC Championship Game.

Some tweaks have been made to the uniform from the 1990s over the years: A solid orange stripe outlined by black up the side of the white pants and jersey was introduced in 2002 and abandoned the following year (home white pants had an orange stripe as well). The orange pants stripes returned in 2006. UT returned to the orange pants and white jersey for its 2008 season opener at UCLA. The Vols donned black jerseys—a first since 1920—and orange pants in a 2009 thrashing of South Carolina at home on Halloween night. And Tennessee was introduced across the chest of the home and away jerseys in 2013.

Tennessee also mixed things up, starting in 2013, with the introduction of Adidas "smoke"-colored jerseys with Vols across the chest (which they wore in a 34–31 overtime loss to Georgia), and all orange unis with white stripes on the pants in a 23–21 home win over No. 11 South Carolina.

With Tennessee's sponsorship change from Adidas to Nike in 2015, more changes should be expected.

19 Tee Martin: Escaping the Shadow of a Legend

Peyton Manning set school records and brought the Vols' first SEC title in seven years. The prodigal son of Tennessee football, Manning's shortcomings were few, but his inability to help UT beat the University of Florida ultimately left the Vols on the outside looking in at conference and national title pictures.

Manning was without comparison as a natural thrower. So when Manning left Knoxville, the question was, how much would Tee Martin be ready to step into the spotlight and take over the Tennessee offense, which still retained a host of stars. Jamal Lewis, Travis Henry, Cosey Coleman, Chad Clifton, Shaun Bryson, Peerless Price, and Cedrick Wilson—all future NFL players— returned on offense.

Manning and Martin couldn't have been more different, from their playing styles to their upbringings. Manning, the son of Ole Miss and New Orleans Saints quarterback Archie Manning, came from football greatness and was rated the consensus No. 1 quarterback recruit in the nation in 1994. Martin, from Mobile, Alabama, came from a background of violence and illness, having lost several friends to both. During his childhood, he changed his address 22 times and was moved between his mother, grandmother, and great-grandmother.

Through his upbringing, Martin maintained an outward nonchalance attitude and charisma that helped win over his teammates.

"You can tell by each personality what his childhood was like," teammate Al Wilson told the Associated Press. "I've never seen Tee Martin nervous, and I think that's one of his biggest attributes. He's always relaxed."

Martin was calm and collected on a cool January 4 evening in Tempe, Arizona. Playing for the national championship that Manning never won, Martin decided the game with two deep balls to Peerless Price, one that hit him in stride for a 76-yard gain, setting up a score, and the other a 79-yard touchdown throw that broke the Seminoles' back.

Beginning in Syracuse, New York, and ending in Tempe, Arizona, Martin took Volunteers fans on the greatest ride of their lives and, in the process, rode out from underneath the giant shadow that Peyton Manning had left behind.

The 1985–86 Sugar Vols

All eyes in the college football universe were on New Orleans and Miami. After all, one of the teams coming out of the Sugar Bowl or the Orange Bowl would be crowned the 1985 national champion by the pollsters on January 2.

There were three teams considered to be in contention, and the Orange Bowl was hosting two of them. No. 1 Penn State was the nation's only undefeated team, having beaten Top 10 opponents Maryland and Alabama, but also surviving scares from unranked Syracuse, Temple, and Boston College. Their opponent, the Oklahoma Sooners, had steamrolled their way to a 10–1 record behind a stifling defense led by All-American linebacker Brian Bosworth. Oklahoma held eight of eleven regular-season opponents to single-digit point totals.

Their only loss? To 10–1 Miami, who came to Norman, Oklahoma, and prevailed 27–14, breaking the ankle of quarterback Troy Aikman in the process. Miami opened the season with a 35–23 home loss to the Florida Gators, then proceeded to rip off 10 straight wins, including a 35–27 win at No. 10 Florida State, in an attempt to duplicate the path to the national championship laid by its 1983 team.

It seemed simple. If Penn State won, they would undoubtedly be crowned the champion. If Oklahoma won, the plot would thicken, and a debate would begin about who deserved the title—Oklahoma, who defeated No. 2 Nebraska, or Miami, who defeated the Sooners head-to-head.

But there was one more one-loss team in the conversation that no one recognized—the 8–1–2 SEC champion Tennessee Volunteers.

It was widely considered a foregone conclusion that Miami would make short work of Tennessee. With skill position players in Vinny Testaverde, Alonzo Highsmith, Warren Williams, Melvin Bratton, Brian Blades, and Michael Irvin—a who's who of future NFL stardom—and a defense laden with size and speed, Miami was expected to wipe the Superdome turf with the less heralded but hungry Tennessee squad.

It was a Tennessee team that had fought and clawed all season long, starting with a season-opening 26–26 stalemate against UCLA. Tennessee quarterback Tony Robinson set single-game school records for passing yards (387) and total offensive yards (417) in leading the Vols to a fourth-quarter 26–10 lead. However, in the final five minutes of the game, UCLA backup quarterback David Norrie connected on two touchdown passes, and the ensuing two-point conversions turned victory into a bitter tie for Tennessee.

Tennessee had not won a conference title since 1969. It had not finished in the AP Top 10 since 1972. The UT program had fallen off the face of the college football map and needed something to breathe life back into the once-proud program. A victory over Heisman hopeful Bo Jackson and the No. 1 Auburn Tigers would be just what the Orange and White faithful needed.

Not intimidated by Auburn's big ranking or its big running back, Tennessee pounced on Auburn early, establishing a 24–0 halftime lead. Robinson threw for four touchdowns on the day with wide receiver Tim McGee pulling in 163 of Robinson's 259 passing yards. The Volunteers defense held Jackson in check. Jackson went for 80 yards rushing on 17 attempts. The Vols allowed a late touchdown in garbage time for a still-convincing 38–20 victory that catapulted them to No. 16 in the AP poll and prompted whispers of Robinson as a possible Heisman Trophy candidate.

It would be short-lived.

After a 17–10 loss at No. 7 Florida, Tennessee traveled the following week to Legion Field for a showdown with the Crimson Tide. Led by quarterback Mike Shula, running back Bobby Humphrey, and defensive lineman Cornelius Bennett, the Tide were looking for revenge against their biggest out-of-state rival one week after suffering a 19–17 loss at Penn State.

Tennessee proved to be up to the challenge.

Tennessee's offense moved the ball in short chunks, leaning on the running and short check-down passes to backs Charles Wilson and Keith Davis. Leading 13–7 to begin the fourth quarter, Robinson scrambled for a first down on second-and-1. Unfortunately, his knee went one direction and Alabama defenders Cornelius Bennett and Curt Jarvis took his body in another. Robinson was helped off the field and was later diagnosed with a torn ACL, ending his season and collegiate career.

1985–86 Orange Crush Defense

The list of the Orange Crush's accomplishments is long and distinguished: Shutting down Bo Jackson and toppling No. 1 Auburn. Thwarting Mike Shula and Alabama to win in Birmingham despite the loss of quarterback Tony Robinson. Pitching three shutouts and allowing only 27 total points over the final six games of the regular season (in which UT went 5–0–1). Shutting down a Miami offense laden with future NFL superstars.

The makeup of the defense might not be as well-known, at least by the fans who weren't around for the team's great run.

Much like the Denver defense from whom it borrowed the name, the Tennessee defense employed a base 3-4 scheme, with three down linemen and four linebackers. The starting defensive linemen in the 1986 Sugar Bowl were Richard Cooper, Robby Scott, and Mark Hovanic. Cooper, a three-year starter at defensive end, would actually flip sides of the ball in the NFL, where he would maintain a nine-year career as an offensive tackle with the New Orleans Saints and Philadelphia Eagles.

Flanking them were a linebacker quartet of Bryan Kimbro, Dale Jones, Kelly Ziegler, and Darren Miller. Kimbro, a freshman in 1985 from Dickson County High School, outside of Nashville, took over the left outside linebacker position after Tyrone Robinson suffered a toe injury against Wake Forest, and he never relinquished the role, earning Football News freshman All-American honors. Jones, captain of the 1986 team, earned first-team All-SEC honors in 1985 and was a Football News third-team All-America selection. Jones sacked Miami quarterback Vinny Testaverde twice in the Sugar Bowl victory.

The Orange Crush secondary was led by starters Charles Davis, Terry Brown, Chris White, and Tommy Sims. Brown, who tallied 47 tackles in the 1985 season, missed the Sugar Bowl with an injury, so reserve defensive back and special teamer Andre Creamer replaced him. Davis, currently a broadcaster with Fox Sports, had an interception with six tackles against Miami.

Inside linebackers Ziegler and Miller led the Vols with 101 and 94 total tackles, respectively. The Vols compiled 25 sacks, with Hovanic accounting for eight of them, and had an incredible 44 takeaways, 22 by fumble recovery and 22 interceptions. Chris White led the team with nine interceptions.

Tennessee still found a way to edge Alabama for the fourth consecutive year behind backup senior quarterback Daryl Dickey and just enough defense. Vols linebacker Dale Jones, who earlier recovered a key fumble that set up the Vols' third field goal, tipped and intercepted a Shula pass in the fourth quarter with UT leading 16–14, helping squelch a potential Bama go-ahead scoring drive. The Tide had one final chance, as Shula drove his offense just past midfield. However, Van Tiffin's 61-yard field goal fell short as time expired.

The next week, the Vols came up with their second tie of the season, against Georgia Tech in a 6–6 defensive slugfest in Neyland. Had it not been for the strong and sure leg of kicker Carlos Reveiz, Tennessee might not have escaped with a tie. The clutch Reveiz drilled fourth-quarter field goals from 55 and 51 yards to preserve the outcome.

It was also against Georgia Tech that the Orange Crush defense made its presence felt.

Over the final five games of the regular season, opponents scored three touchdowns. (One of them had nothing to do with the defense, as Memphis State returned a blocked punt for a touchdown in the first quarter of a 17–7 loss to the Big Orange in Memphis.) The other two scores came in a 34–14 home win over Ole Miss. Wide receiver J.R. Ambrose pulled in a 19-yard touchdown for the final points of the game. However, Rebels quarterback Chris Osgood completed only 4 of 20 pass attempts for 49 yards with two interceptions. The run defense was equally up to the task for Tennessee. Rebels running back tandem Shawn Sykes and Nathan Wonsley combined for 102 yards rushing on 30 carries, less than three and a half yards per touch.

Tennessee posted three shutouts in that stretch: over Rutgers 40–0, Kentucky 42–0, and Vanderbilt 30–0.

Without its leader on offense in Robinson, Johnny Majors' Orange Crush defense had helped clinch the school's first SEC championship since 1969 and a berth in the Sugar Bowl against the seemingly invincible Miami Hurricanes.

While the talk of the week focused on Miami's national championship hopes, given that most pundits had pegged the Vols to lose to the talented Hurricane squad, Tennessee was quietly preparing for a performance that would shock the college football world.

While most felt the Hurricanes—favored by eight and a half points—had the edge between the sidelines, there was no doubt the Volunteers had the edge outside them. Tennessee fans flooded New Orleans the days leading up to the Sugar Bowl, dominating the French Quarter with their shade of orange.

The neutral-site Superdome turned out to be a home-field advantage for the Big Orange, with an estimated 75 percent of the 77,423-strong crowd dressed in Tennessee Orange and White. The crowd roared and sang "Rocky Top" from beginning to end.

It didn't seem to bother the machine-like Hurricanes, at least not at the start. Known for their outwardly confident coin-toss attitude, Miami was no different on this occasion, refusing to even acknowledge their orange-clad counterparts.

"They were very cocky," said UT running back Jeff Powell. "I don't think they respected Tennessee. All this week, Coach [Jimmy] Johnson was talking about the Orange Bowl and who's going to win, and that they should be national champions because they beat Oklahoma. They should have paid attention to Tennessee."

The Hurricanes took the opening possession and, following a successful fake punt, struck first. Testaverde found Irvin for an 18-yard touchdown and a 7–0 lead. The partisan crowd from Knoxville was quieted, but not for long.

Miami would not score again, and the Volunteers offense was about to get started. Tennessee moved the ball into Miami territory on its ensuing drive, highlighted by a Dickey scramble for a first down and a third-down conversion to All-American wide receiver

Tim McGee, who led the Vols with 50 catches for 947 yards and seven touchdowns on the year.

The ensuing drive found pay dirt for the Big Orange. Dickey led the Vols from the Miami 41-yard line down to the 6. On the first play of the second quarter, Dickey rolled to the right away from pressure and lobbed a pass to a wide-open Jeff Smith in the end zone to even the score.

After defensive end Mark Hovanic forced an Alonzo Highsmith fumble, the Orange Crush defense kept the pressure on the Miami offense. With the addition of eight new blitz packages by defensive coordinator Ken Donahue, the Tennessee defense pinned its ears back and came after Testaverde with relentless pressure. A sack by Jones pushed Miami back 20 yards, flipping the field position and putting the momentum squarely in the Vols' corner.

Powell, a senior transfer from William & Mary, put the Vols ahead for good in the second quarter—with a little help from McGee. After gashing Miami for 21 yards, Powell carried eight yards to the 1 and fumbled into the end zone, where McGee recovered for a 14–7 lead.

The rout continued in the second half. Fullback Sam Henderson bowled his way into the end zone for a 21–7 lead early in the third quarter. On the next series, Powell took the handoff from Dickey, sprinted through a hole off left tackle, and raced untouched down the sideline for a backbreaking 28–7 lead, as the roof enclosing the deafening orange ecstasy in the Superdome was ready to explode.

Miami was done, in this game and for the national title. Tennessee tacked on another score in the fourth quarter for a 35–7 shell-shocking victory. Oklahoma defeated Penn State 25–10 for the national title, but it was Tennessee's dominant performance that had the nation abuzz.

Tennessee outgained Miami 342 yards to 269 yards despite running six less plays. Miami was penalized 15 times for 120 yards and allowed seven sacks of Testaverde by the aggressive Tennessee defense.

It was an unforgettable night for Tennessee football. Most of all, it was the heart, intensity, and effort behind a swarming defense, a senior quarterback getting a last shot and making the most of it, and an underdog knocking off a top dog that made the Sugar Bowl win even sweeter for the Tennessee faithful.

The 1985–86 Sugar Vols will go down as one of the most beloved Tennessee teams in school history.

21 Johnny Majors

John T. Majors is the quintessential definition of a Tennessee legend. As a high school and college football player in the Volunteer State before becoming the Vols' head coach in 1977, Majors dedicated much of his life to the University of Tennessee.

Originally from Lynchburg, Tennessee, Majors was a high school player at Huntland High School in Huntland, Tennessee, where he was an outstanding all-around athlete who held the record as the state's overall scoring leader in football for three consecutive years, in 1950, 1951, and 1952.

As a result, Majors was a hot commodity in the recruiting world. The majority of the Southeastern Conference schools contacted him, as did others from Arkansas, Virginia, the United States Military Academy, and several more from across the country. Majors struggled to choose between the home-state Volunteers and Auburn, when his mother, John Elizabeth Bobo Majors, said, "Well, if there's not any big difference between Tennessee and

Auburn one way or the other, I'd just as soon you stayed in the state." Johnny Majors would play football in Knoxville.

As a player at the University of Tennessee, Majors led the Volunteers to an undefeated, untied regular season, an SEC championship, a No. 2 ranking in the AP poll, and an appearance in the Sugar Bowl in 1956. Majors was selected All–Southeastern Conference twice and voted Player of the Year in the Southeastern Conference twice by the *Nashville Banner*, in both 1955 and 1956. Majors' honors during his years at Tennessee also included a selection as a unanimous All-American, United Press International National Back of the Year (1956), Atlanta Touchdown Club's SEC Back of the Year (1956), and he was the Heisman Trophy runner-up in 1956.

While many fans would think the Vols' biggest Heisman snub came in 1997, the reality is that Majors' phenomenal 1956 season was not enough to win the Heisman over a player on a 2–8 team. Notre Dame's Paul Hornung took home the trophy, despite inferior stats on one of Notre Dame's most forgettable teams. Majors' success out of the single-wing formation was undeniable. He completed more than 60 percent of his passes for 552 yards and five touchdowns, with only three interceptions. He rushed for seven more touchdowns and 549 yards at more than five yards per carry. Majors also handled punting duties, and it was his 70-yard punt from Tennessee's own goal line that sealed a 6–0 victory in No. 3 Tennessee's win at No. 2 Georgia Tech.

Like most great head coaches, Majors cut his teeth as an assistant coach before transitioning into a head coach. He began at Tennessee as a student assistant in 1957 and assistant from 1958 to 1959. He then served as an assistant coach at Mississippi State (1960–63) and then at Arkansas (1964–67) under the great Frank Broyles. As head coach at Iowa State Majors made a coaching name for himself, leading the Cyclones to bowl games in 1971 and 1972.

Majors would serve as a college football miracle worker in his next stop, the University of Pittsburgh, where he would make a name for himself on the national stage. He led Pitt to a Fiesta Bowl appearance in 1973. In 1976, he carried the Panthers to the top of the college football mountain, claiming a national championship as well as much-earned National Coach of the Year honors. He came back home to Knoxville in 1977, where he embarked on a career that would span parts of three decades, with 7 bowl wins, 3 SEC titles, and a 116–62–9 record.

Tennessee played many unforgettable games under Majors' watch. Fans celebrated one of the most satisfying wins in school history on October 16, 1982, as Tennessee snapped an 11-game losing streak to Alabama in Bear Bryant's final cameo in the series. The 1985 win at Alabama, with backup quarterback Daryl Dickey taking the Vols home to victory after Tony Robinson's season-ending injury, started a run that ended with a 35–7 Sugar Bowl championship in the Superdome over No. 2 Miami. Majors was there for two of Tennessee's most unforgettable comebacks—on January 1, 1991, against Virginia in the Sugar Bowl and on November 9, 1991, in the 35–34 Miracle at South Bend.

Majors returned to the University of Pittsburgh as head coach in 1993, and in 1997 he became director of athletics and special assistant to the chancellor at the University of Pittsburgh.

22 "I'm Gonna Stay at the University of Tennessee"

Thousands of ears tuned in to cubicle radios, to office televisions, to any place a broadcast could be picked up. They listened intently, waiting for what they thought would be the end of an era, and a sad but memorable day for the University of Tennessee.

It was time for Peyton Manning, with a year of eligibility remaining at UT, to decide if he was going to take his talents to the NFL. And with him already having accomplished so much, many fans anticipated disappointment at his departure. After all, through three years in college, he had already established himself as the best quarterback in recent UT memory. It was academic that a seven- or eight-figure fortune and heightened fame awaited him as the projected No. 1 pick in the 1997 NFL Draft.

With media members from all over the country in attendance, Manning took the podium in the media room inside Thompson-Boling Arena. He began to talk about his experiences at the University of Tennessee. And then: "I also want to have a great experience in the NFL." It seemed like the perfect transition statement from a classy individual looking to the next phase of his life and football career.

Then came the unthinkable words that sent Knoxville into a frenzy: "I've made up my mind; I don't expect to ever look back. I'm gonna stay at the University of Tennessee."

With those words, Manning further deepened his lore in Tennessee history, and further endeared himself to a fan base that will defend him with their last collective breath. Fans would have done that even if the Vols legend had opted for the NFL and the dollars and exposure that followed. Who could've blamed him? Instead, he chose to stay in Knoxville for his final season. And for that, the fans adored him that much more.

At Thompson-Boling Arena on the UT campus in Knoxville, the standing-room-only crowd erupted into wild cheering. As word spread like wildfire across the area (before the invention of Facebook, Twitter, and the world of social media), the excitement and buzz in the Knoxville community spiked. High schools, colleges, factories, and offices across East Tennessee announced the decision.

On the field, 1997 did not quite live up to the hype that Manning's return promised. The Vols went to Gainesville, where Manning fell to 0–4 in his career in a 33–20 loss that again put the Vols behind the proverbial eight-ball in the race to Atlanta.

Manning had led the Vols to their most successful era in many decades, and arguably the best one ever. From 1995 to

Peyton Manning's last game with the Volunteers could have been the 1997 Citrus Bowl, but he chose to remain at Tennessee for his senior year.

1997, Tennessee finished a whopping 21–3 against the SEC. The only losses—to Florida. And along the way, Manning rewrote the Tennessee record book for quarterbacks.

But that's not what endeared Manning to so many Tennesseans. Heath Shuler had rewritten the record book before Manning, and Andy Kelly had rewritten the record book before Shuler. Both of those quarterbacks guided the Tennessee team through successful eras. Kelly even won twice as many SEC championships as Manning.

What endeared Manning to so many Tennesseans was his style and personality. From the moment he announced his decision to sign with Tennessee coming out of high school, Tennessee fans were excited about Manning. Not that Kelly and Shuler (or any of the quarterbacks who came before Manning) were anything less than classy—in fact, they were two of the classiest quarterbacks in the game when they played—but Manning took it upon himself to take the extra step to represent his university with class and character.

But what really endeared Manning to fans was the fact that he stayed. He was the opposite of what Tennessee fans were used to seeing. When Heath Shuler had a chance to earn his payday, he entered the NFL Draft. Chuck Webb, Jamal Lewis, and Peerless Price all did the same. With Manning the almost-certain No. 1 pick, it seemed logical that Archie's son would choose the money over another season of training, school, and college play. Yet he stayed.

Many Tennessee fans will argue that Manning is the best quarterback ever to play college football. That's debatable, with Tim Tebow's great accomplishments in the 2000s to consider.

But with his work ethic and attitude, Manning was destined for greatness. And greatness is what he has accomplished in the NFL. At this point, as Manning enters the twilight of his playing career, it's hard to argue that he isn't one of the top 10 best quarterbacks ever to play the game of football. Given the records he's shattered, his status as a Super Bowl champion, and the class with which he played the game, he will be remembered fondly in the league once his playing days are done.

But you won't find many people who will love him more than those in East Tennessee. In the minds of Tennessee faithful, that was sealed in early 1997. With 20 words, Peyton Manning became a Volunteers legend: "I've made up my mind; I don't expect to ever look back. I'm gonna stay at the University of Tennessee."

23 John Ward

"It's time."

On June 3, 1998, that's basically all that Vol Network broadcasting legend John Ward said at a press conference about his decision to step down following the 1998 football and 1999 basketball seasons.

For those who had listened to him call games for years, one could only chuckle and realize how fitting it was that his curt delivery touched thousands of Tennessee hearts in the deepest ways.

For more than three decades, John Ward delivered football Saturday action from the Neyland Stadium press box with wit, charisma, and a unique style. Ward moved over from stadium PA duties to play-by-play radio broadcasts with his colleague and color man Bill Anderson, and the two combined on calls to make Tennessee football a can't-miss listening opportunity. Before SEC games were broadcast on Jefferson-Pilot Sports, Ward and Anderson served as the eyes and ears for Tennessee fans who couldn't be in Neyland Stadium on game day and had no other way to take in the game.

What those fans heard was a combination of humor, wisecracks, excited outcries, and often painfully slow pauses before announcing the result of a tense play in a crucial situation. While the suspense may have made the occasional fan momentarily irked and impatient, the overall broadcast, win or lose, was almost as enjoyable as the game itself.

John Ward *was* Tennessee football for more than 30 years. Like running through the *T*, checkerboard end zones, Smokey, and "Rocky Top," Ward is a local treasure for Tennessee football. Ward is originally from Knoxville, and graduated from Knoxville High School. He studied political science at UT and went to law school.

Fortunately for Tennessee fans, Ward ended up spending his hours calling games instead of billing for them in a law firm. And it was his trademark calls that made him so popular over the years with fans, such that many would turn down the television broadcast volume and turn on Ward and Anderson on the Vol Network radio broadcast.

- "No, no, no, no, *no*! They *pounded* him!"
- "This is Martin. Looking. Pass downfield is up for grabs. Who's there to grab it? It's Peerless Price. Did he grab it? He grabbed it! Where did he grab it? In the end zone! Give. Him. Six! *Touchdown!* Peerless Price."
- "I do not know, nor care. Touchdown Big Orange!"
- "So the score Tennessee 20, Florida 17. The Gators with a field goal made will tie the game. Snap, the kick is in the air, and the kick this time is... No sirree. No sirree. Final score: Tennessee 20, Florida 17. Pandemonium reigns!"
- "This is [Travis] Henry stutter-stepping—oh, yes, yes, yes. What a move! Touchdown Tennessee!"
- "Wherever you listen, ladies and gentlemen, at Neyland Stadium in Knoxville, Tennessee, *it's football time in Tennessee!*"

While Ward became the Voice of the Vols from the 1960s to the 1990s, his father brought the game to life in a very, very different way.

"My father was a great communicator...much better than I ever was," Ward told WBIR.com.

Ward's father was principal of the Tennessee School for the Deaf. As a child, Ward's earliest memories of Big Orange football were watching his dad interpret the game's radio broadcasts for deaf students.

"Like somebody ran to the 18-yard line, he would draw that," said Ward to WBIR.com.

"And it set up just a rhythm of communication to people who could not hear, but could experience the excitement of Tennessee football."

Besides Ward's broadcasting duties for football and basketball games, he also helped set up the football coach's television show that ran for decades. In his final show with Phillip Fulmer and athletic director Doug Dickey (with whom Ward started the show in 1965) before the 1998 SEC Championship Game, Fulmer recognized the "special chemistry [Ward] brings to Tennessee football."

"Thank you for being our eyes and our ears," said Coach Fulmer.

Attend Your Local Alumni Chapter Gatherings

The opportunities to join up with the Volunteer Nation are endless. If you have left the friendly confines of East Tennessee and no longer can make it to Knoxville with ease, there is inevitably an orange-and-white-hued sanctuary nearby where you can enjoy

Tennessee football and commune with other Vols fans on fall Saturdays.

If you've moved on to the sunny, warm beaches of the Florida Gulf Coast, you can still enjoy the white, sandy beaches, from Pass-a-Grille up through Clearwater, and have plenty of time to make it to Boston's in the heart of suburban Tampa for a 3:30 kickoff against Georgia. Each Saturday like clockwork, chapter president Melissa Vass will make sure you are apprised of the time of each gathering, the opponent (in case you somehow forgot or had a crazy week at work), and any themes for the event.

And if you're new to an area and don't have anybody to watch a game with (and let's face it, watching a game alone is a less appealing prospect for most people), what's better than sitting down to a table with orange-and-white shakers on it, a cold beverage in hand, and meeting some new faces to watch Tennessee play? It's a great chance to meet people living in your area, some of whom may be originally from Kingsport, Clarksville, or your Tennessee hometown. And it's people with whom you share a common bond—you bleed Orange and White, either as a graduate or a lifelong fan.

Of course, those passing through are welcome as well. For example, if you're on vacation in the San Francisco Bay Area, heading out to enjoy the fine wines in Sonoma Valley, make a point to spend your Saturday in San Francisco at Blackthorn Irish Bar, which will be set up with Vols decor, "Rocky Top" playing on the stereo, and drink specials of—what else?—Jack Daniel's and choice beer. Chapter president May Lee and many others will be there to welcome you to the Bay Area and give you tips on where to go and what to do while there.

These are just a couple of the chapters that dot the map, from Boston to San Diego. With more than 356,000 members of the UT Alumni Association, chances are you will run into somebody cheering on the Vols on Saturday wherever you happen to be.

No. 2 Tennessee 6, No. 3 Georgia Tech 0, 11/10/56

The partisan Yellow Jackets crowd roared like a jet engine. The final seconds on the Grant Stadium scoreboard melted away like an ice cube on a Peachtree Street sidewalk in mid-August. Tennessee was cradling a narrow lead. Pinned deep in their own territory, running back Johnny Majors trotted behind the line, setting up for the next play. Except this time, he wasn't ready to take the handoff or pitch and sprint through a hole. This time, he would catch the snap and put toe to leather. In a season when Majors would finish with the most rushing attempts and passing yards on a 10–1 Tennessee team, it was his right foot that helped decide one of the most important games in the immediate post-Neyland era.

On a day that featured a chess match between a former Tennessee great and a current one, youth won out in a battle that shaped the national championship picture in 1956 and produced one of the most hard-fought and memorable games in Tennessee history.

Tennessee, ranked second in the country, traveled to Atlanta to take on the third-ranked Georgia Tech Yellow Jackets, led by head coach and former Tennessee great Bobby Dodd. Tech featured a stable of talented backs in Ken Owen, Dickie Mattison, Paul Rotenberry, Jimmy Thompson, and George Volkert. All five players rushed for more than 200 yards on the season, with Owen leading the way with 497 yards.

But it was a defense that was battle tested and helped carry Tech to a key 9–7 early season road win at No. 3 SMU and set the tone in a 40–0 blowout of No. 15 Tulane. The Ramblin' Wreck defense was firing on all cylinders. Aside from 14–12 loss to Auburn on October 15, 1955, Tech hadn't dropped a game, nor allowed an opponent to reach a double-digit score from 1955 through the first half of the 1956 season.

Meanwhile, Bowden Wyatt's Volunteers were 6–0, coming off a 24–0 win over Alabama in the Third Saturday in October, followed by consecutive poundings of ACC foes Maryland and North Carolina at Shields-Watkins field. The Vols were entering the highly touted matchup against Tech on a 78–7 margin of victory in their last three games.

But points were at the utmost premium on November 10, 1956, in Atlanta. Tennessee found them first. On the arm of Majors, Tennessee made one grand push to pay dirt. Majors connected with Buddy Cruze for a 16-yard completion down to the Tech 46-yard line. On the next play, Majors hit Cruze again, and he dashed and rumbled all the way down to the Tech 1-yard line. As he would for much of the season, bruising fullback Tommy Bronson fought his way over the right side of the line into the end zone for a 6–0 UT lead in the third quarter. Bob Smithers' extra-point attempt sailed wide.

The UT defense bent but didn't break. Tech managed to push its way into Tennessee territory, down to the 21-yard line, but UT defender Jim Smelcher recovered a fumble by Tech fullback Ken Owen to end the drive. Tennessee also ended two drives with interceptions.

But it was the punting game and field position that swung the game in Tennessee's favor…and ultimately made the difference in the final moments of the game. Tennessee averaged around 39 yards per punt, but it was Majors' 70-yard boot from the shadow of his own end zone that, for all intents and purposes, iced the game for the Big Orange. The defense held, and Tennessee escaped Atlanta with a monumental win that bumped them up to No. 1 in the major polls.

Tennessee ultimately fell to No. 2 following a 27–7 win over No. 19 Mississippi at Shields-Watkins Field, in large part after

Oklahoma dismantled Missouri 67–14 on the same day and swayed the voters back to the side of the Crimson and Cream. Oklahoma ended its regular season with a 53–0 thrashing of Oklahoma State, cementing its place as No. 1 in the final AP and UPI polls. Tennessee finished No. 1 in the Sagarin Ratings, although the school doesn't claim a national championship.

26 The 1951 Cotton Bowl

Tennessee entered the 1951 Cotton Bowl with a 10–1 record, having lost only to Mississippi State, 7–0, in the second game of the 1950 season.

On the flight home, General Neyland addressed the team with a short but stern speech.

"On the plane coming back, I recall General Neyland saying, 'Well, we've lost. You don't have a friend in the world outside of what's on this airplane,'" said former Tennessee offensive tackle Bill Pearman.

"Then he says, 'We'll get 'em. But look around you. There are your friends.'"

Neyland's words hit home. The Vols pulled together and finished the 1950 season by outscoring their opponents 315–57, beating then–Top 15 opponents Duke and Kentucky in the process. Tennessee also edged Alabama 14–9 at Shields-Watkins Field.

Despite the nine-game winning streak to end the year, Tennessee finished No. 4 in the major polls, one spot behind the University of Texas. Appropriately, Tennessee found itself accepting an invitation to play the Longhorns in what amounted to their backyard—the Cotton Bowl. It was a battle of Top 5 teams that yielded one of the greatest bowl wins in program history.

In preparation for the Cotton Bowl, Neyland felt his team was getting too uptight.

"The boys were getting keyed up a little too much and Neyland wanted to relax them, but there was nothing to do," said former assistant coach Hugh Faust. "Finally, he said to me, 'Will you open those windows up there?' Just outside the windows was the concourse that went into the stadium, and they had bales of cotton out there, and our [band] members [were] up there playing different songs."

Faust continued, "Just as we pulled the window back and the sound came in, there was the song that all of us in Tennessee were

General Neyland's Biggest Celebration

It was no secret that the general was a reserved man on the sideline. Wild celebrations and outpourings of emotion were not part of General Neyland's makeup.

However, after coming from behind to edge Texas in the Cotton Bowl, the general let out emotion rarely seen by his players in the locker room after the game.

"He wanted to beat Vanderbilt awful bad," said Bob Davis, a center under General Neyland from 1949 to 1951. "He wanted to beat Alabama awful bad. He always was able to get you up for the big ballgame, or [at least] most of the time."

Davis went on, "I remember an incident that happened after we had played Texas and come back in 1951 in the Cotton Bowl, and came back and scored twice in the fourth quarter and beaten them 20–14. Everybody was whooping it up in the [locker] room. It had been raining the entire game, and everybody was muddy and happy. Everybody was hollering for the general. He was whooping around the dressing room, patting everybody on the back. He jumped up on a table that was over there, and he yelled 'I love every one of you!' I think that might have been the happiest I ever saw the general, in my time [at Tennessee], about winning a football game."

fond of: 'Tennessee Waltz.' It was gorgeous music. And, of course, Neyland heard it. He put his hand behind his ear and the boys were all watching him. The music floated in, and Neyland started dancing in front of the boys, back and forth. He did a waltz, the Tennessee Waltz. They boys looked at him in amazement there, and they burst out into great laughter. And it relaxed them. They all talked for a minute or two about it. Then they closed the window and went into their preliminary talks about the game. It was relaxation. It was perfect."

Not one for making brash pregame statements, General Neyland, moved by the music, made a prediction. "When this game is over," Neyland said, "they'll be playing 'Tennessee Waltz.'"

Tennessee scored first, on a five-yard touchdown pass from Herky Payne to John Gruble, set up by a 75-yard run by tailback Hank Lauricella, in which he reversed his field three times and slowed only to allow his blockers to catch up. The run, which set up Tennessee on the 5-yard line, remains one of the most revered runs in UT history, and prompted NBC's Bill Stern to note how Lauricella was able to "stop on a dime and give change." Lauricella went on to finish as a Heisman runner-up in 1951.

Texas trailed 14–7 at the half in a rain-soaked Cotton Bowl stadium. The sloppy back-and-forth play continued through a scoreless third quarter.

Then Tennessee made its charge in the fourth quarter.

The Vols pulled within one at 14–13 on five-yard run by fullback Andy Kozar, who carried 20 times for 94 yards. He proved to be the battering ram that finished off the Longhorns, scoring again in the fourth quarter from one yard out, giving UT the final margin of 20–14 with only 3:11 remaining in the game.

The team was one of the most talented in Tennessee history, led by College Football Hall of Fame members Lauricella, Doug Atkins, and John Michels.

It was the second 11-win season in Tennessee football history to that time, the first having come in 1938 when the Vols finished 11–0. The Vols finished as national champions under the Dunkel rating system, while remaining third and fourth in the UPI and AP polls, respectively, both of which were taken at the end of the regular season.

Riding the upset season-ending victory from a year prior, Tennessee entered the 1951 season ranked No. 1 and ran off 10 wins in a row to claim the consensus national championship.

27 Gene McEver Puts Tennessee Football on the Map in 1928

General Neyland was not really one to sell his team short. But with fellow service member and friend Wallace Wade on the opposite sideline as the coach of Alabama, Neyland and his band of relatively unproven Volunteers entered Denny Field in Tuscaloosa as decided underdogs to the Crimson Tide.

The schools hadn't played since 1914 in Knoxville, a 17–7 Tennessee victory. Before that, Alabama had won seven straight, and most thought Wade's Tide team was in prime position to start a new streak against its border foe. After all, Alabama had won back-to-back national championships in 1925 and 1926 with two Rose Bowl appearances.

General Neyland even approached Coach Wade and asked that if Alabama had a sizeable lead in the final two quarters, that the quarters be shortened to hurry up the game. Wade agreed.

The psychological warfare worked from the start. Taking the opening kickoff on the 2-yard line, Vols halfback Gene McEver raced forward through his blockers, juked the kicker, and raced, untouched, 98 yards for the opening touchdown, stunning the Crimson Tide supporters in attendance.

Coach Wade learned quickly that Neyland wasn't lucky like other coaches, but rather had his players prepared as well as they could be, for any situation.

"One of the things I used to misjudge, I used to think [Neyland] was lucky," said Wade. "But I began to realize after time that luck turns sometimes, but it never did with him because he trained his players to take advantage of opportunities."

And cash in on a huge opportunity the Volunteers did. Tennessee never trailed in the matchup and held on for a stunning 15–13 upset victory, with no shortened quarters. The Third Saturday in October rivalry would help Tennessee make a name for itself as a nationally recognized program—one that was certainly on the rise under General Neyland.

"I suppose the Alabama game in 1928 stands out the most," said McEver. "Not that that was the greatest game, but that was the game that put Tennessee on the map. Naturally, that would make it stand out. But a lot of games were better games than that one, I thought."

Tailback Buddy Hackman, one half of the Hack and Mac backfield with Gene McEver at the time, agreed that the win over Alabama was a shot in the arm for the Tennessee program.

"Especially when you win a big one, that gives you the confidence that you always need. I expect that was our stepping stone," said Hackman.

28 Peyton Manning Leads Big Orange Comeback for 1997 SEC Championship

"It's a cold, glittering night in Atlanta, and [for] the first time in the SEC title game, there are no Gators in the Georgia Dome," said legendary announcer Keith Jackson. "The moat has been forged by Plainsmen and by Volunteers."

Indeed, since the inception of the SEC Championship Game in 1992, the combatants had remained the same. The Florida Gators and Alabama Crimson Tide were mainstays in Birmingham, then Atlanta, with only Arkansas making a quick cameo in a 1995 dismantling at the hands of the national runner-up Gators.

Finally, in Peyton Manning's final season, the Tennessee Volunteers were good enough to play for the SEC championship. As was Auburn. Fans flocked to Atlanta, hoping to see their team claim its first SEC championship in the new divisional format.

Florida's road woes at LSU and in Jacksonville against Georgia opened the door for third-ranked Tennessee to make it to Atlanta. Facing Vanderbilt in the season finale, the Vols just managed to squeeze through said entryway, edging the Commodores 17–10 in Manning's final game in Neyland Stadium. Meanwhile Terry Bowden's Tigers rallied to win at No. 7 Georgia and edge Alabama in the Iron Bowl to finish 6–2 with LSU. Auburn earned the trip to Atlanta over the Bayou Bengals by virtue of a 31–28 win in Baton Rouge.

Tennessee fans hoped to see Manning deliver something that they hadn't had in a long time, a conference title with a chance to compete for a national title, as well as to see him claim the Heisman Trophy, something no Volunteers backer had ever seen.

Their hopes spiked only three minutes into the game. After a long run by Jamal Lewis pushed the UT offense into Auburn territory, Manning launched a deep ball to Peerless Price, who pulled it in at the goal line for a 40-yard touchdown and a 7–0 advantage.

Then Auburn swung the game in its favor. Following a completion from quarterback Dameyune Craig to Hicks Poor for 69 yards, Auburn settled for a Jaret Holmes field goal. But at the end of the first quarter, Brad Ware recovered a Marcus Nash fumble and ran it in from 24 yards out for a 10–7 Auburn lead.

By the time fans had settled into their seats following a quick jaunt up to the bathroom in between the first and second quarter, the scoreboard read: AUBURN 20, TENNESSEE 7. Craig found Tyrone Goodson in man coverage on a deep post, and he hauled it in as he fell across the goal line.

Despite the overwhelming momentum shift in favor of the Tigers, Tennessee chipped in a 27-yard field goal and somehow survived two punt-return fumbles recovered by the Tigers to go into the locker room down 20–10 at the half.

Tennessee made a push early in the second half to get back into the game. Facing third-and-goal from the Auburn 5-yard line, Manning rolled left and fired a dart across his body to a tightly covered Jermaine Copeland. Auburn 20, Tennessee 17.

And when it seemed the Vols were poised to take back the game from Auburn, the Tigers defense made a play to keep UT at bay. On the ninth play of Tennessee's 48-yard late-third-quarter drive, Manning's pass was bobbled up in the air by a wide-open Copeland and intercepted by Jason Bray. Shaun Bryson ran Bray down after a 77-yard return, and Craig's ensuing pass to Fred Beasley pushed the lead back to 10. Auburn 27, Tennessee 17.

But Manning-to-Price was not done for the day. Auburn came on a blitz, leaving Price in one-on-one coverage. Manning hit Price in stride, and Price slipped his defender and ran untouched the rest of the way for a 46-yard touchdown. As mistake-prone as Tennessee had been for much of the day, they weren't quite done.

Jamal Lewis goes over the pile against Alabama. (RVR Photos-USA TODAY Sports)

Jeff Hall's extra point was blocked by Charles Dorsey and scooped up and returned for two points by Quinton Reese. Auburn 29, Tennessee 23.

In the longest play of the day, Manning found senior Marcus Nash to give the Vols their first lead since 7–0, and the game's winning points. With less than 12 minutes to play, Manning went to Nash, being given a generous cushion, on a quick hitch route. Nash turned up the field, beat his defender to the sideline, and raced 78 yards untouched to the end zone. Hall's extra point was good.

Tennessee 30, Auburn 29. Despite two interceptions—one of which was bobbled by the intended receiver—Manning had carried a turnover-prone Tennessee team to a slim lead. And Tennessee's defense, led by future NFL first-round draft pick Leonard Little, finished the job. On Auburn's last drive, facing third-and-23, Little sacked Craig, forcing a punt that allowed Tennessee to bleed the clock to all zeros.

Fulmer and Manning had finally reached the top of the SEC mountain together. There would be no jabs from Spurrier that day. Tennessee was the cream of the SEC for the first time since 1990.

Manning by the Numbers

Manning rewrote the Tennessee record book by the time he left school. Some of his records and most impressive accomplishments:

Manning's Highest Single-Game Passing Totals

1. 1997 vs. Kentucky—523 passing yards
2. 1996 vs. Florida—492 passing yards
3. 1996 vs. Northwestern—408 passing yards
4. 1997 vs. Southern Miss—399 passing yards
5. 1995 vs. Arkansas—384 passing yards
6. 1997 SEC Championship Game vs. Auburn—373 passing yards

UT Single-Season Passing Records

- Yards (1997)—3,819
- Yards per game (1997)—318
- Lowest interception percentage (minimum 200 attempts)—1.05%

UT Career Passing School Records

- Completions—863
- Attempts—1,381
- Completion percentage (minimum 400 attempts)—62.5%
- Yards—11,201
- Touchdown passes—89

Record as starting quarterback: 39–5

Combined record versus historical rivals Alabama, Vanderbilt, Kentucky, and Georgia: 15–1

The Vols went on to lose to Nebraska in the Orange Bowl, and despite completing 25 of 43 passes for 373 yards and four touchdowns in Atlanta, Manning would lose out to Woodson for the Heisman Trophy. However, the 1997 SEC Championship Game was a microcosm of the talent and heart on the Tennessee roster, which would raise the national championship trophy one year later.

29 Little Man, Big Heart

Those who watched him play knew that he was anything but his nickname. James "Little Man" Stewart ran with the physicality and the style of a back much bigger than his frame would indicate. The intensity and effort made Stewart, Tennessee's former all-time leading rusher and future NFL mainstay, a fan favorite in the early 1990s.

And where did the nickname Little Man come from? Stewart's own father.

"My dad gave it to me when I was five years old," Stewart told VolQuest.com. "I was bouncing on his knee and he started calling me 'little man' and it took off from there. I never really got called James by anyone. My family was calling me 'little man' and then my teachers started doing it and it really just took off. Everyone knew me as 'little man' and it even followed me to Jacksonville."

Stewart committed to Tennessee out of Morristown West High School, being in an apparent position to eventually succeed the bruising Chuck Webb. It was a short-lived plan, as Webb announced his eligibility for the NFL Draft. What was left behind was a competition between Stewart and fellow freshman Aaron Hayden for the starting tailback role in 1991.

The Vols' season opener against Louisville, who had finished 1990 on an eight-game winning streak, provided a stage for Stewart and Hayden to show off their abilities. Both did, each scoring a touchdown and rushing for more than 100 yards in UT's 28–11 win.

Stewart pulled away early in the season and won the battle with Hayden, finishing the season with a team-high 190 carries for 939 yards and eight touchdowns. But Stewart's opportunities became limited in the coming seasons, when he and Hayden were joined by Charlie Garner, creating a three-headed monster at the tailback spot that was led by Garner. The touches became few and far between from 1992 to 1993, with Stewart gaining just 923 yards on 171 carries in that span, although he scored an incredible 16 touchdowns. In 1993, although Garner rushed for more than twice the yardage of Stewart on nearly twice the carries, Stewart scored more touchdowns (nine, to Garner's eight).

In 1994 Garner announced he would leave for the NFL Draft, in which he was selected by the Philadelphia Eagles with the 42nd overall pick. At last, the spotlight was back on Little Man, and Stewart took full advantage, putting his stamp on the Tennessee record books and using the season as his personal audition for a future NFL career.

His peak performance came in a 41–23 win at Georgia. In a game featuring future Super Bowl MVP Terrell Davis, it was Stewart who stole the show. Little Man tore up the Bulldogs defense for 211 yards and four touchdowns, the latter matching the UT modern-era record for touchdowns and points in a game.

Leading 27–15, Stewart put the game away with one of the signature plays of his career—and one of the most memorable runs for UT fans. Taking a pitch, Stewart twisted out of the tackle of a linebacker in the backfield, slipped around an attempted tackle from safety, and sprinted up the sideline for a 71-yard game-sealing touchdown.

"He was absolutely stopped," exclaimed Vols radio announcer John Ward. "But no. He goes 71 yards. Was hit at the 5. Breaks the tackle. Carries her home, and Tennessee's James Stewart has had a monumental run to give Tennessee a 33–15 advantage."

Stewart finished that season with 170 carries for 1,028 yards with 11 touchdowns. In the season finale against Vanderbilt, a 65–0 pasting of the Commodores in which he rushed for 121 yards, Stewart passed Johnnie Jones to become Tennessee's all-time leading rusher, with 2,890 yards.

He now ranks third all-time behind Travis Henry and Arian Foster. Stewart also accounted for an astonishing 40 total touchdowns (35 rushing, 4 receiving, 1 passing), only 4 short of Gene McEver's total of 44 from 1928 to 1931.

A first-round draft pick of the expansion Jacksonville Jaguars in 1995, Stewart played five seasons as a running back in Jacksonville before playing out the remaining four years of his career with the Detroit Lions. He finished with 5,841 rushing yards on 1,478 carries (4.0 yards-per-carry average) and 48 touchdowns. His best season was in 2000, when he rushed for 1,184 yards with Detroit. He still holds the Jaguars' single-game record with five touchdowns against the Philadelphia Eagles in 1997.

For Tennessee fans, it was Stewart's physical running style, his penchant for making key plays, and the patience he showed in his sophomore and junior seasons that won them over and made him one of the most popular and productive players in Tennessee history.

30 Learn the Words to "Down the Field"

The words to "Rocky Top" will always be known, cherished, and sung across the Volunteer Nation countless times over on fall Saturdays. After touchdowns, turnovers, and big plays, the Pride of the Southland Marching Band will boom the strains of Tennessee's most popular (unofficial) school fight song.

As for the *official* fight song, "Down the Field"—which is played both when Tennessee runs through the *T* at Neyland Stadium and immediately after a touchdown is scored—leaves many fans smiling and clapping without adding the words that were initially written for the song. The fact is: many fans don't even know there are words to "Down the Field," much less what the words actually are.

"Down the Field" is eerily similar, if not basically identical, to the fight songs of the Yale Bulldogs and Nevada Wolf Pack. (A Google or YouTube search and comparison between the three schools' fight songs will confirm that.) What can't be denied is that the song is a strong part of Tennessee's traditions, and sadly it's one that most schools don't know. As fans recite, "On a hallowed hill in Tennessee, like beacon shining bright" or sing "Wish that I was on old Rocky Top, down in the Tennessee hills," it's the other song that leaves fans voiceless in the stands and in front of television screens across the country.

So for those who don't know the words, take some time to find the song, either on UT's official website or on YouTube, and practice singing the following lyrics with each turn in the song:

Here's to Old Tennessee
Never we'll sever
We pledge our loyalty

Forever and ever,
Backing our football team,
Faltering never,
Cheer and fight with all of your might,
For Tennessee.

The words don't always seem to fit up with the tune coming from the band (i.e., the "we pledge our loyalty, forever and ever" takes some practice to work into the music in this part of the song). Yet when you stop and sing the words—which are surprisingly simple but inspiring—enough times, the song comes together well.

The next time Tennessee takes the field at home or carries the ball into the checkerboard, sing the words as loudly as you can, whether jammed into Section GG in Neyland Stadium or in front of a big-screen with a group of friends. Chances are you will surprise your fellow fans, and might earn a slap on the back or two.

The 1997 Heisman Trophy Race

Charles Woodson and Peyton Manning will both be enshrined in the hallowed walls of the Pro Football Hall of Fame in Canton, Ohio, likely five years after they hang up the cleats. Manning is a clear first-ballot Hall of Famer, having garnered 14 Pro Bowl selections and five league MVP awards. He shattered vaunted NFL passing records such as career touchdowns, single-season passing yards, and single-season touchdowns. Woodson likely will be a first-ballot inductee as well, having earned eight Pro Bowl selections and seven All-Pro honors. He became the first player in NFL history to record at least 60 interceptions and 20 sacks. Both men have helped their teams achieve the highest success in their sport: a

Super Bowl victory. Manning won the MVP award in the Colts' 29–17 win over the Chicago Bears in Super Bowl XLI. Woodson, despite leaving Super Bowl XLV with a collarbone injury, helped anchor a Green Bay defense that allowed only 17 points per game in the NFC playoffs en route to a Super Bowl title.

So much has happened for both men since the 1997 college football season. But that doesn't mean Tennessee fans have completely forgotten about Woodson claiming the Heisman Trophy over Manning.

Manning is one of those generational players whom people talk about for decades—the Joe Montanas, Ronnie Lotts, Billy Simses, Tim Tebows, Bo Jacksons of the college football pantheon. At the time, no one questioned his accomplishments, and the numbers were there—his 3,819 yards passing and 36 touchdown passes still rank No. 1 in school history through the end of the 2014 season. The dominating performances were there too, as fans saw against Kentucky (a then–school record 523 passing yards and five touchdowns) and Southern Miss (399 yards passing, four touchdowns).

That vaunted "Heisman moment" never came when it needed to: against Florida. To the contrary, it may have been Manning's undoing, even if those who credit Woodson's own performance as his reason for winning won't admit it. In a pivotal point of the game (and a seminal moment in Manning's season), Manning was intercepted by Tony George, which George returned 89 yards for a 14–0 lead from which Tennessee never recovered.

Conversely, that "Heisman moment" came for Michigan's Woodson in a 23–7 win over in-state rival Michigan State, which also happened to be a clash of two teams ranked in the Top 15 of the polls. With 2:12 left in the third quarter, leading Michigan State 13–7, Woodson had his moment. He leaped high in the air near the sideline and snared a Bill Burke pass with one hand for a highlight-reel interception.

Manning vs. Woodson: Remembering the Vitriolic Aftermath

The venom rained down from the throng of Tennessee fans surrounding the *College GameDay* set inside Sun Devil Stadium following the Vols' 23–16 win over Florida State to seal the national championship. Some stayed to celebrate the win in all sincerity and try to get a little bit of face time on TV. Others stayed to get in a pot shot or two at the ESPN villains they felt had cost their favorite player the Heisman Trophy just a season earlier. In reality, Chris Fowler can't be held solely responsible for Woodson's win, even if those still screaming about his "trailer park frenzy" comment would like to pin the loss on him. (ESPN's Fowler, who officiated the Heisman ceremony, became persona non grata in Tennessee after making this colorful description of Vols fans on a radio broadcast.) However, it remains open for debate whether ESPN's coverage of a "race" between Manning and Woodson added fuel to Woodson's chances while diminishing Manning's.

In James Andrew Miller's 784-page book, *Those Guys Have All the Fun: Inside the World of ESPN*, Fowler wants to make it very clear, for the record, that he is not responsible for costing Manning the Heisman Trophy. Even though he believed Woodson would get it, he asserts that he voted for Manning himself. "See? It was nothing personal, you guys," he insists.

As the hype machine for Woodson geared up, so did Manning's late-season production. In the regular season's final five games, Manning put together three of the best statistical performances in Tennessee history. In a 44–20 dismantling of No. 25 Southern Miss on homecoming, Manning completed 35 of 53 passes for 399 yards and four touchdowns with no interceptions.

"If there's a better player than Peyton Manning in this country, I'd like to see him," Vols coach Phillip Fulmer told the media after the game. "He's a phenomenal player. He took over the football game."

Another record fell in Lexington, Kentucky, when Manning became the first Tennessee quarterback to surpass 500 yards passing in a single game (523) in UT's 59–31 romp in Commonwealth Stadium. The win moved the Vols up to No. 3 in the AP poll, behind Woodson's Michigan squad and Nebraska.

Finally, with a long-sought-after SEC championship on the line, Manning rallied the Vols from a 20–7 first-half deficit to a thrilling 30–29 victory in the Georgia Dome. Manning threw for 374 yards, including the winning touchdown.

But was it enough? Woodson had gained popular media attention for leading Michigan to an undefeated regular season and a berth in the Rose Bowl against Washington State. Manning's Vols had an outside chance at the national title if they could beat second-ranked Nebraska in the Orange Bowl.

Still, no purely defensive player had ever won the award, and Manning's season, aside from the loss to Florida, was a record-setting monster of a year. For a position—quarterback—that was a traditional favorite to win the award, history, production, and a sense (among some fans) of Archie Manning's career accomplishments would give him the nod for the trophy.

The votes came in. At the Downtown Athletic Club, Manning, Woodson, Ryan Leaf, and Randy Moss waited for the winner to be announced of the two-man race everybody knew was at its conclusion.

It was Woodson. Manning politely clapped, as outrage slammed the Knoxville-area radio airwaves like Jamal Lewis running over a would-be tackler.

Woodson compiled 481 first-place votes and 1,815 total votes to Manning's 281 and 1,543.

It has been nearly 20 years since the 1997 Heisman Trophy vote, the anger and hostility has subsided in East Tennessee, but the confusion and disapproval of the results remain with almost any fan who followed the events.

32 Vols 41, Bama 14, 10/14/95

Joey Kent sprinted away from the Alabama defense. For bruised and battered Tennessee fans, it marked the beginning of the Volunteers sprinting away from the Crimson Tide for years to come.

Finally, Tennessee would conquer the longtime nemesis Alabama, against whom a streak of futility had reached nine. As quickly as the raucous crowd had turned Legion Field into a deafening, intimidating monster, it would take only one play for Tennessee to silence it.

Peyton Manning dropped back to pass on the game's first play and found his favorite target, Joey Kent—who had pulled in 13 passes the previous week in a win against Arkansas. Kent had run a simple streak past the Alabama linebackers sitting in zone coverage, and split the safeties to the end zone.

It would be the signature play of the game, and one of the most unforgettable plays in the collegiate careers of both Manning and Kent.

Peyton's father, Archie, put up 540 yards of offense against Alabama, with 104 yards rushing and three touchdowns, in a 33–32 Ole Miss victory in 1969. The not-so-fleet-footed Peyton, who completed 20 of 29 passes for 301 yards and three touchdowns on the day, ironically helped put away the Tide with his legs, fooling the entire Alabama defense on play action and trotting into the corner of the end zone for a 21–0 lead.

Alabama made a push to get back in the game late in the first half after Freddie Kitchens, who took over for an ineffective Brian Burgdorf, found receiver Chad Key for a three-yard touchdown to draw within 21–7 midway through the second quarter.

But Peyton Manning made sure Tennessee would stay in cruise control for the second half. After pushing UT into Alabama territory by finding Joey Kent on a fade route, Manning punctuated a dominant first half by hitting Marcus Nash for a 30-yard touchdown with seconds remaining in the half, for a 28–7 lead.

"These seniors are guys I really wanted to win for," said Manning after the game. "They've been here four or five years. Haven't beaten Bama. This is special for them. It means a lot for this program... It's a big day in Tennessee."

And for Tennessee fans, it couldn't have come any sooner. Having endured a painful nine-season winless streak at the hands of the Tide, Tennessee's 41–14 victory was a belated blessing from the football gods. The victory, which remains Tennessee's largest margin of victory in the series through the 2014 season, proved a spark for both the 1995 season and for the short-term future of the Tennessee-Alabama rivalry.

The Volunteers put the second-half collapse of the Florida game in the rearview mirror, outscoring the Tide 13–7 in the second half. It would be an emphatic punch in a stretch of nine straight wins to end the season on the way to a No. 2 final ranking in the coaches poll and No. 3 in the AP poll after stopping Heisman Trophy winner Eddie George and Ohio State 20–14 in the Citrus Bowl. Alabama reeled off four straight wins before losing a controversial 31–27 contest at Auburn when wide receiver Curtis Brown was ruled to have been out of bounds on a potential game-winning touchdown catch.

It was also the reversal of fortunes for Tennessee against its historical rival to the south. The win marked a change in paths for both programs. Tennessee, which had not won a conference title since 1990 and had yet to play in an SEC Championship Game, was in the early stages of a 45–5 run from 1995 to 1998 that would end with the program's first national title in nearly half a century. Alabama had been placed in probation by the NCAA less than a month before the season started and was forced to miss a bowl, forfeit 11 games from 1993, and give up 25 scholarships over the next three years.

The resulting turn in the series was all roses for the Orange and White faithful. Tennessee went on to win seven straight in the series. Alabama eventually snapped the streak in Knoxville in 2002, 34–14, but it lasted through three Alabama coaches: Gene Stallings, who retired following the 1996 season, Mike DuBose, and Dennis Franchione.

Phillip Fulmer finished with a record of 10–5–1 against the Crimson Tide (not counting the 1993 game forfeited by Alabama as part of their 1995 probation sanctions), making him the most successful coach in UT history against its chief rival.

Vols Stop Bo Jackson, No. 1 Auburn in 1985

He slashed. He streaked. He trucked over hapless defenders. It was a case of an unstoppable force without an apparent immovable object capable of stopping him.

The Orange Crush proved to be a more-than-capable impediment.

Bo Jackson entered the third week of the season as a truly deserving Heisman front-runner, having torched SW Louisiana and Southern Miss to the tune of 247.5 yards per game on the ground. The hype machine trumpeting Jackson didn't hurt Auburn's placement in the polls, as the Tigers came into Knoxville as the nation's top team in the AP poll.

Tennessee had just managed to hold No. 10 UCLA at bay in their season opener in Knoxville in a 26–26 tie. The result was heartbreaking for UT fans, as UCLA scored on a 25-yard touchdown pass with less than a minute remaining in the game and got the two-point conversion to deny Tennessee a statement win to start the year.

The statement would come two weeks later in the Vols' following game.

Jackson and Auburn entered Neyland Stadium having won three straight against UT, including a 37–14 trip to Knoxville in 1983. Jackson, a senior in 1985, who had helped carry Auburn in the streak, would ultimately become a nonfactor in the Tigers' worst performance of the regular season.

Tennessee jumped out to a 7–0 first-quarter lead, capping off a 76-yard drive with a Charles Wilson four-yard touchdown on a toss sweep.

Little did anyone know then, but the rout was on in Knoxville. Terry Brown recovered a fumble by quarterback Jeff Burger, and quarterback Tony Robinson immediately made the Tigers pay. Dropping back, he found a streaking Tim McGee for a 37-yard touchdown and a 14–0 lead.

Tennessee extended its lead to 24–0 by halftime.

Meanwhile, Jackson and the Auburn ground game was no help to the shell-shocked Tigers. Jackson had averaged roughly 10 yards per carry in his first two games. He gained about half that for the game, going for 80 yards on 17 carries. Against Tennessee, the Tigers had just 88 yards rushing at the half.

Meanwhile, it was Robinson who emerged as the star player of the game. He threw for 259 yards and four touchdown passes of 37, 4, 10, and 30 yards. He threw two fourth-quarter touchdowns to keep UT comfortably in front, one on a lob to wide receiver Joey Clinkscales from 10 yards out and the other to wide receiver Eric Swanson, who outfought the Auburn defender for the football in the end zone, from 30 yards.

If Robinson needed a co-MVP for the game, it was a fast and physical Tennessee defense. Not to mention opportunistic, as it recovered two pitched fumbles by Auburn starting quarterback Jeff Burger that turned into Tennessee touchdowns.

Bo Jackson's 1985 Heisman Run by the Numbers

Bo Jackson's 1985 run to the Heisman Trophy was impressive in all respects. As the workhorse back for the Tigers, Jackson racked up six games with at least 150 yards rushing and an incredible 17 touchdowns. His numbers from his Heisman Trophy–winning campaign:

Jackson's 1985 Game-by-Game Statistics

	ATT	YDS	AVG	TD	LG	1ST Down Runs	More Than 10 YDS	TD Runs by Yards
Southwestern Louisiana	23	290	12.6	4	76	10	6	7, 47, 76, 12
Southern Mississippi	30	205	6.8	2	34	9	4	2, 2
At Tennessee	17	80	4.7	0	17	2	3	—
Ole Miss	38	240	6.3	2	25	16	9	3, 3
Florida State	30	176	5.9	2	53	9	3	54, 35
At Georgia Tech	32	242	7.6	1	76	9	5	76
Mississippi State	28	169	6.0	2	40	9	5	22, 4
Florida	16	48	3.0	0	12	3	1	—
East Carolina	14	73	5.2	0	16	6	2	—
At Georgia	19	121	6.4	2	67	4	2	67, 6
Alabama (Birmingham)	31	142	4.6	2	20	4	2	7, 1
1985 Totals	**278**	**1,786**	**6.4**	**17**	**76**	**81**	**42**	—

The Vols' Orange Crush defense was one of three teams to keep Jackson to less than 100 yards rushing. Although Jackson left in the third quarter against Tennessee with the game well in hand for the Volunteers, he left in the second quarter with an injury against then–No. 2 Florida, when Jackson was held to his lowest total on the season. Still recovering from injury the following week, his presence was not needed in the 35–10 whipping of East Carolina.

As such, while Tennessee shut down talk of an Auburn national championship season early, it only put a dent in the Bo Jackson hype train that would eventually claim the trophy. But the UT defense still left one heck of a mark in Jackson's season numbers.

"We played awfully, awfully hard and awfully, awfully well," Coach Majors said. "This was one of our biggest wins at UT."

As well as Tennessee played in its head coach's eyes, the 1985 Volunteers saved their best for last, literally. Following its only loss of the season, 17–10 at Florida, Tennessee lost Robinson to a knee injury for the season in its 16–14 win at Alabama. Daryl Dickey spelled him, and helped Tennessee to a 6–0–1 record down the stretch in claiming the SEC championship. In a game that remains unforgettable in Tennessee lore, the Vols went on to dominate No. 2 Miami 35–7 in the Superdome, Tennessee's largest margin of victory over a No. 2 team in the country in program history. The win likely denied Miami its would-be second national championship, as then–No. 1 Penn State fell to Oklahoma in the Orange Bowl 25–10.

It would also be a memorable run for the Orange Crush defense. Starting with a 6–6 tie against Georgia Tech and ending with the Sugar Bowl rout, Tennessee allowed only 34 points in its last seven games of the season, pitching three shutouts in the process. Not since Tennessee's string of defensive superiority from 1938 to 1940 had Tennessee fans enjoyed such a run of defensive success in one season.

The Sugar Vols finished 9–1–2 and No. 4 in both major polls.

Despite only gaining 80 yards and leaving the game in the third quarter with a knee injury, Jackson went on to a tremendous season. He finished the year with 1,786 yards rushing, 17 rushing touchdowns, and one Heisman Trophy.

Auburn went on to drop three of its last five games to finish 8–4 and out of the polls.

Chuck Webb Shreds Rebels for School-Record 294 Rushing Yards

Many very talented running backs have come through the University of Tennessee. Hank Lauricella, Gene McEver, Johnny Majors, and George Cafego earned All-America honors in the single-wing attack of Tennessee's earlier days. James "Little Man" Stewart, Aaron Hayden, and Jay Graham helped carry the load in the 1990s, turning Tennessee into a national power. Jamal Lewis, Travis Stephens, and Travis Henry helped Tennessee get to the top of the mountain in 1998; Lewis would become an NFL stalwart for many years, while Henry and Stephens shattered school records. Recently, Arian Foster has become one of the most dangerous runners in the NFL in the past few seasons.

But it was on November 18, 1989, that Volunteers fans were wowed with the most incredible statistical performance by a Tennessee running back in school history.

Tennessee was sitting at 7–1, ranked No. 9 in the AP poll, and still in the hunt for the SEC championship. Having lost 47–30 at Alabama, Tennessee had to be perfect in their final three games to have a chance.

Ole Miss was first up, and the Rebels, at 6–3, were the toughest test remaining for head coach Johnny Majors' squad. And it was the Rebels who put the Vols behind the eight-ball early, after tailback Randy Baldwin scored on a pitch to give Ole Miss a 7–0 lead after one quarter. Tennessee answered quickly, as quarterback Andy Kelly hit wide receiver Alvin Harper for a seven-yard touchdown.

Tennessee pushed ahead; the historical day of redshirt freshman running back Chuck Webb was just getting started. After an interception by wide receiver and occasional two-way star Carl

Pickens, Webb bulled his way over center from five yards for a 14–7 Tennessee lead.

Ole Miss answered with a nine-play, 70-yard drive to bring the score even at 14. But Majors called on Webb on the next drive, and he ripped off a 22-yard gain that set up a 49-yard field goal, giving UT a 17–14 halftime lead.

Whatever momentum UT had summoned up was squelched before the fans returned to their seats from the halftime bathroom break. Rebels wide receiver Tyrone Ashley returned the second-half kickoff 90 yards for a 21–17 lead. These would be the last points of the day for the Rebels, but not for Webb and the Vols.

Webb responded on the next drive with a 19-yard run through a host of would-be Ole Miss tacklers before getting forced out of bounds, drawing a loud roar from the Tennessee fans. Although trailing, Webb's sledgehammer running style was energizing the Neyland Stadium crowd—and wearing down a Rebels defense that

UT's Best Single-Game Rushing Performances

Chuck Webb's record-setting performance against Ole Miss isn't the only performance by the Cobb-Webb combination on UT's all-time single-game rushing list. Along with Webb and Reggie Cobb are a who's who of great running backs in recent Tennessee history:

Rank	Player	Yards	Year	Opponent
1.	Chuck Webb	294 yards	1989	Ole Miss
2.	Chuck Webb	250 yards	1989	Arkansas (Cotton Bowl)
T-3.	Tony Thompson	248 yards	1990	Mississippi State
T-3.	Johnnie Jones	248 yards	1983	Vanderbilt
5.	Tony Thompson	236 yards	1990	Vanderbilt
6.	Johnnie Jones	234 yards	1983	Rutgers
7.	Jamal Lewis	232 yards	1997	Georgia
8.	Travis Stephens	226 yards	2001	Florida
9.	Reggie Cobb	225 yards	1989	Auburn
10.	Arian Foster	223 yards	2005	Vanderbilt

had little answer for the more physical back. Tennessee managed a field goal—Ole Miss 21, Tennessee 20; end of third quarter.

As Tennessee pushed into field-goal range on its first drive of the fourth quarter, Webb broke through the line, finally going down 26 yards later at the Rebels 12-yard line after fighting through the contact of six Ole Miss defenders. On fourth-and-1 from the 2-yard line, Majors called Webb's No. 44 again, and Webb followed his blockers and dove just across the goal line for a 26–21 lead.

"Touchdown, Chuck Webb!" exclaimed radio play-by-play announcer John Ward. "That Tennessee offensive line just bowed out Ole Miss defensively! [Charles] McRae, [Tom] Myslinski, [John] Fisher, [Eric] Still, [Antone] Davis, and here comes Webb! Riding right behind All-American Eric Still and big 306-pound Antone Davis, crashing, not only for the first, but also for the touch[down]!"

After Tennessee's defense held Ole Miss, Webb delivered another long run late that helped put away a Tennessee victory—and his place in Tennessee and SEC record books. From his own 32-yard line, Webb broke free up the right side and was pushed out of bounds by the last defender back for the Rebels for a 38-yard gain. Running back Greg Amsler finished the 11-play, 82-yard drive by diving in from three yards out, for the final margin of Tennessee 33, Ole Miss 21. Webb accounted for 62 of those 82 yards on only five carries.

Webb had literally carried Tennessee to a victory it needed to keep its hopes of an SEC title alive. On 35 carries, Webb finished with 294 yards rushing and two touchdowns. The 294-yard performance eclipsed Johnnie Jones' 248 yards against Vanderbilt in 1983 and still stands as the school's single-game record for rushing yards through the 2014 season.

Although a 10–1 finish was not enough to give Tennessee the outright SEC title (UT finished in a three-way tie with Auburn and

Alabama at 6–1 in the conference, with the Tide getting the nod to play in the Sugar Bowl), Tennessee still had the opportunity to do something special on New Year's Day—topple a Top 10–ranked opponent and finish with 11 wins. No. 10 Arkansas entered the game at 10–1, its only loss to Southwest Conference rival Texas.

In a 31–27 win, Webb rushed for 250 yards on only 26 carries, ripping off a 78-yard touchdown run that put the Vols ahead 31–13 in the third quarter. Webb's 1,236 rushing yards were the second-most in the SEC in 1989, and his 250-yard performance was the second-most in the bowl game's history.

Join the Vol Navy on a Game-Day Flotilla to Neyland Stadium

Game days in Knoxville are just a little bit different from the rest of the SEC.

Ask 14 graduates of the 14 member institutions of the SEC, and you might get 14 different responses as to whose tailgates and pregame traditions are the best.

While that debate is too subjective to fairly decide, it's more than fair to say the Vol Navy cruising the Tennessee River to Neyland Stadium is a sight rarely seen in the college football world, and not elsewhere in the conference.

Fans sport short-sleeved orange-and-white apparel and enjoy cocktails and sharing stories of good tailgating and football times while they enjoy the slow cruise into Knoxville, past the beautiful park grounds of the Sequoyah Hills neighborhood, past sorority row and the agricultural campus, and just past Neyland Stadium on the north bank of the river. Vol Navy flags—blending the Power T into a boat anchor in the foreground of an orange background—fly

The tailgating flotilla assembles for game day.

proudly from the armada forging its way up the river. Luxury yachts cruise slowly with dozens of guests taking in the view from the aft, waving to the passing driver of a center-console fishing boat hauling a small group of friends with cozie-covered drinks in hand. Houseboats, sailboats, cruisers, and luxury yachts of all shapes and sizes convene at the docks near the popular Calhoun's on the River restaurant.

But getting there is literally half the fun of traveling by boat with the Vol Navy to Neyland Stadium. Once docked, those grills that haven't already been fired up and smoking on the backs of the yachts and cruisers are lit. The mouth-watering aroma of racks of ribs, steaks, and burgers wafting from nearby grills combined with the faint smell of whiskey being generously poured into plastic cups means that the tailgating aspect is being taken almost as seriously as the game itself.

The congeniality of the fans in the Vol Navy is unmistakable. While some folks may be satisfied with the trip and de-board their boat for the delicious cuisine at either Calhoun's or a nearby tailgate, many others will remain on the boat until kickoff.

And it might be worth your while, if you walk along the docks, just to admire the fleet of ships that have gathered to have a great time. If you can hear between the strains of "Rocky Top" and country music blaring from the stereos aboard the boats, you might hear a voice calling to you, inviting you aboard. It's no secret that the Vol Navy waygoers are generally as hospitable as any bunch in the SEC. You may step onto a yacht, meet some new friends, try some incredible Southern recipes, and be handed an ice-cold beer or maybe even a flaming Dr. Pepper on one particular vessel.

And while there may be an opportunity to be invited aboard a boat and take in the scenery of the river, part of campus, Neyland Stadium, and downtown Knoxville all in one fell swoop with some new friends on their boat, you can also enjoy the trip on the river with the right group of your choice *and at the right price.*

If you're not fortunate enough to own a boat or have a friend in the local Knoxville area that does who can enjoy the journey with you, you can still find a way to get on the water and enjoy the festivities. USCG-certified captains offer a scenic game-day cruise, for a price, on the river.

There may be other ways to take in a ballgame in an SEC venue. RV trips are certainly fun and are a staple near any stadium across the country. But the Vol Navy's combination of food, beverage, scenery, and good company makes the trip by boat (or yacht, houseboat, cruiser, etc.) arguably the most entertaining way to travel to a game and tailgate in the country.

36 Vols Snap 11-Game Skid to Bama in '82

Fans flooded the field and orange-clad players picked up Johnny Majors like he was a sack of potatoes. With smiles as wide as the Tennessee River, they carried him to midfield, where the sour face of the legendary Bear Bryant sat beneath his customary houndstooth hat, waiting for the customary postgame handshake.

This time, things were finally different for the entire Tennessee program. It had been many years since Bryant's postgame greeting was humbling for Alabama's legendary coach. Since 1971 Alabama had left the field victorious, starting with a 32–15 win at Legion Field in 1971. What followed was an 11-year stretch of dominance by the Crimson Tide, and complete misery for Tennessee.

Eleven straight wins seemed almost certain to stretch to twelve in Knoxville on October 16, 1982. A week prior, the No. 4 Crimson Tide had just annihilated No. 3 Penn State 42–21 at Legion Field. The Tide picked off Nittany Lions quarterback Todd Blackledge four times and blocked a Penn State punt.

Meanwhile, Tennessee entered the game in Knoxville at 2–2–1, coming off a 24–24 tie at No. 18 LSU, where Fuad Reveiz's 53-yard field-goal attempt had fallen short with two seconds remaining. Quarterback Alan Cockrell threw for 213 yards but couldn't quite move Tennessee deep enough to get in Reveiz's range on its final three plays from the LSU 45-yard line.

So that seemingly average Tennessee team would face off against an SEC juggernaut that had lost only four SEC contests in the previous 11 seasons.

But, as with any upset-minded team, Tennessee needed to make an impact play early—and they did on defense. Alabama quarterback Walter Lewis' pitch was deflected backward and recovered by Tennessee at the Tide 11-yard line. Tennessee's offense couldn't punch it in against a Bama defense that was allowing only 14 points per game coming in. A Reveiz chip-shot field goal gave Tennessee a 3–0 lead.

Tennessee's offense compounded its inability to score in the red zone by turning it over. Cockrell's pass near his own end zone was picked off by Jeremiah Castille. Bama led 7–3 after the first quarter when Joe Carter beat the UT defense to the pylon on second-and-goal.

The Tide continued to roll in the second quarter, as Lewis, after faking the option, stepped back and found split end Jesse Bendross for a 35-yard touchdown strike, making it 14–3 Crimson Tide.

In one play, Tennessee swung the momentum of the game back in its favor. Wide receiver Willie Gault sprinted past the Alabama secondary, and Cockrell found him in stride as Gault strolled into the checkerboard. Alabama 14, Tennessee 10. The 95,000-plus in attendance were on their feet and turning Shields-Watkins Field into a virtual jet engine.

There was belief. This could be the year. Tennessee's Vince Clark intercepted Lewis and returned it to the Bama 20-yard line, but all the Vols could manage was another Reveiz field goal to pull within one, at 14–13. Alabama pushed the lead to 21–13 by halftime after Castille picked off his second pass of the game and Lewis hit Joey Jones for a 38-yard score in the waning moments of the half.

Tennessee slowly forged ahead in the second half. Down 21–16, Tennessee's defense forced a second turnover, as Lee Jenkins recovered a fumble on the option by Ken Coley. Two plays later, Cockrell fired a 39-yard touchdown pass to Mike Miller, who made the reception on the Alabama 13. Cockrell then connected with Kenny Jones on a two-point conversion, and the Vols grabbed a lead they would not relinquish, 24–21.

But the final minutes were, as Majors called it after the game, an "eternity" as Tennessee tried to protect a lead after UT running back Chuck Coleman pushed the margin to 35–21 with 7:21 remaining after a 34-yard touchdown run. Alabama quickly drove 79 yards to score on Linnie Patrick's 14-yard sweep.

Tennessee 35, Alabama 28, with 5:04 left to play. Tennessee fans, elated with what seemed like a kill shot from Coleman on his touchdown run, nervously looked on as Alabama got the ball back with a last chance to tie. Taking over at their own 35 with less than two minutes remaining, Lewis guided the Tide down the field, in large part to a huge catch and run by Bendross inside the UT 20-yard line.

With seconds remaining, Lewis lofted a pass into the end zone that was tipped by Jenkins. Defensive end Mike Terry cradled the ball as he went to the ground. The back judge waved his arm over his head: touchback.

The crowd and sideline were in a frenzy, as teammates hugged each other on the field and the student section began to flood down the steps toward the field. Tennessee had snapped a painful 11-game losing streak to its biggest rival, beaten the No. 2 team in the land, and defeated legendary coach Bear Bryant in his last game on the sideline for the Third Saturday in October.

Without question, although Tennessee went on to finish 6–5–1 in 1982, the win over Alabama still ranks as high as any single victory in UT history in many Tennessee fans' minds.

37 Learn, Remember, and Appreciate the Retired Numbers

Their heroics left Vols fans speechless throughout the decades. Very few times in a program do players come through that have the impact of the eight former Volunteers whose jersey numbers have been retired.

For the legends of the Tennessee Volunteers program, the best of the best make their way onto the upper deck facing inside Neyland Stadium, their names and numbers to remain forever associated with each other exclusively. Tennessee's No. 16 will always be the number of Peyton Manning. Johnny Majors will always be No. 45. Reggie White (No. 92), Doug Atkins (No. 91), Bill Nowling (No. 32), Rudy Klarer (No. 49), Willis Tucker (No. 61), and Clyde Fuson (No. 62) are forever intertwined with the numbers they wore with pride, spilled blood on, and represented the University of Tennessee in.

The club is as exclusive as it is diverse. Johnny Majors was the heart and soul of Tennessee football in his 16 seasons as head coach of the Tennessee Volunteers. Like Phillip Fulmer, he devoted his life, both as a player and coach, to the school he loved.

Also among the group are three of the most dominant players in the history of the NFL at their respective positions. Manning, entering his 18th pro season, has shattered some of the most hallowed passing records in the NFL: career passing touchdowns (530), single-season touchdown passes (55), and most passing yards in a season (5,477). Through the 2014 season, he has thrown for 69,691 yards.

Reggie White was one of the most fearsome defensive linemen in the history of the NFL. Virtually unblockable by a single player, White recorded 198 sacks in his career, second-most in NFL history. He was selected for an incredible 13 Pro Bowl appearances and received All-Pro honors 12 times. He was also named to both the NFL 1980s and 1990s All-Decade Teams. White tragically passed away in December 2004 from complications related to sarcoidosis. His number was posthumously retired by the University of Tennessee in 2005, and he received posthumous induction into the Pro Football Hall of Fame in 2006.

A fellow Pro Football Hall of Fame inductee, Doug Atkins helped revolutionize the defensive end position during a 17-year NFL career in Cleveland, Chicago, and New Orleans. At 6'8" and with the wingspan of a stork, Atkins was a terror to opposing quarterbacks. In addition to using his massive frame and long arms to get to opposing quarterbacks, Atkins, an SEC champion high-jumper, even leaped over opponents to get into the backfield. Atkins was selected to eight Pro Bowls and was named All-Pro four times. He was ranked as the ninth-best pass rusher by the NFL Network.

These men were some of the greatest Volunteers at the professional football level. However, the remaining four men represented the Volunteers spirit in the most personal and grandest of ways: by making the ultimate sacrifice in the name of the United States of America.

Nowling, Klarer, Tucker, and Fuson all lost their lives on the battlefield in World War II. Far too often, words such as *battle*, *warrior*, *life*, *death*, and *war* are used by fans and sports media without a second thought as to their true meaning. These four Volunteers represent the truest meanings of these words. They are Volunteers in every sense of the word and unquestionably deserving of their places of honor amongst the greatest Volunteers in the history of the University of Tennessee.

The 1991 Miracle in South Bend

As the snap was put down, the clock ticked down to all zeros, and the kick sailed off the toe of Irish kicker Rob Leonard, as both Tennessee and Notre Dame fans held their breaths.

For the first hour and a half of Tennessee's game against Notre Dame, it was the Irish who dominated play, turning three Tennessee turnovers into a 21–0 first-quarter lead, including a 79-yard interception return for a touchdown by Irish cornerback Tom Carter. The lead swelled to 31–7, and Notre Dame looked to tack on a Craig Hentrich field goal at the end of the first half.

The game switched decisively on the foot of Hentrich, who was injured on the play.

Tennessee senior linebacker Darryl Hardy broke through the line and blocked Hentrich's attempt. Out of the ensuing scrum, UT's Floyd Miley emerged with the ball and cut across the field ahead of the pursuing Irish defenders and into the end zone to cut the halftime margin to a more manageable 17 points.

The score sparked the Tennessee offense in the second half, prompting them to improve on their first-half performance, which had produced only a 21-yard score from quarterback Andy Kelly to wide receiver Cory Fleming. In the third quarter Kelly led the Vols on an 11-play drive, culminated by a three-yard touchdown pass to tight end Von Reeves to pull the Vols to within 10. Notre Dame pushed its lead to 34–21 with two minutes left in the third quarter on a 20-yard field goal by a gimpy Hentrich, who left the game after the kick.

The fourth quarter belonged to Tennessee.

Facing a fourth-and-9 at the Irish 29-yard line, Kelly dropped back and found wide receiver Cory Fleming near the sideline for

Andy Kelly set a new school record for career passing yards against Notre Dame in 1991, with 5,885. It was later broken by Peyton Manning. (RVR Photos-USA TODAY Sports)

a first-and-goal. The completion gave Kelly 5,885 career passing yards, moving him ahead of Jeff Francis as the school's new leader in career passing yardage.

But it was Aaron Hayden who emerged as the hero of the day, or at least the fourth quarter. On the ensuing play, Hayden took a toss sweep pitch, stepped through a would-be tackler, and trotted into the end zone.

Notre Dame 34, Tennessee 28, with 9:03 remaining.

Notre Dame's Rick Mirer inexplicably was called on to move the sticks with his arm, rather than work down the clock behind the bruising running of Jerome Bettis and Tony Brooks. Three passes led to three incompletions—and a near pick-six by defensive end Chuck Smith—and the Irish were forced to punt. The Irish converted just one of eight third downs and were held to 162 yards of total offense in the second half.

It seemed temporarily as if Notre Dame may have dodged a bullet thanks to their defense. Facing a fourth-and-9 again, the Irish secondary denied Carl Pickens in the end zone to give the ball back to their offense.

But the Tennessee defense rose to the occasion again. Mirer's third-down pass was intercepted by safety Dale Carter, a future four-time Pro Bowler in the NFL, and the Volunteer offense had one last chance to pull off a miracle with just more than five minutes remaining.

It didn't take Kelly and Hayden nearly that long to put the Vols ahead for good.

Moving down to the 26-yard line, Kelly waited for the right side of the Notre Dame defensive line and the blitzing safety to push past Hayden, who caught the screen pass with two blockers ahead of him and joyously trotted into the end zone with not a Notre Dame defender in sight.

Tennessee 35, Notre Dame 34, with 4:03 left.

The Irish weren't finished yet. Starting at their own 25-yard line, the Irish drove all the way to the Tennessee 9-yard line, including a Mirer scramble that put the Irish inside the 15. Confident waves to the television camera transformed into nervous swaying by some on the Volunteers sideline, as Leonard—who had kicked only an extra point in his ND career—trotted onto the field with four seconds remaining for a 26-yard, game-winning field goal.

As the ball thumped off Leonard's foot, there was a second thump—off Tennessee's Jeremy Lincoln, one of several Tennessee defenders who broke through the line and had a chance to block it. In fact, the thump was off Lincoln's rump.

"I thank my mom for giving me a big butt," Lincoln said after the game. "When I go home she says, 'You've got a big butt.' I tell her, 'I can't help it. You gave it to me.'… I put it to good use this time."

Lincoln's rear end deflected the ball wide to the right, setting off a wild celebration on the field and in the pockets of orange inside Notre Dame Stadium.

For Tennessee, it was another terrific late-season story, as the Vols improved their record to 28–1 for games played in November and December since 1985. The Vols finished the 1991 regular season at 9–2 and earned a trip to play Penn State in the Fiesta Bowl, where the Vols fell 42–17.

39 Wilhoit Shanks, Then Boots UT to Victory vs. Florida in 2004

The Volunteers faithful fell back in their seats, shocked by what they had just seen.

Trailing 28–21, Tennessee quarterback Erik Ainge fired to an open Jayson Swain for 13 yards, and Swain leaned forward and broke the plane. Neyland Stadium erupted, as the Pride of the Southland Marching Band blared "Down the Field" while the field goal team trotted onto the field for the game-tying extra point.

High fives turned to palms on faces as kicker James Wilhoit's boot sailed wide right, setting off a wild celebration among the pockets of Gators fans. Wilhoit trotted off the Neyland Stadium field; after drilling 47 extra points in a row, he had flubbed arguably the most important extra point the Vols had attempted in so many games.

With only 3:25 remaining, the chances of getting the ball back and finding the decisive points seemed slim for the Big Orange.

Tennessee, who had been playing a glorified game of chase with coach Ron Zook's Gators all evening, seemed like they would come up painfully short after battling back all game. The Vols pulled even at 21 with 13 minutes left in the game after wide receiver Bret Smith outleaped the Gators defender for the ball and trotted into the end zone.

Then the Gators pushed back in front by seven with only 7:43 left to play. Chris Leak lobbed a deep ball that safety Brandon Johnson jumped for too early. The ball sailed over his fingertips and into the waiting arms of Gators receiver Chad Jackson, who trotted in for an 81-yard touchdown.

And with three minutes and change left, all the Gators needed to do was bleed out the rest of the clock. After Ciatrick Fason carried the Gators for a first down, it seemed the team would be able to wind the clock down inside half a minute before punting. However, a late flag was thrown following a third-down stuff of Fason by the Tennessee defense. Wide receiver Dallas Baker, the recipient of a slap by cornerback Jonathan Wade, smacked Wade back in the face. The official caught Baker in the act and penalized the tall wideout for a personal foul.

Suddenly, the clock stopped at 55 seconds, and the Gators had to punt from their own 23-yard line. The Vols had a final chance.

Wilhoit, who was shown receiving pats of confidence from his teammates on the sideline during Florida's last drive, would get a shot at redemption...if his team could get him into position.

It didn't take long to get in Wilhoit's range. On second down, Ainge spun out of a would-be sack and threw a dart to wide receiver Chris Hannon for a gain of 21 yards, putting the Vols at the Florida 40-yard line. Ainge and his linemen sprinted to the line of scrimmage as Coach Fulmer and his staff vehemently implored the quarterback to spike the ball.

Ball spiked. First-and-10 at the 40-yard line with 29 seconds remaining.

Wilhoit, who was 17 of 25 on field goal attempts with a long of 51 yards, trotted up and down the sideline, waiting for his chance. Another first down would put the Vols in range.

A seven-yard catch and a spike left the Vols in a second-and-3 position at the 33 with 13 seconds left. And with a major decision to make.

Coach Fulmer called for the field goal unit. Wilhoit trotted to his position on the field, and players offered encouragement as he lined up for his chance at football's rare gift of redemption.

The snap was good. The hold was down, laces spun out. Wilhoit's foot met the ball, which cleared the line and sailed high in the air.

James Wilhoit: from goat to hero.

If anyone wanted to be the first to know the result of the kick, all he or she had to do was look at the joyous Wilhoit. Several seconds before the kick split the uprights and cleared the crossbar with room to spare, the redeemed Wilhoit was sprinting from the elated Tennessee sideline back onto the field, dodging would-be gleeful tacklers like Barry Sanders in his prime.

Tennessee 30, Florida 28. After an excessive celebration penalty, Wilhoit was able to boom the kickoff well inside the 10-yard line. After a couple laterals, the clock read zero, and Tennessee had won at home against Florida for the first time since the goal posts fell in 1998.

The improbable comeback win was meaningful for Tennessee, as it allowed the Vols to take early control of the SEC East. Featuring two true freshmen quarterbacks in Brent Schaeffer and Erik Ainge, it appeared unlikely that Tennessee would claim the East and a berth in the SEC Championship Game. But that's just what they went on to do. Disappointing home losses to Auburn and Notre Dame knocked Tennessee out of the national championship picture, but Tennessee earned its second trip to Atlanta in four years. It would be the fourth of Phillip Fulmer's five SEC East titles.

Seeking to avenge a 34–10 dismantling by Auburn in Neyland Stadium on October 2, Tennessee nevertheless dropped the SEC Championship Game as well, 38–28. Auburn completed a perfect 13–0 season with a win over Virginia Tech in the Sugar Bowl.

It was also the third win over the Gators in the past four seasons, something Tennessee had not done in many years.

And for Wilhoit, it was a metamorphosis from goat to hero in just more than three minutes of game time.

40 Condredge Holloway: The Artful Dodger

He cut right, ducked his head, and pirouetted away from another would-be tackler. Finding an alley up the middle, he burst ahead and slipped through a pair of Georgia Tech defenders reaching for his legs.

Fingertips met the thigh pads of the elusive 5'11" ball carrier. And as quickly as they touched the white pads, they slipped off into nothingness, as if they had passed through the legs of a ghost.

Condredge Holloway would not be denied, not on this play.

Rumor had it that all 11 defenders achieved varying levels of contact with the Tennessee quarterback on the play. That became verifiable, thanks to modern technology, and the myth was dispelled—10 different players touched him but poor No. 42 missed him...twice. Still, the run helped earn Condredge Holloway the moniker the Artful Dodger from legendary Tennessee announcer John Ward.

The last of the players to try to stop Holloway, defensive back Randy Rhino, was trucked and flattened. He could only look straight up to see Holloway run past him and gleefully jump across the goal line. Rhino was inducted into the College Football Hall of Fame and remains the Yellow Jackets' only three-time first-team All-American in program history.

That's what Holloway could do: make the best look foolish. There was no question that his athleticism helped define the unique skill set Holloway possessed as a quarterback.

Holloway was the first African American quarterback in the history of the Southeastern Conference. Because Holloway hailed from Huntsville, Alabama, it was believed that either Auburn or Alabama would win his services. The problem was that neither program believed in Holloway at the game's most visible and difficult position—quarterback. Bear Bryant even admitted to Holloway that Alabama was not ready for a black quarterback.

Holloway at least appreciated the honesty.

Meanwhile, Tennessee coach Bill Battle had no such reluctance to play a black quarterback. Three years earlier, a black wide receiver named Lester McClain had entered the program and been accepted by fans.

Holloway credited McClain for making the transition to Tennessee easier.

"He took a lot of stuff for all of us, and he made it possible," Holloway said. "We're all on somebody else's shoulders."

On the field, Holloway was smart with the football and knew where to go with it. He ended his career with the best interceptions-to-attempts ratio in Tennessee history, throwing just 12 interceptions in 407 collegiate attempts.

But even when Holloway threw an interception, he could make up for it. In one case, he made up for it on the very same play. In one of the most unforgettable plays in UT history—and in Holloway's first game in 1972—Holloway dropped back and threw an out pattern, which was picked off by Georgia Tech's Mike McKenzie going the other direction; McKenzie streaked down the sideline in what seemed to be a certain touchdown.

Long before Alabama's George Teague ran down Miami's Lamar Thomas in the 1993 Sugar Bowl and stripped the ball away, there was Holloway's less-heralded rundown of McKenzie. Holloway caught up with McKenzie around the 20-yard line and brought him down.

"If I don't catch him and we don't win that game, I get labeled as an athlete trying to play quarterback and can't win," said Holloway in the 2011 ESPN documentary *The Color Orange*.

Tennessee would ultimately roll to victory 34–3 in Atlanta.

Craig T. Smith

But there were reports that Holloway had hurt his shoulder on the play, that it was separated or maybe even broken. It seemed the worst could be in store for Tennessee fans, as they would have to finish their season-opening matchup with No. 12 UCLA without

George Wallace's and Bear Bryant's Recruitment of Condredge Holloway

Former UT quarterback Dewey Warren had to see it to believe it. When watching Condredge Holloway account for all 49 points of his team's scoring in a Friday night victory during the high school season, Warren was blown away, and he gave his full endorsement to UT assistant Frank Trail, who was recruiting Holloway.

But not to be outdone, both Alabama and Auburn (not to mention Major League Baseball's Montreal Expos) were hot on Holloway's trail, trying to keep the exceptionally gifted athlete in-state.

In fact, Holloway was contacted by one of the least likely individuals an African American athlete in the late 1960s could ever expect to hear from—former Alabama governor George Wallace, the man who staged the infamous "Stand in the Schoolhouse Door" in a stubborn and pigheaded attempt to prevent segregation at the University of Alabama.

"The phone rings, it's George Wallace on the phone, wanting him to go to Alabama," Trail told AL.com. "He came back and he said, 'Coach, can you believe that? George Wallace, the guy that stood on the steps of the university and said there'll never be a black guy [to] enter the University of Alabama, calls me.'"

From a more traditional sense, Alabama head coach Bear Bryant recruited Holloway as well, but his cautionary words came across to Holloway as sincere and diplomatic tact in his recruiting. He told Holloway straight up that the University of Alabama was not ready for a black quarterback.

"I respect Bear Bryant for telling me the truth," Holloway said. "I'm not mad. Why would I be mad? A 17-year-old kid from Huntsville, Alabama, he told me the truth. So what do I have to be mad about?"

Tennessee fans certainly aren't mad at Alabama's failed recruiting attempts at landing Holloway. Otherwise the Artful Dodger may have starred in crimson rather than orange.

their star quarterback. Holloway had gone to the hospital and had his shoulder X-rayed.

After a gain of a yard or two, the Neyland Stadium crowd erupted as if the Big Orange had just found the end zone. Holloway was jogging across the end zone and back to the Tennessee sideline. He made it back just in time for the fourth quarter in a 10–10 tie. And it couldn't have been any sooner for UT fans.

With three minutes left and the Vols threatening at the UCLA 12-yard line, Holloway took the snap and rolled right, looking to throw. Seeing nothing open, he cut around the right end and toward the goal line, where two UCLA defenders were waiting. Holloway leaped high, plowed into both defenders, and landed on his shoulder in the end zone. The game went on to end in a 17–17 tie.

Holloway's heroics and groundbreaking legacy extend beyond the football field. Besides being the first black quarterback at Tennessee, Holloway was also the first black player in the Tennessee baseball program. He garnered All-SEC and All-America honors as a shortstop in 1975 and finished with a .353 career batting average. His 27-game hitting streak still ranks as the school's longest. In fact, Tennessee is fortunate that Holloway did not choose professional baseball out of high school. The Montreal Expos drafted Holloway with their first pick, but Holloway heeded his mother's advice and went to Tennessee instead.

Holloway was a pioneer. Leaving his home state (and football factory) of Alabama, he became the first black quarterback in SEC history. He was one of the first players to combine a strong and accurate arm with good decision-making skills and a pair of legs that could take off like a running back's when necessary.

Holloway's career record at Tennessee as a starting quarterback was 25–9–2. He led the Vols to three bowl games from 1972 to 1974. Although he wasn't drafted until the 12th round of the NFL Draft, by the New England Patriots, he turned in an impressive

13-year career in the Canadian Football League, where he passed for more than 25,000 yards and rushed for 3,167 more, throwing 155 touchdown passes. He was the Most Outstanding Player of the league in 1982 with the Toronto Argonauts.

Holloway, currently UT's assistant athletic director for student-athlete relations and lettermen, is in his 17th year on the Tennessee staff. He has been inducted into the Alabama Sports Hall of Fame, Tennessee Sports Hall of Fame, Tennessee Baseball Hall of Fame, and Canadian Football Hall of Fame.

He and his wife, Courtney, have two children: Jasmine and Condredge III.

41 The 2005 Comeback on the Bayou

When the Golden Band from Tigerland fires up the four-corners salute and the Tigers take the field through the band to a deafening roar from the Purple and Gold faithful at dusk, the hair on a visitor's neck will raise up. Trying to call an audible is a points-worthy accomplishment in itself for a quarterback, given the near impossibility of hearing anything over the din from the crowd.

And if the pressure of 100,000 screaming fans wasn't enough, the eyes of the entire nation were looking on the Tigers and Volunteers on September 26, 2005, as the game had been moved to Monday night due to regional devastation from Hurricane Katrina and the aftereffects of Hurricane Rita.

For a night, it seemed like it was the entire state of Louisiana versus the Tennessee Volunteers. For the nearby city of New Orleans and the emergency-stricken state, the fourth-ranked Tigers

Gerald Riggs carries the ball—and the team—to pay dirt.

could provide an uplifting moment for the region by knocking off the 10th-ranked Vols.

And for a half, it seemed like Tennessee was to suffer the fate of a lamb thrown into a lion's den—or in this case, a tiger's. After seeing LSU score on its first carry of the game, Tennessee quarterback Erik Ainge compounded the problem late in the half by blindly tossing an underhanded lob from his own end zone while under pressure that was picked off on the Tennessee 3-yard line and jogged in by LSU's Kenneth Hollis for a TD.

Rick Clausen vs. Erik Ainge: A Failed Experiment in 2005

The Vols entered the 2005 season ranked third in the AP poll and with the sky as the limit. Five wins turned out to be the actual limit, and few things can crumble the foundation of a team and a season faster than a rotating quarterback controversy.

Ainge was anointed the starter for the season-opening 17–10 win against UAB. After a largely pedestrian performance against Florida, in which Ainge completed 14 of 29 passes for 147 yards and a touchdown in the Vols' 16–7 loss, Coach Fulmer stuck with Ainge going into Baton Rouge. After one of the most embarrassing plays of Ainge's career—a spinning underhanded lob pass that was picked off and returned for a score—Fulmer tapped Rick Clausen, who led the Vols to a 2005 Cotton Bowl victory. Clausen fueled the Vols' comeback victory in Baton Rouge, completing 21 of 32 passes for 196 yards with a touchdown and an interception.

As a result, Clausen went on to start the next four games, commencing with a 27–10 win over Ole Miss and followed by three listless losses against Georgia, at Alabama, and against South Carolina. Clausen threw for one touchdown pass against three interceptions while averaging less than 180 yards passing per game.

On UT's trip to Notre Dame, Coach Fulmer reinserted Ainge as the starter. If the hope was to provide a spark, it didn't work, as Ainge completed only 13 of 32 passes and threw two interceptions in the 41–21 loss.

Still, looking for some level of consistency from the position, Fulmer kept Ainge as the starter the following game against Memphis. It didn't work, as Ainge was benched after throwing two first-quarter interceptions. With the Vols trailing Memphis 13–0 even though the Tigers were playing without leading rusher DeAngelo Williams, who was out with an ankle injury, Clausen was reinserted. Just like in Baton Rouge, Clausen led the Vols back, throwing second-quarter touchdown passes to Josh Briscoe and C.J. Fayton to give UT a slim lead at the break. Clausen threw for 209 yards, and Tennessee held on to win 20–16 and avoid postseason elimination.

Clausen earned the start against Jay Cutler, Earl Bennett, and a talented Vanderbilt team on Senior Day. With more ineffective play from the quarterback position (11 of 26 for 125 yards, one touchdown, and two interceptions), Tennessee's offense couldn't put away Vandy, as the Commodores scored with less than two minutes to play to snap a 22-year losing streak and end the Vols' bowl hopes.

With live game reps for the 2006 squad the only issue of significance in the season finale at Kentucky, Ainge again got the start, completing 17 of 25 passes for 221 yards and two touchdowns in an efficient and clean performance to end the season.

For those scoring at home: Clausen starts–5; Ainge starts–6. Offensive coordinators resigned–1 (Randy Shannon). Wins–5; Losses–6.

But as much as the game was about a region, it was about a young man from the bayou who flipped the script on the evening and brought Tennessee to life.

Quarterback Rick Clausen, who transferred to Tennessee following the 2002 season, entered the game following the Ainge interception in the second quarter and almost immediately brought a spark to the Tennessee offense. With the coaching staff keeping the play calling manageable, Clausen threw darts to his wide receivers on short out routes, moving the Tennessee offense for the first time of the day. Although a fumble at midfield ended the drive, the Volunteers offense had finally shown up at Tiger Stadium.

And the defense showed up right before the half.

After stopping a scrambling JaMarcus Russell inside the 10-yard line on a second down run with 15 seconds left, Les Miles inexplicably ran his field goal team on the field as the final seconds ticked off the clock rather than spiking the ball.

LSU 21, Tennessee 0. Halftime. Those missed three points would prove ruinous for the Tigers in the second half.

After the defense forced a Tigers punt to start the second half, it was Clausen who returned to the field instead of Ainge. Ainge was 7 of 19 for 54 yards passing with an interception in the first half.

Clausen and the UT offense wasted little time marching the field for their first touchdown in 17 offensive possessions going back to the previous game against Florida. Clausen capped off the opening drive of the second half with a eight-yard touchdown pass to Bret Smith, and the Vols were on the board at 21–7.

After LSU pushed the lead back out to 24–7, and with one quarter remaining, the Volunteers offense turned in one of its best performances of any quarter in years…and not a moment too soon.

After finding a crossing Robert Meachem to bring the offense into the red zone, UT faced a fourth-and-goal inside the 1. Coach Fulmer decided to go for it. As the deafening Death Valley crowd roared like a jet engine, Clausen surged forward into a scrum of bodies. The linesman raised his arms high.

LSU 24, Tennessee 14, with 9:35 remaining.

Down two scores, Tennessee still needed an impact play to catch up. They would get it from their defense 90 seconds later.

Russell dropped back and tossed a gift into the waiting arms of UT cornerback Jonathan Hefney, who returned the ball to the 3-yard line. "Rocky Top" blared. Two plays later, Gerald Riggs was in the end zone, nodding at the legion of Purple and Gold sitting in silence.

LSU 24, Tennessee 21, with 7:15 remaining.

After an LSU three-and-out, Riggs continued his takeover of Tiger Stadium, breaking free for 22 yards to put UT in field goal range.

Tennessee 24, LSU 24. End of regulation.

Tennessee won the toss and elected to send its defense out first. UT continued what it had done for the entire second half: shut down the volatile LSU offense. Facing a third-and-9 from the 14, Russell fired into the end zone. Incomplete. Colt David's 31-yard field goal flirted with the upright and snuck inside.

LSU 27, Tennessee 24.

On UT's first play, Clausen found Riggs out of the backfield, and Riggs fought up the sideline for 10 yards. Riggs then took a draw for seven yards on the next play. Another Riggs draw put the Vols at the 3, first-and-goal.

After being down 21–0 at the half and 24–7 in the fourth quarter, Tennessee was three yards away from an incredible victory. As LSU fans played with their hair and chewed their nails, Riggs drove the Vols down to the 1-foot line.

Two plays later, against a tired Tigers defense, Riggs powered through an attempted tackle by LSU linebacker Cameron Vaughn. The officials signaled touchdown, orange-and-white jerseys sprinted toward the end zone, and LSU fans slunk toward the exit. Coach Fulmer flashed a grin as he welcomed embraces from his elated staff while walking to midfield to shake hands with Coach Miles.

Entering the season ranked No. 3 in the nation, the 5–6 finish proved to be one of the more deflating seasons in recent Tennessee history. However, Tennessee's resurgence in Baton Rouge proved to be a bright spot, as well as one of the most memorable games of the 2000s for Tennessee fans. Down 24–7, the game stands as the biggest fourth-quarter comeback in school history.

Riggs was the coup de grace for the Tennessee offense, seemingly running harder as the game went along. He carried 24 times for 89 yards and two touchdowns.

Clausen, who was booed by his former supporters when he entered the game in the second quarter, found his own storybook ending, completing 21 of 32 passes for 196 yards and a touchdown, with another score on the ground.

"Getting done what he got done, coming back here to win this football game at a place where he had been, I don't know if there is a better story in the world than what this guy has done," Coach Fulmer said after the game.

Vols Overwhelm Franco Harris, Penn State in 1971

The Orange and White faithful streamed onto Shields-Watkins Field, eager to soak up every ounce of the energy that permeated Neyland Stadium. Through the crowd, a shocked and dejected Penn State squad filed off the field.

Losing was an unfamiliar feeling for head coach Joe Paterno and his Nittany Lions. Not since a 24–7 loss to Syracuse on October 17, 1970, had Penn State walked off the field in defeat. During the 15-game winning streak, Penn State had turned into an unstoppable force, with only Air Force being able to come within single digits of the Lions.

But Penn State ran into a proverbial buzz saw in Knoxville on November 27, 1971. Tennessee had won five straight games since a 32–15 loss at No. 4 Alabama, allowing only 30 points in that stretch.

The day began with festivities celebrating Coach Johnny Majors—the football patriarch of the state of Tennessee—and his family. As the Pride of the Southland Marching Band formed a block *M* on the field in honor of the Majors family, Bobby— Johnny's brother, and the youngest of Shirley and John Elizabeth Majors' five children—stood in uniform alongside Johnny.

Minutes later, Bobby fielded the opening kickoff and raced 54 yards to give the Volunteers an early spark. Although a fumbled pitch ended the drive deep in Penn State territory, the Tennessee defense made sure the turnover battle swung heavily in favor of the Big Orange.

The first step was to prevent the white-clad juggernaut Penn State offense, which averaged 463 total yards per game and 320 rushing yards per game, from parading up and down the field. The

Vols accomplished that by slowing down future Pro Football Hall of Fame running back Franco Harris and putting the game, and the ability to carry the Lions, onto the shoulders of quarterback John Hufnagel.

Tennessee forced the game onto the arm of Hufnagel, and he completed 19 of 29 passes—but four of his incompletions were pulled in by Tennessee defenders. Tennessee defensive back David Allen returned a pick 15 yards for a 14–3 lead.

The defense and special teams weren't done finding the end zone. Conrad Graham scored on a 76-yard fumble return for a touchdown. Bobby Majors returned two punts for 82 yards, one for a score, and returned two kickoffs for 113 yards.

The game proved a microcosm of Bobby Majors' memorable career. He excelled as a defender and on special teams. He set the school record for interceptions in 1970, with 10. He also set school career marks that stand today for career punt returns (117) and punt return yardage (1,163). He earned consensus All-America honors in 1971.

Against a Top 5 team, the third time would be the charm for the 1971 Vols. Having lost to No. 5 Auburn 10–9 and at No. 4 Alabama 32–15, Tennessee finished its season with a win over the previously 10-0 Nittany Lions and edged No. 18 Arkansas in the Liberty Bowl to finish its season at 10-2. Penn State, already locked into the Cotton Bowl to face Texas before coming to Knoxville, clobbered the Longhorns 30–6 to cap an 11–1 season.

43 Erik Ainge / Brent Schaeffer QB Combo Yields '04 SEC East Title

Although they came from completely different worlds, they seemed to be perfect complements to each other.

Erik Ainge, nephew of Boston Celtic great Danny Ainge, committed to the Vols out of Glencoe High School in Hillsboro, Oregon. Tall and lanky at 6'6" and around 200 pounds, Ainge had the length and arm strength most coaches would drool over.

While Phillip Fulmer was able to go to one coast to get his prototypical pocket passer, he went to the other coast to pluck a dual-threat signal caller who could beat teams with his arm and legs. Fulmer got that in Brent Schaeffer out of Deerfield Beach High School in Florida. At 6'3" and 190 pounds, Schaeffer accounted for 36 touchdowns his senior year, throwing for 24 and running for 12. It was actually a step down from his junior year, when he threw for 31 scores and ran for 15 more.

Despite the varying skill sets, Tennessee would be without something they'd enjoyed at the quarterback position since the early 1990s: consistency and experience.

Tennessee had been somewhat fortunate with its quarterbacks going back more than a decade. Andy Kelly had given way to Heisman Trophy runner-up Heath Shuler. Shuler gave way to Peyton Manning, who emerged quickly from the three-headed quarterback competition with Jerry Colquitt and Todd Helton. Manning, the greatest quarterback in school history, gave way to Tee Martin, who guided the Vols to an SEC and national championship, as well as to two BCS bowl appearances. After A.J. Suggs' brief cameo in 2000, Casey Clausen took over as a freshman and held the position through 2003.

Clausen proved to be one of the most successful road quarterbacks in Tennessee history, going 14–1 as a starter in true road contests and helping the Vols claim the 2001 SEC East title and a share of the 2003 East title with Florida and Georgia.

But then before the 2004 season the Vols suddenly had a competition between two true freshman candidates for the starting job, something never before seen in Knoxville. The talented freshmen had an immediate edge on returning quarterbacks C.J. Leak and Rick Clausen.

After battling through fall practice in August, Phillip Fulmer announced the Friday before the season opener against UNLV that Schaeffer would get the nod as starter, but that Ainge would also play and was effectively a "co-starter." Schaeffer became the first true freshman to start a season-opening game for an SEC team since September 22, 1945, when Georgia's John Rauch started the Bulldogs 49–0 win over Murray State.

But Ainge made a statement the following game against Florida, putting together one of the strongest performances by a Tennessee freshman quarterback ever. He went 16 of 24 for 192 yards and three touchdowns against Florida, and led touchdown drives of 80, 80, and 96 yards. On the final touchdown drive, Ainge converted third-and-9, fourth-and-6, and third-and-8. With 55 seconds left and the Vols down a missed extra point, Ainge moved the Vols 28 yards with two completions to set up Wilhoit's redeeming 50-yard field goal with seven seconds remaining.

Ainge started his first game on October 2—a 34–10 home loss to Ronnie Brown, Cadillac Williams, Jason Campbell, and the Auburn Tigers. Ainge's growing pains were evident, as he completed fewer than half of his 35 pass attempts and threw four interceptions—all to defensive back Junior Rosegreen. Schaeffer completed one of five passes in relief, also throwing a pick.

Ainge immediately bounced back to lead the Vols to a shocking 19–14 upset at No. 3 Georgia. Schaeffer played only one series in

Athens, with Ainge completing 12 of 21 passes for 150 yards and, more important, no turnovers. He threw two touchdowns, the latter to Chris Hannon for the winning points.

Ainge had begun to take control of the quarterbacks race, which was exacerbated by Schaeffer suffering a season-ending collarbone injury in a 43–29 win at South Carolina.

The next week, injury again changed the face of the season for UT. With seconds remaining in the first half and the Vols leading 10–7, Ainge was sacked by Notre Dame defensive lineman Justin Tuck on the final play of the first half while attempting to throw a Hail Mary pass of some 60 yards. The resulting shoulder injury ended Ainge's freshman season and cost the Vols the game in a 17–13 loss, as Rick Clausen could only engineer three points in the second half in relief.

Still, Ainge was the freshman quarterback most responsible for Tennessee's success going into November. Thanks to his steady play, the Vols were in position to clinch the SEC East division crown the next week at Vanderbilt, which they did, 38–33.

Although UT fell to Auburn in Atlanta 38–28, the Vols fought and stayed in the game, mostly behind the 182 rushing yards from Gerald Riggs. Tennessee rallied to tie the game at 21 and in the second half to pull to 31–28 before finally losing 38–28.

Although the 2004 season didn't result in a conference championship, it remains one of the most memorable of the decade for Vols fans, given the dramatic wins over Florida and Georgia and the winning of the Eastern Division. And it was the start of a four-year UT career for Ainge, who would help guide the Vols back to the SEC Championship Game in his senior season.

Schaeffer transferred to the College of the Sequoias after being arrested for a fight in a dorm lobby in May 2005. After earning first-team All-America junior college honors, he transferred to Ole Miss for the 2006 and 2007 seasons and earned the starting job for Rebels coach Ed Orgeron.

44 Casey Clausen: Road Warrior

Although Casey Clausen emerged as the starter midway through the 2000 season, he was thrown into a four-man quarterback competition to replace Tee Martin during fall practice that year. Joey Matthews from nearby Sevier County High School was the favorite, having been in the program the longest. To make matters worse for the true freshman Clausen, a shoulder injury in fall camp put him further behind the other candidates. A.J. Suggs eventually earned the starting job in the first game of the season, but by October the Vols were 2–3 in an admitted rebuilding year.

After taking a handful of snaps against Louisiana-Monroe and Georgia, Clausen was named the starter in the off week before the Alabama game, as Coach Fulmer decided to go with his talented but developing young star in a move geared for the future. Clausen's first start came against Alabama in Knoxville, where Clausen directed the Vols to their sixth straight win in the series, 20–10.

Clausen assumed command of the team the following week in Columbia, against a 7–1 South Carolina team that had been winless the season before. Down 14–10 in the fourth quarter, Clausen led a 16-play, 68-yard drive for the win, a march that included a third-and-14 completion to Donté Stallworth and culminated in a one-yard Travis Henry leap over the goal line for the game-winning score.

The Vols rolled through their final six games with the freshman Clausen at the helm, finding a late-season offensive rhythm behind the steadily improving Clausen and the Travises—Henry and Stephens. Though Kansas State handled the Vols 35–21 in the Cotton Bowl that year, things were looking good for Clausen

Casey Clausen's Stats in His 14–1 Road Record

Without question, Casey Clausen showed as much poise and composure in a hostile SEC environment as any Tennessee quarterback in program history. Twice he won at the Swamp. Twice he won at Bryant-Denny Stadium. Fifteen times he took the starting snaps in a true road game. Fourteen of those times he left the field of battle with a smile and with the Pride of the Southland Marching Band blasting out "Rocky Top."

How good was Clausen, statistically? Here's a look at his career statistics on the road as a starter:

- Tennessee 17, South Carolina 14 (10/28/00); 19 of 31, 152 yards, 1 interception
- Tennessee 19, Memphis 17 (11/4/00); 19 of 30, 224 yards, 1 interception
- Tennessee 28, Vanderbilt 26 (11/25/00); 14 of 30, 158 yards, 1 touchdown, 2 interceptions
- Tennessee 13, Arkansas 3 (9/8/01); 13 of 17, 136 yards
- Tennessee 35, Alabama 24 (10/20/01); 21 of 28, 293 yards, 2 touchdowns, 0 interceptions, 1 rushing touchdown
- Tennessee 28, Notre Dame 18 (11/3/01); 17 of 29, 228 yards, 1 touchdown, 1 interception, 1 rushing touchdown
- Tennessee 38, Kentucky 35 (11/17/01); 20 of 30, 285 yards, 4 touchdowns, 0 interceptions
- Tennessee 34, Florida 32 (12/1/01); 17 of 25, 168 yards, 1 touchdown, 2 interceptions
- Tennessee 18, South Carolina 10 (11/2/02); 17 of 23, 175 yards, 1 touchdown, 0 interceptions, 1 rushing touchdown
- Tennessee 24, Vanderbilt 0 (11/23/02); 12 of 22, 120 yards
- Tennessee 24, Florida 10 (9/20/03); 12 of 23, 235 yards, 1 touchdown, 1 interception
- Auburn 28, Tennessee 21 (10/4/03); 30 of 47; 355 yards, 2 touchdowns, 1 interception
- Tennessee 51, Alabama 43 (10/25/03); 23 of 43, 283 yards, 4 touchdowns, 0 interceptions, 1 rushing touchdown
- Tennessee 10, Miami 6 (11/8/03); 11 of 18, 81 yards, no touchdowns
- Tennessee 20, Kentucky 7 (11/29/03); 11 of 27, 110 yards, 1 touchdown, 1 interception

and the direction of the Tennessee program. Clausen was named to the freshman All-SEC and freshman All-America teams. For the season, he finished 6–1 as a starter, and 3–0 in true road games. As the unquestioned starter in 2001, Clausen passed for 2,969 yards and the Vols went 11–2. He helped Kelley Washington get the school record with 256 receiving yards against LSU, extended the Vols' winning streak over Alabama to seven, gutted out a win at Notre Dame, and upstaged Jared Lorenzen in a 38–35 nail-biter at Kentucky.

But Clausen was at his best when it mattered most: on the road against the No. 2 team in the country. Behind the strong running of Travis Stephens, Clausen guided the 17½-point-underdog Vols to their first victory in the Swamp in 30 years, a 34–32 win over Rex Grossman and the Gators that claimed the SEC East title and put the Vols one step closer to playing Miami in the Rose Bowl for the national championship (ultimately Nebraska played Miami). After losing 31–20 to LSU in the SEC Championship Game, Clausen played arguably the best game of his career against Michigan in the Citrus Bowl, completing 26 of 34 attempts for 393 yards, three passing touchdowns, two rushing touchdowns, and no interceptions.

The Vols were preseason No. 5 in 2002, and expectations were high for Clausen and the team. Instead, Clausen was at the center of the moment it all went wrong: in the final five minutes of the first half against Florida, the Vols turned the ball over three times, including three consecutive fumbled snaps in the downpour, and Florida built a stunning 24–0 lead.

Clausen bounced back to lead the Vols to a six-overtime win over Arkansas but was injured in overtime. As a result, he missed the following game, an 18–13 loss against UGA. When Kelley Washington's UT career ended with a neck injury in that game, Clausen was without his best weapon at wide receiver in pivotal home games, and both Alabama and Miami took advantage, winning 34–14 and 26–3, respectively. After starting a 2002 season with such high hopes after narrowly missing the 2002 BCS National Championship Game, the Vols finished a disappointing 8–5 after getting blasted 30–3 by Maryland in the Peach Bowl.

In his senior season, Clausen helped cement his legacy as one of the most undaunted players in a hostile environment in SEC history. In what would be the Vols last win in the Swamp through the 2014 season, Clausen led the Vols to a 24–10 conquest. A subsequent road loss at Auburn served as Clausen's only road defeat in his four-year career as a starter. He more than made up for it in Tuscaloosa. Clausen led an 80-yard touchdown drive in the final minutes to tie it, then connected on a fourth-and-19 conversion in overtime to extend the game. Tennessee finally won, 51–43, after five overtimes.

Clausen finished with 2,968 yards in his senior season, with 27 touchdowns to 9 interceptions. He finished 34–10 as a starter, compiling the most wins by a UT quarterback other than Peyton Manning. Clausen's record on the road was an incredible 14–1, including two wins in Gainesville and two in Tuscaloosa. Clausen is second in several major passing categories in the UT record books, trailing only Manning.

Travis Stephens Helps Drain Swamp 34–32 in 2001

A jubilant Will Bartholomew directed the Pride of the Southland Marching Band, blaring strains of "Rocky Top" across the emptying Florida Field. Orange-and-white shakers flailed above the heads of strangers high-fiving strangers, wives hugging husbands, and kids being swept up off their feet by their excited parents.

Minutes earlier, the 2001 Tennessee-Florida game came down to one play: a two-point conversion attempt. The SEC East championship hung in the balance. Perhaps Florida quarterback Rex Grossman's Heisman Trophy chances did as well.

The question "What if the biggest game in the SEC East was played at the end of the year?" was, unfortunately, answered by the postponement of the original September 15 date due to the devastating aftermath of the events of September 11. Both teams entered the game at 9–1 and 6–1 in the SEC. A de facto SEC East Championship Game had come to fruition.

There was little doubt in the minds of the oddsmakers as to which team held the perceived edge. The 2001 Gators, thought by Steve Spurrier to be one of the best Florida squads, were able to turn their season around after a 23–20 loss at Auburn on October 13. Double-digit dismantlings of Vanderbilt and ranked Georgia, South Carolina, and Florida State teams, plus a week off, was all the oddsmakers needed to see to anoint the Gators as 17½-point favorites over the Volunteers.

It mattered little to the oddsmakers that Tennessee had run off six straight wins since Georgia's David Greene found Verron Haynes in the back of the checkerboard end zone for a 26–24 Bulldogs win on October 6. But the size of the line was not lost on the players. Defensive tackle John Henderson reportedly flipped over a couch in the hotel room when the line was shown on ESPN's *College GameDay*, which was broadcasting from Gainesville for the showdown.

And a memorable pregame speech by Phillip Fulmer had the white-clad Volunteers energized as they took the field for the night contest that would decide the SEC East, and possibly the national championship picture.

"I don't know how many people in this country believe," Coach Fulmer said. "That really doesn't matter either. It only matters what the men in this room believe.... Those guys put their jocks on just like you do. Those guys like the same girls that you guys like. Everything's the same. It gets back down to who wants to win it the most."

"That stadium is the loudest stadium, college or pro," UT running back Travis Stephens told SI.com. "I've never been in a stadium as loud as Florida's stadium.... LSU is pretty loud. Georgia is pretty loud. But there's nothing like Florida."

The noise energized Stephens, who put the Vols on his back and carried the offense to the tune of 226 yards and two touchdowns. The Tennessee passing attack featured breakout star wide receiver Kelley Washington, future Dallas Cowboys standout Jason Witten, and future New Orleans Saint Donté Stallworth, but it was the running game that carried Tennessee to victory.

The Tennessee defense made the plays it needed to make to give Stephens and the offense the chance to take over the game. Clinging to a 23–21 lead with a minute left in the third quarter, Spurrier rolled the dice on a fourth-and-6 from the Tennessee 36-yard line. Defensive end Will Overstreet sacked Grossman, swinging the momentum in Tennessee's favor.

On the ensuing drive, Travis Stephens burst through the right side of the line and down the sideline to the 2-yard line. Bulky reserve tailback Jabari David dove over the line for a 27–23 lead. On the ensuing drive, UF's Jeff Chandler drove in a 52-yard field goal to make the score 27–26.

Then it was Stephens, who already had eclipsed 150 yards on the ground, who put the Volunteers in command of the game. On the first play of the next drive, Stephens drove through the left side of the line, cut right, broke through a couple tackles, and ripped off a 68-yard run that put the Vols on the doorstep of a suddenly silent Orange and Blue house. Jabari Davis finished off the drive with his second dive-into-the-line touchdown of the day, and the Vols led 34–26 with just more than eight minutes to play.

Unable to run out the clock, Tennessee punted back to Florida with five minutes left, and a battered Grossman led the Gators down the field. Henderson, Overstreet, and the Tennessee front accumulated more than 30 quarterback pressures, nearly as high as the total number of yards the Tennessee defense allowed rushing (36). A two-yard touchdown pass to Carlos Perez with a minute left brought Florida to within two, at 34–32, as a somewhat muted cheer resonated throughout the Swamp. Everybody knew what was at stake on the following play.

Again under pressure, Grossman released the ball just before getting flattened from behind. The pass sailed wide of intended target Jabar Gaffney, who had made the controversial "catch" to beat Tennessee the year prior.

All Tennessee needed to do was field the onside kick. Chandler's kick fluttered and bounced high toward his charging teammates. But it was UT reserve tight end John Finlayson who ended the Gators' hopes. With only four catches on the season, his fifth touch of the year was his most impressive, as he rose high to snare the ball and held on through a jarring blow and a tangle of clawing arms.

As Clausen took the final knee, a sea of orange Gatorade—ironically concocted on the very same campus where the Vols were celebrating jubilantly—rained down on Coach Fulmer, who jumped with arms raised in the air. Not in 30 years had Tennessee celebrated a win over the Gators in Gainesville, since back when Fulmer left the field as a guard on the 1971 team.

Although the joy of the win would be dampened a week later in a 31–20 loss to LSU in the SEC Championship Game, the 2001 Tennessee-Florida matchup showed that Tennessee could rise to the occasion against, literally, overwhelming odds. It was also the final game Spurrier coached at Florida Field before resigning in January 2002.

A happy send-off for Tennessee fans, undoubtedly.

46 Cherish the Voice of the Late Bobby Denton

If you were headed to a Tennessee game, and shuffling slowly through the sea of orange and white outside Gate 21 or along Phillip Fulmer Way, you hoped not to hear the voice of Bobby Denton belt out a familiar phrase. At least not yet.

While the longtime UT stadium announcer would announce pregame items, such as the starting lineups and opposing team's fight song, it was a catchphrase Denton would boom through the speakers at Neyland Stadium that let fans know their beloved football team was taking the field—and that they'd better hurry up and get to their seats: "It's football time in Tennessee!"

With the emphasis on the "seeeeeee" of the phrase, the band would form a *T* and the Tennessee state flag and the Power T flag would be paraded forward with the cheerleaders, ahead of the players taking the field. Denton's deep yet soothing voice was one of the components that caused the hair to rise on spectators' necks as the team made its famous run through the *T*.

But Bobby Denton, who passed away on April 9, 2014, was so much more to the University of Tennessee than just its longtime stadium announcer. He was a local legend and a regional treasure. He made his life in front of a microphone in the Knoxville area, serving as a local radio DJ at WIVK for 36 years and helping to make the country music station one of the most popular in the area.

His voice was synonymous with the University of Tennessee. Even after retiring to Florida, Denton returned to Neyland Stadium each home game weekend to assume his duties as the stadium announcer.

Denton would also remind fans that the concession prices were listed in the souvenir program before proclaiming, "We urge you to pay these prices and please pay no more!" The now-renowned line comes as a result of the addition of concession prices in the game programs in the 1970s. When they were added, a line persuaded fans to avoid falling trap to stadium concession vendors who looked to make an extra buck or two off unwary customers. Though not an issue at the stands in later years, the line endured as a Tennessee tradition.

"Bobby Denton is a true treasure of Tennessee football," head coach Butch Jones said to UTSports.com. "Hearing him say 'It's football time in Tennessee' is one of the greatest traditions in the history of college football. His voice is as synonymous with Neyland Stadium as the checkerboard end zones, and everyone in the Tennessee family will miss him greatly."

Denton also had a laid-back approach that was entertaining and amusing at times. The University of South Carolina was facing a third-and-33 in 2001, and Denton announced that the Gamecocks were facing "third down and the river," referring to the Tennessee River outside the stadium.

Denton took over stadium PA duties from John Ward, legendary voice of Tennessee football and basketball, in 1967.

"Bobby Denton was a true radio professional in every way," Ward said. "He had a great hobby like I had, and his was the PA at Neyland Stadium. But he was first and foremost a true professional radio man. He was an on-the-air radio personality before getting into management and sales, and he understood what you had to do to answer to the audience.... His PA effectiveness came...from the fact that he...could anticipate what people in the stadium wanted to hear. His timing was done so that he would set the stadium crowd up, and then when they were collectively saying 'He's going to say it,' he said it, and they reacted. He was very, very effective, no question."

47 Vols 51, Bama 43, Five Overtimes

The crowd at Bryant-Denny Stadium rose to their feet, bringing a deafening roar over the two longtime rivals that had spellbound a national television audience. The Third Saturday in October had brought about the first overtime between Tennessee and Alabama.

And as the stadium groaned to contain the shaking and shouting from the partisan crowd, a man who earned the nickname the Iceman proved that moniker was well deserved.

The situation seemed dire for the Vols. Tennessee's offense had sputtered for most of the second half, with quarterback Casey Clausen completing only two passes before the final drive. However, Clausen and the offense came to life in the final two minutes of the game, moving 81 yards to tie the game with 25 seconds left. After the first overtime elapsed, Tennessee found itself facing a fourth-and-19 in the second overtime, down 34–27.

At the snap, Tennessee quarterback-turned-receiver James Banks already was given 15 of those yards via a massive cushion from opposing defender Charlie Peprah. Although Banks wouldn't catch the pass, he served a big role on the play, running the defender out of his zone. Receiver C.J. Fayton ran into the vacated space and caught the ball for a 28-yard gain.

With 90,000-plus crimson jaws lying on the ground, it was easy for Clausen and the Tennessee offense to snatch life—and ultimately victory—from them.

One play later, Clausen rolled right and, committing the cardinal sin of quarterbacking, threw the ball against his body into coverage. The ball tipped off an Alabama defender and into the hands of Banks in the end zone.

Alabama 34, Tennessee 34. Starting third overtime.

And once again, it took only one play for Clausen to find Banks. Off a play-action fake, Clausen lofted a pass into the corner of the end zone, where Banks had beaten his man and pulled it in for a 40–34 lead. Having to go for two points under the overtime rules, Clausen rolled right and fired incomplete.

Alabama could win with a touchdown and a two-point conversion. Then it was Tide quarterback Brodie Croyle who made a game-saving play, dodging pressure and dumping a pass to running back Ray Hudson, who scampered for a first down. One play later, Alabama was in the end zone.

Alabama 40, Tennessee 40. Again, the Tennessee faithful were chewing their fingernails, hoping this time that the defense could make an impact play to keep the game alive. Their prayers were answered when future New Orleans Saint and Super Bowl champion Jabari Greer intercepted Croyle's pass.

In the fourth overtime, a 29-yard Brian Bostick field goal pushed the Tide ahead 43–40. Tennessee quickly moved to the 9-yard line on a Clausen scramble and Antwan Odom personal foul penalty. Two Clausen incompletions resulted in James Wilhoit booting through a 25-yard field goal to move the game into a fifth overtime.

Two Corey Larkins runs pushed the Vols down inside the 4-yard line, where the Vols eventually faced a third-and-1. Clausen rolled right and dove for the pylon, where the officials ruled him out of bounds inside the half-yard line. Fortunately for Tennessee, they picked up a first down on the effort. Clausen lined up the team and pushed into the mass of white jerseys. Touchdown.

On the two-point conversion, Tennessee went back to where its bread had been buttered earlier. Clausen lobbed a ball in the direction of Banks, who outjumped the defender and fell to the ground with the ball.

Tennessee 51, Alabama 43.

And finally Tennessee made its stand. On fourth down, needing two yards to convert, Croyle opted to lob a pass into the end zone to receiver Dre Fulgham. UT cornerback Jason Allen, a Muscle Shoals, Alabama, native and future first-round pick of the Miami Dolphins, batted the pass away, sending orange-and-white-clad revelers streaming from the UT sideline to the end zone, where the Vols celebrated with the faithful who had made the trip from Knoxville.

The longest and most grueling contest in the Tennessee-Alabama series had ended. First-year head coach Mike Shula struggled in his first year in Tuscaloosa, going 4–9 and ending the probation-shortened season with a 37–29 loss at Hawaii. Meanwhile, Tennessee paired its win in Tuscaloosa with a win at Florida and finished the season 10–2 with a share of the SEC East title with Georgia and Florida. Snubbed by the BCS bowl selection committees, the Vols accepted a bid to return to the Peach Bowl for the second straight year, where they lost 27–14 to Clemson.

48 Learn About Lester McClain, Tennessee's First African American Football Player

The dazzling play of Condredge Holloway, the first African American quarterback in Tennessee history, left Tennessee fans incredulous, and Holloway in high esteem with the Volunteers faithful to this day. His bravery in a time when integration was still a struggle with many major college football programs and their fan bases—especially in the South—was commendable. Even Bear Bryant told Holloway that the University of Alabama wasn't ready for a black quarterback.

Lester McClain (center) at the University of Tennessee reunion in 2004.

But there was another man who had already stepped into uncharted territory in the world of race and sports in the state of Tennessee: Lester McClain.

Kentucky's Nat Northington receives the credit for being the first African American to play in an SEC game, entering the game as a wide receiver on September 30, 1967, in Lexington in the Wildcats' 26–13 loss to Ole Miss. Nonetheless, McClain's journey from Nashville to the dog-eat-dog world of competitive college football in Knoxville—then an all-white football program—was groundbreaking in East Tennessee.

And while McClain did not play in 1967, he made his impact known early in 1968. With the Vols trailing 17–9 with two minutes to go against rival Georgia in Neyland Stadium, quarterback Bubba Wyche engineered a game-tying drive with less than three minutes to play. Having completed only 7 of 22 passes on the day, the task seemed daunting. However, a 14-yard pass to McClain helped bring the Vols down to the Georgia 9-yard line, where Wyche found Gary Kreis for a touchdown to make it 17–15 with no time remaining on the clock. On the ensuing conversion, Wyche struck Ken DeLong for the two points.

Tennessee 17, Georgia 17. The elated fans in the stadium felt like they had come away with a win.

While the score was a tie, the game itself was a win for racial relations. McClain, who played a significant role in the final touchdown drive, had shown in front of a national television audience that the color barrier in the South was starting to fall. In front of Tennessee governor Buford Ellington, US senator Albert Gore Sr., and US representative Bill Brock from Chattanooga, who were all in attendance that September afternoon, McClain showed that an African American athlete could perform just as well as his white counterpart.

McClain, wearing No. 85 during his time at Tennessee, went on to provide a solid career as a wide receiver for the Orange and White. From 1968 to 1970, McClain caught 70 passes for 1,003 yards and 10 touchdowns.

But more than ability, what McClain brought to the field was courage, and each week he donned the No. 85 for the Volunteers he showed other young African American men that times were beginning to change. Slowly, but change was happening. When McClain caught that fourth-down pass, he wasn't black or white. He was Orange and White.

Attend an SEC Championship Game

Since the East and West divide starting in the 1992 season, the SEC Championship Game has proved to be one of the marquee events in college football. Aside from deciding combatants for the national championship game, the scene itself provides a spectacle, for both the fans and the players.

For some schools, trips to Atlanta, the host since 1994, have been almost regular—Alabama and Florida in the 1990s, for example. The Tide and Gators clashed in the first two championships in Birmingham, splitting the matchups. In 1994 Florida edged an undefeated Alabama to keep the Tide out of the national championship picture. Florida also toppled Arkansas and Alabama in 1995 and 1996, respectively, to ultimately play for the national championship in their bowl games.

The Gators lead all teams with 10 appearances in the SEC Championship Game, one more than second-place Alabama's nine. LSU, Auburn, Georgia, and Tennessee all claim five appearances. Arkansas represented the West three times, Missouri won the East in 2013 and 2014, and both South Carolina (2010) and Mississippi State (1998) have earned a single trip to Atlanta. Vanderbilt and Ole Miss are the only members existent prior to the 2012 expansion not to have played in the game through the 2014 season.

Tennessee's recent trips to Atlanta have not been particularly memorable for the right reasons. After beating Florida to win the 2001 SEC East, the Vols followed it with a come-from-ahead loss to an underdog LSU squad in front of a highly partisan UT crowd, knocking the Vols from the national championship game. Appearances in 2004 and 2007 ended in painstakingly close losses to Auburn and LSU that kept Vols fans in their seats until the final drive, only to be sent home disappointed.

But that shouldn't discourage any future trips. Trips to Atlanta are hard-earned for the players, and given the parity in the SEC, it's hard to say when a team will make it back. So if you get the opportunity to go, by all means do so. Hartsfield-Jackson Atlanta International Airport is one of the biggest and most accommodating airports in the nation. Atlanta is also one of the more centrally located cities to the majority of the teams in the conference. Renting an RV and cruising down I-75 from Knoxville through Chattanooga and into the Atlanta metro area with a beverage of choice and a couple of friends is a great way to get to the big game with built-in accommodations (especially if there's a grill or smoker attached to the back). If you're displaced from East Tennessee and hoping to drive, I-20, I-75, I-85, I-16 into I-75, and I-24 into I-75 are all roads that lead from numerous populated Southern locales into Atlanta.

And when you get there, make sure to check out the SEC Football Fanfare event in the nearby Georgia World Congress Center. Tens of thousands of fans show up to enjoy the festivities in the spacious facility. If you're lucky, you might wind up in a contest throwing or kicking a football, or swept up in a game of flag football with a former SEC great, a number of whom make cameo appearances at different events at Fanfare.

Between the World Congress Center and the Georgia Dome, RVs, trailers, tents, smokers, and throngs of people holding red Solo cups filled with a variety of mind-altering liquids will be jammed together. The tales of past road trips, the smell of slow-cooked barbecue, and the chant of fight songs from the overserved will swirl together to create the familiar feel of a Southern football pregame vibe. Except this time sprinkle in the anticipation of each side preparing to watch their team do battle for one of the most coveted prizes in college sports: the SEC football championship.

50 Johnny Majors: Tennessee's Biggest Heisman Snub

The Heisman Trophy has eluded the University of Tennessee in its great football history. It seemed as though Peyton Manning had the advantage in 1997. Fair or not, many fans and talking heads who considered the award to be a career award saw Manning as a shoo-in. From 1995 to 1997, during which Manning started three full years under center, Tennessee lost a total of just five games, three of them against Florida. Following a 33–20 loss to Florida, Tennessee cruised to an 11–1 regular season, the SEC championship, and an outside shot at a national title. It wasn't quite good enough, as the first-ever true defensive player to win the award—Charles Woodson—turned in an incredible season for the Michigan Wolverines, who claimed a share of the national championship.

Indeed, fans still hold a grudge over the voting. But the Vols arguably had another runner-up to the trophy who had a far greater claim than Manning or any other Volunteer in program history—Johnny Majors in 1956.

Majors was the featured back in Tennessee's single-wing offense, and led the team with 549 yards on a team-high 108 carries for seven touchdowns. Majors and the run-oriented offense created opportunities down the field in the passing game, where Majors showed a dual-threat potential. He completed 61 percent of his passes for 552 yards and five touchdowns, with only three interceptions. As impressive as his balanced game was, Tennessee was equally impressive as a team, fluctuating between No. 1 and No. 3 in the AP poll for the majority of the season. The Vols went the final seven games of the season allowing opponents to score either seven or zero points each game. The Vols finished an undefeated regular season 10–0 and were a contender for the national championship. Majors was the main reason why.

Yet it was the star player on a beloved football program with a 2–8 record who took home the Heisman Trophy. Notre Dame's senior quarterback, Paul Hornung, took home the hardware despite the Irish finishing with one of the worst winning percentages in team history. Hornung completed only 53 percent of his passes for a career-high 13 interceptions to only three touchdowns for 917 yards. The Irish beat Indiana 20–6 and North Carolina 21–14. They got blasted by Iowa 48–8, Navy 33–7, Oklahoma 40–0, and Michigan State 47–14.

Despite the divergent team and individual results, both tilting strongly in Majors' favor, Hornung totaled 1,066 points to Majors' 994. Oklahoma running back Tommy McDonald, the 1956 Maxwell Award winner, totaled 1,135 yards from scrimmage and a whopping 16 touchdowns. He finished third in the voting with 973 points. Syracuse running back Jim Brown finished third in the nation in rushing yards (986) and total touchdowns (14), while leading the nation in rushing touchdowns (13). He finished a distant fifth in the voting.

While McDonald and Brown had outstanding seasons, what is undisputed is that Majors had a better statistical season that paced a team that was in prime contention for the national championship. No matter how one argues the matter—statistics, team performance, what each player meant to his team—the scales tip strongly in favor of Majors over Hornung.

Undoubtedly, McDonald and Brown were each deserving of top consideration in their own rights, and both should have finished higher than Hornung as well. But it was Majors who finished second to Hornung and was the most immediate snub for college football's highest honor. Woodson snared the Heisman Trophy from Manning in 1997 with a highlight-reel "Heisman moment" interception against Michigan State on the way to a national title.

Hornung had no such moment, or relative level of play. For this reason, folks should remember Majors' Heisman snub as the worst in Tennessee history, and arguably one of the worst in college football history.

51 Know the College Football Hall of Fame Inductees

The best of the best in the history of college football have their names enshrined in Atlanta, Georgia, home of the College Football Hall of Fame. The Hall of Fame serves as a shrine to these players and the impact their outstanding contributions have made on the collegiate game.

The University of Tennessee is well represented in Atlanta. Twenty former Volunteers players have been inducted into the Hall of Fame as of the end of the 2014 season, as have four former coaches.

The first player inducted in 1954 was the Bristol Blizzard, Gene McEver—one-half of the Hack and Mac backfield in the late 1920s, along with fellow halfback Buddy Hackman. McEver had a number of great accomplishments in his time at Tennessee, including returning the opening kickoff 98 yards and catching a touchdown pass from fellow inductee Bobby Dodd in a 15–13 Tennessee win over Alabama in 1928. McEver also still holds the Tennessee record with five touchdowns in a single game—a 1929 win against South Carolina.

Other players inducted during the 1950s were Dodd (1959); Herman Hickman (1959), who plowed the road for McEver and the UT running backs; and Beattie Feathers (1955), who succeeded McEver in the backfield from 1931 to 1933. Nathan Dougherty, after whom an engineering building on campus is named, and who, as UT chairman of athletics, was responsible for hiring General Robert Neyland as a Tennessee assistant coach in 1925, was inducted in 1967. George "Bad News" Cafego, the team's leading rusher during the first two year of Tennessee's 31–2 run from 1938 to 1940, was named SEC Player of the Year in 1938 and was a two-time All-American from 1938 to 1939. He was inducted in 1969.

Bowden Wyatt was the school's first former coach and player inducted, as a player in 1972 and as a coach in 1997. As a head coach, Wyatt led Wyoming, Arkansas, and Tennessee to championships in their respective conferences from 1949 to 1956.

After 1981, when Heisman runner-up and 1951 Cotton Bowl star running back Hank Lauricella was inducted, Tennessee continued to place former players in the Hall of Fame as almost an annual occurrence. Doug Atkins, a defensive lineman on the 1951 national championship team and Pro Football Hall of Famer, was inducted in 1985. 1956 Heisman runner-up and Tennessee legend Johnny Majors followed suit in 1987, as did Joe Stefy, who lettered with the Volunteers in 1944 before transferring to Army, where he won the Outland Trophy his senior season.

A run of offensive linemen came next for Tennessee. Bob Johnson, center of the 1967 national championship squad; Ed Molinski, a guard during UT's 1938–40 run under General Neyland; and John Michels, a guard on Neyland's 1951 national championship team, were inducted in 1989, 1990, and 1996, respectively. Steve DeLong, a terror of a defensive tackle who won the Outland Trophy in his senior season, was inducted in 1993.

Linebacker Steve Kiner, coach Doug Dickey's first and only player to earn two-time All-America status (1968 and 1969) entered the Hall in 1999. The Vols went 26–6–1 during his career and claimed two SEC championships.

The Tennessee "Minister of Defense" Reggie White was inducted in 2002. Linebacker Frank Emanuel and guard Chip Kell, both of whom played under Dickey, were the most recent player inductees, in 2004 and 2006, respectively.

As mentioned, four former Tennessee coaches are members of the College Football Hall of Fame, including Bowden Wyatt, who was already discussed. General Neyland was inducted in 1956, four years after his final season as head coach. Neyland remains one of the most accomplished coaches in college football history, having amassed a record of 173–31–12. His single-wing formation was studied and copied by coaches around the country, including Darrell Royal, Frank Broyles, and former Volunteers player and Georgia Tech coach Bobby Dodd.

Doug Dickey received induction in 2003. Compiling a 104–58–6 record during his time as head coach at Tennessee and Florida, he is credited with Tennessee's return to national relevance in the mid to late 1960s, including a claimed 1967 national championship. He also served as athletic director at UT from 1985 to 2003, during which time Tennessee rose to prominence under Phillip Fulmer in the 1990s. Dickey's son, Daryl, led the Vols to a 1986 Sugar Bowl victory over No. 2 Miami in one of the most memorable wins in school history.

Phillip Fulmer is the most recent Volunteers member in the College Football Hall of Fame. For years, Coach Fulmer's winning percentage ranked among the highest in the country, with his final coaching record 152–52. His teams from 1995 to 1998 won 45 games and lost only five. He was named the National Coach of the Year in 1998, the year in which the Volunteers won their first consensus national championship since 1951.

52 Make Your Mark on "the Rock"

If you've spent more than a few days on the University of Tennessee campus, you almost certainly have seen it. More likely, you've driven by and chuckled at some late-night message written by a group of students whose pyramid of stacked beer bottles served as their motivation, or creativity, in proclaiming a political, personal, or sports-related message. Invariably, if you drove by again an hour later, a different group of students were likely reclaiming the school's unofficial message board for their own personal broadcast.

Many have been to the Rock, driven past the Rock, maybe even thought about actually writing something on the Rock but never did.

You should. The Rock is as much an actual piece of rock as it is a time capsule capturing countless thousands of messages through thousands of layers of paint. Each layer holds a personal, amusing, inspiring, crude, or congratulatory message that has helped define the times at the university. Wedding proposals (as one UT official joked—who could say no to a rock that big?), birth announcements, encouragement to the football team, and political messages lie forever stuck together, one after the other. Capturing the excitement of students from one generation to the next. So drag your spray-paint cans (with or without a beverage of choice) over to its current location in front of the Natalie L. Haslam Music Center (the Rock was previously located across the street, near fraternity row, for decades until it was moved in 2009).

And what is the Rock, actually? It's an enormous chunk of Knox Dolomite that was unearthed in the 1960s. Shortly thereafter, the Rock became a "canvas" for student messages...or even a literal canvas for the next aspiring Bob Ross or Picasso. For

A Local Icon Moved, but Not Removed

When construction plans for a new student health center were announced for the former site of the Rock in 2009, fear spread among students and alumni that one of the school's proudest traditions was in danger of being removed from campus. But during the summer of that year, UT officials announced that the Rock would not be hauled off, but rather would be relocated diagonally across the intersection in front of the Natalie L. Haslam Music Center. Plans for the center were even created to provide for a small courtyard around the Rock.

"For generations, the Rock has been an unofficial message board for our campus," Chancellor Jimmy G. Cheek stated to the media prior to the move. "Over the years, tens of thousands of students and others have painted it with their messages—from proposals to birthday wishes, from rallying cries to protest notes. It's a UT-Knoxville icon. Knowing that, we've worked hard to come up with a plan that allows us to preserve tradition as we expand our campus facilities."

During the short move across the intersection, the Rock was estimated to weigh more than 80 tons. Of course, much of that weight can be attributed to the thousands of layers of paint that have coated its surface and slowly increased its size.

years the university sandblasted away the messages but eventually deferred to students' artistic endeavors. The *Daily Beacon*—UT's student newspaper—has editorialized: "Originally a smaller rock, [t]he Rock has grown in prestige and size while thousands of coats of paint have been thrown on its jagged face. Really, its function is as an open forum for students."

And an evolving, never-ending chance to add your name or message to the amalgam of pictures, paintings, announcements, and late-night parties that the Rock has become.

The Kentucky Streak: 1985–2010

Though they came from a state known for its breed of grass, the Kentucky Wildcats experienced a seemingly never-ending nightmare playing on the surface against their border rivals. Kentucky's trip to Knoxville served as an exercise in futility for almost three decades. Until the streak was broken in 2011, it ranked as the nation's ongoing second-longest winning streak.

Tennessee and Kentucky began playing each other in 1893, making the series one of the oldest in college football history (Kentucky is the opponent Tennessee has played the most in its history, with 110 meetings as of the end of 2014). The string of success by Tennessee from 1985 until 2011 was far and away the longest streak in the series.

Kentucky edged Tennessee 17–12 in 1984 in Neyland Stadium. Tony Robinson's frantic last-minute drive put the Vols at the Kentucky 13-yard line after a long completion to Tim McGee. But Robinson could not kill the clock before it hit all zeros, sending Kentucky players running off the field in a wild celebration.

The rivalry produced a number of close calls, but Tennessee started its winning streak in 1985 with a 42–0 trouncing of the Wildcats in Lexington. Tennessee squeaked by in a rain-soaked affair in Neyland Stadium in 1988, after which they rolled to victory from 1989 through 1994 by a combined point differential of 165. UT shut out Kentucky in 1993 and 1994 by scores of 48–0 and 52–0, respectively.

The year 1995 was one of Tennessee's best and most dominant years in recent memory. Kentucky arguably provided the Vols' biggest challenge of the season outside of the Florida game. Trailing 31–16 in the second half, Manning rallied the Vols in the chilly

Close Calls in the Tennessee-Kentucky Series

Although Tennessee's domination over Kentucky seemed, especially for Kentucky fans, like it would never end, there were several opportunities for Kentucky to end it. Some of the most memorable and tense chapters in the rivalry during the streak:

- **1987:** UT 24, Kentucky 22. The Wildcats needed a sixth win to qualify for bowl contention, and early they played like they wanted it, leading 17–7 in the second quarter. Tennessee rallied to take the lead 24–20 with 6:25 to play. Kentucky drove the field and set up first-and-goal at the 5. On fourth-and-goal at the 1, Mark Higgs was stopped short, and the Vols took a safety to preserve a 24–22 win, knocking Kentucky out of a bowl game.

- **1995:** UT 34, Kentucky 31. With snow flurries blowing through Commonwealth Stadium, Kentucky QB Billy Jack Haskins and running back Moe Williams led Kentucky to a 31–16 lead in the third quarter at Commonwealth Stadium against the fourth-ranked Vols. But behind Peyton Manning, Tennessee scored the game's final 18 points, surviving its biggest scare of the season and paving the way to a No. 2 finish nationally.

- **2001:** UT 38, Kentucky 35. On the arm of hefty quarterback Jared Lorenzen, Kentucky soared to a 21–0 second-quarter lead in Lexington. Tennessee fought back to tie it at 21 in the third quarter, and snuck ahead in the fourth quarter on a field goal with 2:49 remaining. As Kentucky would often do, it found a way to lose, with Chase Harp fumbling away the ball inside the Tennessee 30-yard line in the waning moments.

- **2004:** UT 34, Kentucky 31. It seemed like Kentucky was about to spoil Senior Day in Knoxville, jumping out to a 31–22 lead going into the fourth quarter. But the Vols used a trick play, with C.J. Fayton passing to Robert Meachem, to engineer a touchdown, and Gerald Riggs scampered for 12 yards with seconds remaining to break hearts in Lexington yet again.

- **2007:** UT 52, Kentucky 50, seven overtimes. This might have been Kentucky's best chance to win. In the third overtime, Knoxville native and UK kicker Lones Seiber had to make a 38-yard field goal to win the game. As Kentucky fans prepared

> to flood the field in excitement, Tennessee blocked the kick. Tennessee's two-point conversion to Austin Rogers in the seventh overtime proved to be the difference, when Andre' Woodson was tackled on the Wildcats' attempt, securing the SEC East title for UT.
>
> - **2009:** UT 30, Kentucky 24, overtime. With victory only six yards away, Tennessee's defense held at the end of regulation, forcing Seiber to bang through a 23-yard field goal to force overtime. His 49-yard kick sailed wide left, and Montario Hardesty burst straight up the middle on Tennessee's first play to end the game and, yet again, send the big blue nation home beaten and disappointed.

weather inside Commonwealth Stadium, raising the beer barrel trophy in celebration at the end.

Even while Kentucky celebrated its best quarterback in recent memory in Tim Couch, Coach Fulmer's squad was superior to Hal Mumme's in every way in the late 1990s, rolling up a final point total of either 56 or 59 points in each contest from 1996 to 2000.

Tennessee survived a number of close calls in the 2000s, starting in Lexington in 2001 (38–35) after Kentucky fumbled away the ball while in field goal range in the final seconds. A Gerald Riggs 12-yard touchdown run with seconds remaining gave the Vols their first lead of the day in a 37–31 thriller in 2004.

Trips to Lexington in 2007 and 2009 saw the Vols and Wildcats go into overtime, both with Kentucky inside the Tennessee 10-yard line in the final moments of the game. Lones Seiber was forced to kick field goals to put both games into overtime. In 2007 Seiber's would-be winning field goal was blocked, and Tennessee escaped 52–50 when quarterback Andre' Woodson was sacked on the tying two-point conversion attempt. In 2009 Montario Hardesty rumbled 20 yards to end the game and continue the streak.

The Vols handled the Wildcats 24–14 in Neyland Stadium in 2010 but, as the saying goes, all good things must come to an end. The Vols' streak ended on their next trip to Lexington, in 2011, and at the hands of the most unlikely of players. Matt Roark, a reserve wide receiver for Kentucky, was called upon to start for the 4–7 Wildcats, and he responded with 124 yards rushing on 24 carries. His 15 passing yards were the fewest against a Tennessee squad since the days of leather helmets. Still, behind a stout Kentucky defense that forced three turnovers, Kentucky was able to run its four-minute drill to perfection late in the game, bleeding out the clock and celebrating with its legions of fans who stormed the field, hoisting Roark up on their shoulders.

Twenty-six years of dominance was, for Kentucky fans, at long last over.

54 Experience the Vol Walk

As far as the eye can see, orange-and-white jerseys, shirts, dresses, and hats merge together into a near-mob, with shakers waving overhead, as UT fans try to catch a glimpse of their heroes as they march to Neyland Stadium to do battle on a sunny Saturday afternoon. Parents hoist kids onto their shoulders. Almost as if trying to avoid a Big Orange flood, people try to find higher ground to get the best views. Police officers try their best to make a clear path for the suit-clad players to maneuver down Peyton Manning Pass, on to Phillip Fulmer Way, and into the stadium.

The Vol Walk is, without question, a spectacle and a Tennessee tradition. Many schools have some form or fashion of "the walk" and claim it to be their own. While the tradition did not start at

Tennessee, it has grown into an adored and passionately followed game-day event of its own.

The Vol Walk officially became a part of the pregame festivities on October 20, 1990, when Alabama came to town. Before 1990 players traversed from Gibbs Hall down to Gate 21 at Neyland Stadium, with little fanfare as a logistical part of game day. According to an article by UTSports.com, a trip to Auburn early in the 1990 season changed everything:

> Tennessee team busses were delayed in arriving at Jordan-Hare Stadium because the team bus route had to cross the path of Auburn's Tiger Walk. The delay gave head coach Johnny Majors the idea of formalizing his players' journey from their dorm to Neyland Stadium and three weeks later, the tradition was born.

The Vol Walk tradition has evolved over the years with changes in its path and length. When the Tennessee Lettermen's Wall of Fame was erected outside the Neyland-Thompson Football Complex in 2000, Phillip Fulmer had the walk begin with players running their fingers along the wall's marble surface that bears the name of every Tennessee letter winner in every sport in the program's history.

The route of the Vol Walk was shortened in 2009, when team busses dropped the players and staff off at the head of Peyton Manning Pass to make the walk through thousands of fans. The route down the street named for the Tennessee legend leads past the Pride of the Southland Pep Band, before turning left on Phillip Fulmer Way to the cheers of more fans and a right hand turn into Gate 21A for a quiet final journey down the ramp to field level. In 2010, Derek Dooley added a team gathering around the Torchbearer statue to coincide with his inaugural year as Vol head coach. The famous symbol of the University stands tall at the corner of Volunteer Blvd. and Peyton Manning Pass where the walk still begins. Players and coaches, clad in suits and ties, get off the buses to the cheers of fans all around and greet family, friends and fans as they make the walk.

Today, players passing along Phillip Fulmer Way take part in a new addition to the walk: the statue of General Robert Neyland. Revealed as part of homecoming festivities against Ole Miss in 2010, the general's statue kneels over the crowd from its spot inside the stadium, just as Neyland used to kneel on the sideline.

The Vol Walk gives fans from all generations the opportunity to get up close and personal with the players, and the two groups feed off each other. As the players listen to their headphones and get fired up for the game by high-fiving and nodding at adoring fans, the fans ride the excitement of being near their favorite players.

If you have the chance to sneak away from your tailgating and get to the area near the *Torchbearer* on campus about 2 hours and 15 minutes before kickoff, you might have the chance to catch the Vol Walk, a newer but electric Tennessee tradition.

The Best Block That General Neyland Ever Saw

It took a lot to get a superlative compliment from the reserved General Neyland. Yet there were certain things Neyland believed in, certain fundamentals and parts of the game that carried a lot of weight in his mind. Net punting, the amount of yardage gained over the opponent in the kicking game, was one important factor Neyland put a lot of focus and emphasis on.

Another, as one can imagine in a single-wing offensive system, was assignment blocking. In 1947 offensive lineman Denver Crawford flattened a host of Vanderbilt would-be tacklers and made way for a kick return that pushed the Vols ahead for good.

Leading 7–6 late in the game, Vanderbilt punted the football to Hal Littleford, a 1991 inductee into the Tennessee Sports Hall of Fame.

Littleford fielded the punt at the UT 35-yard line and took off to the right. With a host of Vanderbilt defenders closing in between him and the sideline, it seemed he was going to be forced out of bounds near midfield. Suddenly, Crawford dove in front of the lead Vanderbilt defender, sending him flying into the two defenders flanking him, and a lane opened up at the Vanderbilt 45-yard line. Littleford turned up the sideline and strode into the end zone for the game-winning touchdown in a 12–7 final.

"Vanderbilt had me cut off to the sideline," said Littleford. "I didn't see Denver's block until the following week when I saw the film. I had ducked my shoulder and was resigned to the fact that they were going to knock me out of bounds. I was just waiting for the impact, and it never did come. I went about another 10 yards and looked back to see what was happening, and I didn't see a football player for a good 20 yards. So I just went on in, and I'm lucky I didn't fall flat on my face."

As three black-jerseyed defenders prepared to pounce on the cutting Littleford, Crawford came across the face of the closest defender and drove him away from the ball carrier. The force of the impact and direction of the block also took out the other two defenders in pursuit.

"As I got down on the wall, and I saw Hal, I knew it was going to be timed just right," said Crawford. "I could see three Vanderbilt players converging on Hal, and I thought, *Man, they're going to knock him out of the stadium.* And I just laid out with a body block, and I got that lead man. The other two were so close that it got those two. There was a lot of luck involved, and old Hal sailed on for the winning touchdown!"

Tennessee's win ended a disappointing 1947 on a positive note, with the Vols finishing 5–5. Littleford eventually became the head football coach of the East Tennessee State University program, winning the Volunteer State Athletic Conference Championship in 1954. Crawford was drafted by the Green Bay Packers but played a season for the New York (football) Yankees of the All-America Football Conference instead. The AAFC merged with the NFL in 1950.

56 Pride of the Southland Marching Band

From blasting out "Rocky Top," "Down the Field," the alma mater, and many other game-day favorites to serving as the *T* through which the Volunteers players flood onto the field, the Pride of the Southland Marching Band has become as much a tradition as any associated with the Tennessee football program.

The band's history is a long and rich one, as it has represented both the school and state since its initial formation after the Civil War, making it one of the oldest and most prestigious collegiate band programs in America. Starting as a part of the university military program, the Pride of the Southland has morphed over the years into a 300-member university marching band.

The Pride of the Southland Band was born as a group of cadets back in 1869. The band was made up most of cornet players, headed up by a single cadet leader. It wasn't until 1892 that there was an official "bandmaster," who was Ernest H. Garratt. Charles P. Garratt, and William Knabe succeeded him in leadership, as the band began to make appearances at football events. In fact, the band made its first appearance in 1902, where Tennessee took on Sewanee.

By 1917 the band, wearing military-style uniforms, had increased in size to 30 members, and following a change in leadership in 1925, it began a gradual increase that would put it at 80 members.

The 1940s saw a number of changes to the marching band program. Women were finally included and marched in the band. The halftime shows were lengthened and themes were introduced for each performance. Major Ryba, former member of the John Philip Sousa Band, served for two decades as UT's director. It was also during the 1940s that the Pride of the Southland moniker was born, courtesy of former *Knoxville Journal* sports reporter Ed Harris.

Under bandmaster W.J. Julian (1960–93), the Pride of the Southland Band flourished and continued to grow in both sheer numbers and by reputation. The band was relocated from the Reserve Officers Training Corps to the College of Education. Dr. Julian was also responsible for ushering in the bands' uniforms, which they still wear today. In 1972, Dr. Julian created one of the more important and longstanding traditions, as he unveiled the now-classic "Rocky Top" to the fans at Neyland Stadium.

In July 1997 the Pride of the Southland introduced its ninth director, Dr. Gary Sousa. Under Dr. Sousa's leadership the marching band has continued to honor its rich traditions as well as begin new and lasting traditions for the University of Tennessee.

The Pride of the Southland Marching Band has bolstered its prestige and sterling reputation through numerous television and public appearances in the last 40 years. It has represented the state of Tennessee at one of the nation's most prestigious events of the last half-century by appearing at the last 12 consecutive presidential inaugurations. The band has also attended more than 40

The Pride of the Southland Marching Band arrives on game day.

bowl games, including the Rose Bowl, Cotton Bowl, Sugar Bowl, Orange Bowl, Citrus Bowl, Sun Bowl, Outback Bowl, Gator Bowl, and the 1998 national championship in the Fiesta Bowl.

Aside from being a symbol and an ambassador for the state of Tennessee, it serves as a reminder that, as Bobby Denton would say, no matter where you, here in Neyland Stadium, "it's football time in Tennessee!"

57 The Jabar Gaffney "Drop" in 2000

They sat stunned in disbelief at what they had just seen. The officials huddled up, and after tense seconds, referee Al Ford raised his arms to signal a touchdown. The extra point sailed through, and the outcome was all but settled. Florida 27, Tennessee 23, with 14 seconds remaining. As the Florida travel band pounded out the Gators' fight song while the pockets of orange-and-blue-clad fans celebrated wildly, a furious Orange and White crowd turned into an angry mob, raining unrelenting boos down on the officiating crew that had, in their minds, altered the outcome of the game in favor of the Gators.

The call is one that will live in Tennessee lore forever. On first-and-goal from the Tennessee 3, UF quarterback Jesse Palmer threw a quick strike to wide receiver Jabar Gaffney just over the goal line. Gaffney trapped the ball against his chest for an instant and then it was immediately knocked loose by UT cornerback Willie Miles. But line judge Al Matthews ruled Gaffney had made the catch, and the call stood after a brief conference with referee Ford. What further fueled the ire of Vols fans was that Matthews was a player on the last Vanderbilt team to beat the Vols, in 1982.

The pain for Tennessee fans was magnified by the fact that Tennessee had outgained Florida and generally outplayed the Gators on both sides of the ball for most of the contest. But they settled for four first-half field goals and a 12–7 lead instead of a much bigger margin, especially given the vast discrepancy in yardage. Florida managed only 79 total first-half yards, while Tennessee rolled up 226.

Much of that was on the back of Travis Henry, who finished with 175 yards on a whopping 37 carries with a touchdown. The irony for Tennessee fans, as will be discussed momentarily, is that if Henry could have finished with 176 yards, Tennessee would have toppled the No. 6 Gators in a supposed rebuilding year for Tennessee and would have gained the rare leg up on Spurrier and Florida in the SEC East race.

After all, with the departures of offensive stars such as Tee Martin, Jamal Lewis, Cosey Coleman, and Chad Clifton to the NFL, it was going to be a struggle for Tennessee to keep pace with Florida's Fun 'n' Gun offense. New quarterback A.J. Suggs, who beat out local star Joey Mathews as Tee Martin's replacement, earned the start in the Vols' second game of the season and had performed adequately into the fourth quarter, completing 17 of 29 passes for 140 yards and an interception.

Yet, with just more than two minutes remaining, there the Vols were, holding a 23–20 lead and a dominating 203–39 edge on the ground. With only 2:25 left in the game, all they needed to do was push ahead for one more yard to move the chains and put the Vols in victory formation. Henry took a pitch from Suggs but was slowed by Florida defensive lineman Buck Gurley, who burst past lineman Anthony Herrera and helped gang-tackle Henry for a two-yard loss.

With a chance to clinch the game, Tennessee was stuffed and forced to punt, pinning Florida at its own 9-yard line. Palmer, who finished 20-of-43 for 290 yards, began what felt for Tennessee fans like General Sherman's march to the sea. He completed four passes, including a 33-yard strike to Gaffney, to put Florida at first-and-goal at the 10-yard line. After a catch and run to the 3-yard line, Florida faced a second-and-goal with 20 seconds left. Gaffney ran a quick hitch in front of Miles, who hit him almost as soon as the ball arrived. The ball squirted out, Matthews the ref raised his arms, Florida celebrated, and a potential Big Orange upset that could have jump-started a surprise season fell by the wayside.

Tennessee's 23-game home winning streak was over, and despite the controversial ending, the Vols had no one to blame but themselves. Specifically the aforementioned third-down conversion that could have been. Or the five field goals that Alex Walls booted through, including three chip shots where the Volunteers offense had reached the 6-, 1-, and 2-yard line of the Gators.

The threat of the Tennessee passing game just wasn't there yet with Suggs at quarterback, and Florida was able to bow its collective back and limit Tennessee in key short-yardage running situations. Would a victory have helped Suggs' cause to keep the starting quarterback job over Matthews and eventually Casey Clausen? Unlikely, given Clausen's far superior ability. Suggs transferred to Georgia Tech and started 13 games for the Yellow Jackets in a 7–6 campaign in 2002 before being replaced.

Still, any time you outplay your opponent and lose, it stings. And it stung even more for Vols fans, who felt they had had one taken away by the officiating.

"I saw the ball fall," said Miles. "I'm not a ref. What I think doesn't matter. The Gators won, but the world knows about the last play. I thought they were going to overrule. I don't think they were sure."

Not one to be gun-shy with the barbs, even Spurrier recognized when his team was outplayed, and when fortunes were in his team's favor.

"No question, God was smiling on us, because the other team outplayed us," Spurrier said. "And somehow we got more points."

Florida claimed the SEC East at 7–1 in the conference. They won the SEC championship 28–6 over Auburn. UT finished in a three-way tie for second with Georgia and South Carolina at 5–3.

Two Knee Injuries and a Star's Emergence in 1994

In 1994 Tennessee fans were faced with a quandary that, today, would seem like the punch line of a joke. But a now-long-forgotten quarterback controversy truly divided the Volunteers fan base. The question: Peyton Manning or Branndon Stewart?

Looking back, the incredible success of Manning's collegiate and professional careers makes it easy to forget there was once another freshman quarterback in 1994 whom many UT fans wanted to play instead of Peyton Manning. The fight came down to No. 16 Peyton Manning and No. 6 Branndon Stewart from Texas.

Manning's legacy has been well etched into football history, but some fans may have forgotten the esteem and hype that Stewart brought with him from Texas to Knoxville. Stewart was a consensus high school All-American out of Stephenson High School, where he was coached by eventual Baylor head coach Art Briles, won a state championship, and was named the Texas High School Football Player of the Year. The result was a flood of offers from most major college football programs, including Nebraska and Florida State. Stewart stood 6'3" and sported the combination of athleticism and throwing ability that gave fans visions of championships.

Despite their respective hypes, Manning and Stewart went into the 1994 season fighting for the third-string job. The anointed starter, senior Jerry Colquitt, suffered a torn knee ligament in the first half of the season opener against UCLA. For a guy who had

Branndon Stewart's Career at Texas A&M

After leaving Knoxville for more playing time in his native state of Texas, Stewart found the sledding a bit tougher on a Texas A&M program that was down when he arrived in 1995. After sitting out a year due to NCAA transfer rules, Stewart earned the starting job for the Aggies going into the 1996 season. With four running backs who rushed for 598 yards or more each (Sirr Parker, Eric Bernard, D'Andre Hardeman, and Dante Hall), head coach R.C. Slocum opted a ground-and-pound offensive attack. Stewart finished with only 1,904 yards passing, while the Aggies rushed for more than 2,700 yards as a team. The Aggies finished 6–6, missing a bowl game after a 51–15 thrashing at the hands of intrastate rival Texas.

In 1997 Stewart struggled, finishing with 1,429 yards passing and completing only 56.6 percent of his passes. Reserve quarterback Randy McCown began to cut into his playing time, and by 1998, McCown had ripped the starting job away from Stewart. However, Stewart started the final two games of his career—against No. 2 Kansas State in the Big 12 Championship Game, a 36–33 overtime win, and against Ohio State in the Sugar Bowl.

While Stewart's muted time at Tennessee and subsequent mixed results in College Station are a disappointing result for a player with so much hype coming out of high school, Stewart came through for Tennessee one more time when it mattered most for the Volunteers: with a trip to the national championship on the line. Even though Miami had shocked UCLA in the Miami Orange Bowl to make it a two-horse race to the Fiesta Bowl, Stewart knocked out the Wildcats with the performance of a lifetime. Completing 11 of 20 passes for 245 yards with two touchdowns in the fourth quarter and overtime, Stewart crushed the Wildcats' championship hopes while ensuring Tennessee would be the only remaining undefeated squad left going into the night's last game, the SEC Championship Game. Tennessee rallied for 14 late points to win 24–14.

waited behind Heisman Trophy candidate Heath Shuler, it was a quick and sad end to his career. Then a knee injury sidelined backup Todd Helton in Tennessee's loss at Mississippi State. Helton was a two-sport star who helped lead the Tennessee baseball team to the 1995 College World Series and went on to fame as an All-Star Major League Baseball player.

Suddenly, two freshmen were in a true battle for the starting spot. Despite their respective successes, they couldn't have been more different. The tall, lanky Manning, the immobile-yet-strong-armed beanpole, had the hype as the top quarterback recruit in the country by most major recruiting syndicates. Yet Stewart's athleticism was intriguing. Fans were generally divided on who they wanted to see take over the reins.

Out of necessity, both players were pushed right into the deep end of the pool. Manning earned the start the following week in Knoxville against No. 17 Washington State, a 10–9 Tennessee win. Although Manning got the start, Stewart and Manning took turns alternating a few series each half moving forward the rest of the season.

By the end of the 1994 season, Stewart may have been the fan favorite, but the coaches had given the nod to Manning. In the 45–23 Gator Bowl win over Virginia Tech, Manning played the vast majority of the game, and it seemed the writing was on the wall for Stewart's chances of continuing to play regularly at UT. Stewart quarterbacked just three drives in the Gator Bowl, two at the end of the first half and a third at the end of the game with the victory already in hand.

A couple weeks later, in January 1995, Stewart transferred back to his home state to play for Texas A&M. In a twist of irony, Stewart quarterbacked the 1998 Texas A&M team that won the Big 12 South title and defeated No. 2 Kansas State in overtime in the Big 12 Championship Game to keep the Wildcats out of the BCS National Championship Game in Tempe against Tennessee.

Thus, given Tennessee's victory over Florida State for the national championship, Vols fans can thank Branndon Stewart for helping deliver the Fiesta Bowl matchup that ultimately left Phillip Fulmer, Tee Martin, and elated Tennessee fans holding the national championship trophy. And Vols fans can certainly thank Peyton Manning for the tremendous run from 1994 to 1997, the likes of which UT fans may never see again.

59 Johnny Butler's Run vs. Tide in 1939

Most folks who remember the early glory days against Alabama still remember the stunning 15–13 victory the Vols laid on Wallace Wade's Crimson Tide in 1928, sparked by Gene McEver's opening kickoff return for a touchdown.

Fast-forward to 1939, and Tennessee was in the midst of its perfect, clean-sheet season. On October 21, 1939, No. 5 Tennessee invaded Legion Field for a contest with No. 8 Alabama, having beaten NC State, Sewanee, and Chattanooga by a combined score of 81–0. Led by halfbacks Paul Spencer and Jimmy Nelson, Alabama entered the game after relatively tight matchups with Howard College (now Samford University), Fordham, and Mercer.

The key play in the game came from Tennessee halfback Johnny Butler in the second quarter with the ball on the Tennessee 44-yard line. Butler took the handoff, running to the weak side of the formation. Then he cut back and down the field. He reversed his path two more times before ending the exhausting run in the Alabama end zone. Following the extra point, it was 7–0 Tennessee.

"I was especially pleased with Butler's play and thought his touchdown run was one of the prettiest I ever saw," said General Neyland to reporters after the game. "Our line also did a fine job."

Tennessee wasn't done putting points on the board. In the second half, from the Alabama 11-yard line, halfback Bob Foxx scored on a reverse to push the lead to 14–0. The coup de grace came from Buist Warren, who scored on a fake reverse from 13 yards out.

Led by Ed Molinski, Bob Suffridge, and Abe Shires, Tennessee bludgeoned Alabama to the tune of 190 yards rushing for its backs. Conversely, Nelson and quarterback Sandy Sanford found the Volunteers defensive front to be a brick wall, combining for 60 yards rushing on the day and sustaining only one potential scoring drive, which fell short on Sanford's missed field goal attempt from 37 yards.

It was a dominating victory for the Big Orange, arguably the most impressive performance in what was becoming a bitter rivalry against its highest-ranked opponent of the season. Tennessee completed its run of absolute perfection, winning its final six regular-season games by shutout, including a November 4 trip to Baton Rouge against No. 18 LSU, which Tennessee beat 20–0.

The 1996 Citrus Bowl

The 1995 Tennessee Volunteers and Ohio State Buckeyes arrived on the Florida Citrus Bowl field having a lot in common with each other. Both programs had taken their schools to the brink of a conference championship, led by a future NFL great in the backfield, but failed in gut-wrenching fashion after falling to their

Steve White (left) and Leonard Little (right) sack Ohio State quarterback Bobby Hoying in the 1996 Citrus Bowl.

biggest rivals. Yet, despite both being ranked in the AP Top 5, both programs had taken a different route to the game.

Tennessee and Ohio State started the year in the Top 15, with the Buckeyes ranked 12 and the Vols sitting at No. 8. After putting away East Carolina 27–7 in the opener, Tennessee fought past an unranked but scrappy Georgia team 30–27. Peyton Manning threw for 349 yards and two scores, and freshman kicker Jeff Hall drilled home a 34-yard field goal with 10 seconds remaining to overcome Georgia tailback Robert Edwards' 156 yards rushing.

For a half in Gainesville, it seemed the battle with Georgia had the Vols well positioned for an upset over the fourth-ranked Gators. Safety Raymond Austin returned a Danny Wuerffel fumble 46 yards for a score and Manning was razor-sharp in the pocket, completing 13 of 16 passes for 216 yards and two touchdowns as Tennessee headed to the locker room with a 30–21 advantage. However, an Orange and Blue storm emerged in the second half, burying the Vols under 41 unanswered points in a 62–37 shaming that dropped the Vols to 15th in the polls and an apparent footnote in the 1995 college football season.

But Coach Phillip Fulmer would not let his team fold the rest of the season. Dominating road wins over No. 18 Arkansas and No. 12 Alabama pushed the Vols back into the national conversation. In fact, from the third week of September until the first week of November, no team stayed within a single score of the Vols.

Ranked fourth, Tennessee finished the regular season with rivals and traditional season-ending doormats Kentucky and Vanderbilt. The Vols were in for a fight. Trailing 24–9 in the third quarter in Lexington, the Vols see-sawed ahead of the Wildcats for good on a touchdown strike to Greg Kyler in the fourth quarter and blocked a late field goal to escape victorious.

The following week at home against Vandy would prove even more of a battle. After seeing Vandy march 80 yards on the opening drive for a 7–0 lead, the Tennessee defense held Vandy to 112 yards the rest of the game. But it was the Tennessee offense, despite amassing 455 yards of total offense, that sputtered for most of the game. Trailing 7–6 with minutes left on the clock, Manning engineered a season-saving drive that was capped off by a one-yard dive over the top of the line by Jay Graham for a 12–7 lead and final margin with three minutes left.

With Florida having clinched the SEC East and a trip to Atlanta to play for the SEC title, the Vols accepted the first of consecutive bids to play in the Florida Citrus Bowl. The Vols entered the game on an eight-game winning streak, with Manning setting school records for completions (244), attempts (380), and passing yards (2,954) in a season.

With Tennessee rising, Ohio State landed in Orlando with a resounding *thud*. Led by Heisman Trophy–winning running back Eddie George and Fred Biletnikoff Award winner Terry Glenn, the Buckeyes trounced the competition en route to an 11–0 start, beating six teams ranked in the AP poll. Only one team had come within a touchdown of the Buckeyes—the Nittany Lions in a 28–25 loss in Happy Valley.

In what would be a recurring nightmare for Ohio State fans, a John Cooper–led team—and a more talented team on paper—stumbled against "that school up north." That year's version of Scarlet and Gray heartache came at the hands of an 8–3 Michigan team with only pride left to play for.

Pride carried the day for the Wolverines over the second-ranked Buckeyes. That, and a dominating rushing attack. While Eddie George and the Ohio State offense went for 106 yards on the ground, Michigan's Tshimanga Biakabutuka nearly tripled that total himself with 313 yards rushing on the day. Glenn's Rose Bowl guarantee had wilted. Senior QB Bobby Hoying's hopes for a Big Ten championship were gone. The loss ensured 10–1 Northwestern would be representing the Big Ten in the Rose Bowl. A John Cooper–led team would instead wind up in Orlando for a second straight season.

That one was arguably the toughest for Cooper to swallow. "I'm obviously disappointed," said OSU coach John Cooper. "I don't know if I've ever been as disappointed in my life as I am right now."

The Buckeyes got the early jump on Tennessee, capped off by a two-yard run by their Heisman Trophy back George for a 7–0 lead. Game MVP Graham's 69-yard run in the second quarter tied the score at seven. The Vols would not trail again.

Despite holding the hardware, the Buckeyes offense was no match for a Tennessee defense that more than answered the bell in one of their toughest challenges of the season. George and the Buckeyes offense were held to a season-low rushing output of 89 yards on 36 carries. The highlight of game came on a fourth-and-goal from the 2-yard line with the Buckeyes leading 7–0. Tennessee defensive lineman Bill Duff broke through the middle of the line and collapsed the running lanes, stifling George and giving a joyous Tennessee group a shot in the arm. Minutes later, Graham would score, and a confident Volunteers team was on its way to a 20–14 victory.

Tennessee finished the season 11–1 and ranked No. 2 in the Coaches Poll, the highest ranking for a Tennessee team since finishing No. 2 in 1967.

Certainly, 1995 marks a season to be appreciated for Vols fans, and the Citrus Bowl victory was one of the shining moments of the decade for a program on the rise.

The Transition from Johnny Majors to Phillip Fulmer

Moving from a Tennessee legend, who arguably had earned the right to step out on his own terms, in favor of a young and rising head coach–in-waiting could not have been an easy decision to consider for athletic director Doug Dickey.

The decision wasn't even that ripe for consideration, as the 1992 season approached. In fact, the talk of replacement wasn't even in the conversation, given the Vols were coming off a nine-win season, Fiesta Bowl appearance, and Top 15 finish.

But shortly before the 1992 season opener against SW Louisiana, Coach Majors underwent open-heart surgery. Although the circumstances were not one in which anyone would have preferred to see Tennessee try out a new coach, Fulmer was given the opportunity some felt the longtime Tennessee Volunteer from Winchester, Tennessee, was suited for.

And Dickey had a very tough decision to make. This was not just any coach who lay on the operating table for more than three hours and was returning. This a man who, next to General Neyland, was the closest thing to royalty there had been in the history of the University of Tennessee football program. When Coach Majors was well enough to return to the program, which Dickey thought would be around the Alabama game, he could come back in a limited fashion and assist with recruiting or, with the doctor's blessing, he could return to his full-time duties as head coach. Or he could take the entire year off to focus on improving his health.

With Fulmer running the team, the Vols responded, winning their first four games, including a thrilling 34–31 last-minute win at Georgia and a 31–14 trucking of Florida in a driving rainstorm, the program's last true blowout win against the Gators. Tennessee, at 4–0 and having beaten two of its three chief rivals for a trip to the first-ever SEC Championship Game in Birmingham, made Volunteers fans excited about the direction in which the program had shifted.

Suddenly, the day after the Florida win, Coach Majors was back in his office, and there were more than a few confused people inside and out of the program as to who was to be calling the shots.

Still, Majors returned to the sideline, and Tennessee seemed to be returning to its winning ways, shutting out LSU the next week in Death Valley. At 5–0 and No. 4 in the nation, Tennessee seemed to be in prime position to make a run to the Alabama game undefeated. After all, they only had to get past a 1–4 Arkansas team to do it.

They didn't. Arkansas rallied from a 24–9 deficit and stunned Tennessee on a last-minute field goal after recovering an onside kick in the final seconds. Arkansas was supposed to have been no more than a warm-up before the Vols faced Gene Stallings' Crimson Tide, and since Tennessee had lost this "no-count" game, their season was suddenly damaged goods. It felt even more so after a 17–10 setback to the Crimson Tide on October 17.

With a week off, the talk show airwaves filled with calls looking to return to the winning ways of weeks before, under Coach Fulmer, suggesting an if-it-ain't-broke-don't-fix-it mentality and that Tennessee's chemistry was affected by Majors' return and self-insertion back into the program.

Still, Tennessee had the tiebreaker over Georgia and Florida. All they needed to do was go to Columbia, South Carolina, and do what Tennessee almost always has done: win. Trailing 24–23 and needing a two-point conversion to escape with the lead in the SEC East, Majors called a flood right from the left hash mark. Shuler dumped the ball underneath to a running back, who was dragged down at the 3-yard line. The Vols were all but eliminated from the SEC race on one play.

If the controversy between Fulmer and Majors had been a narrow divide in the football program before the loss, it was the size of the Grand Canyon afterward. Fulmer suddenly was, naturally, the green grass on the other side of the fence—a young talent who Tennessee didn't want to let get away. He was already drawing strong interest from Arkansas and South Carolina for head coaching jobs.

Thus, Dickey and the university trustees had an extremely difficult and uncomfortable decision to make. Although rumors and chatter flew about backroom dealings between Fulmer and the athletic department, no such talk was ever substantiated. More likely, the Volunteers brain trust saw new blood that could take the program in a new and higher direction and didn't want to lose that.

Whatever their ultimate reason, the end result was Majors reading a prepared statement in Memphis shortly before the Vols took on Memphis State.

"I played hard," said Majors. "I coached hard. I demanded a lot of myself and [of] those who surrounded me. Sometimes in the heat of battle, I've occasionally said things that upon reflection I wish I hadn't. But that's been my style, and it's brought me more success than failure. I still love the game of football, and if there's an opportunity to coach elsewhere, I certainly would consider it."

The national media mainly came down on the side of the long-time Volunteers coach and school legend Majors. The day after the announcement, ESPN commentators Lee Corso and Craig James responded with the following criticism of the university:

"It's a sad situation, though, when a man who has basically given his entire life to a university is forced out of the system based on one lousy month on a football field," said Corso.

"It really shows you how far college athletics have [regressed] when a virtual living legend like Majors is forced out because he didn't win the SEC in a year that his football team was supposed to be rebuilding," said James. "They weren't even supposed to win this year."

Yet, despite the criticism and the hurt felt by fans and those inside the program and university who felt hurt by the decision to part with Majors, Tennessee had to move forward. And they did so with a coach they believed would be the future of the program.

The university bought out the last two years of Majors' contract for $600,000. Majors coached the Vols in their final three games against Memphis State, Kentucky, and Vanderbilt—all wins—before bowing out. Fulmer coached Tennessee to a 38–23 win over Boston College in the Hall of Fame Bowl.

Now that both men have retired from coaching—Fulmer himself was unceremoniously terminated in 2008, one year after winning the SEC East crown—each has his name on a street on campus: Phillip Fulmer Way and Johnny Majors Drive. Both men are College Football Hall of Fame inductees, and both brought championships to Knoxville. Both men made great strides in improving the University of Tennessee program and left it a better place than when they took over.

Hopefully that will be how folks look back on the 1992 controversy and one of the most difficult months in the history of the football program.

Vols, Tide Return Series to Tuscaloosa in 1999

The pep rally in Tuscaloosa was furious. "Yea Alabama" was blaring from the Million Dollar Band, who encircled the Crimson Tide football players and coaches amid crimson-and-white shakers wildly flailing above the legions of adoring fans.

Finally, the Third Saturday in October had returned home, to the campus of the University of Alabama.

From 1932 to 1997, Tennessee traveled to Birmingham, Alabama, to take on the Crimson Tide. The teams' last matchup in Tuscaloosa had been in 1930, an 18–6 Alabama victory. For decades, Legion Field in Birmingham—known over the years as the Old Gray Lady—hosted Crimson Tide clashes with its longest-played rivalry (Tennessee), and became a staple of great matchups in college football, including many memorable Iron Bowl contests with intrastate rival Auburn.

However, once the mid-1990s rolled around, stadium issues began to surface, necessitating that the rivalry—and Alabama football—needed to move in a new direction. Trustees of the university agreed with the cities of Tuscaloosa and Northport and of Tuscaloosa County on an expansion of Bryant-Denny Stadium. The localities footed a combined $4.65 million for the renovation that ultimately brought the creation of an upper deck to the north end zone of the stadium.

The trade-off was too enticing for the localities to pass up: all home games would be played in Tuscaloosa.

As a sea of orange and crimson spilled onto the streets of Tuscaloosa the night before the game, it was obvious that the move was a gold mine for the regional economy. Co-eds and alumni shuffled from fraternity row to the campus bar scene, which had been, in part, barricaded to allow for the (over)consumption of alcohol.

The matchup proved to be as enticing as the aroma of barbecue ribs wafting from a nearby tailgating tent. Tennessee and Alabama entered the game with one loss apiece, both ranked in the Top 10 of the AP poll. Tennessee had fallen 23–21 in its road opener at Florida, snapping a 14-game winning streak dating back to the start of the 1998 season. Meanwhile, the Tide had won an overtime 40–39 thriller in Gainesville but dropped a head scratcher in Birmingham to Louisiana Tech, 29–28.

An Alabama native led the Vols to their first win in Tuscaloosa since 1928. Tee Martin, from Mobile, flashed the athleticism and skill set that had taken him to 17–1 as a starter entering the game. He scrambled into the end zone from six yards out late in the second quarter to tie the game at seven.

Early in the third quarter, Martin delivered the decisive blow, hitting wide receiver David Martin in stride on a fade route for a 43-yard touchdown. Martin finished the game 11 of 17 for 147 yards and a touchdown, with 49 yards rushing on 9 attempts.

He finished the Tide with a play-action bootleg run for a game-clinching 21-yard touchdown.

Tennessee won the game 21–7, but it was the Tide who made the bigger splash in 1999. After beating Auburn in the Iron Bowl, Mike DuBose's team beat Steve Spurrier and the Florida Gators for the second time that season, this time in a 34–7 rout for the SEC championship.

Bryant-Denny Stadium, like Neyland Stadium in Knoxville, now holds more than 100,000 fans and is one of the loudest and most intimidating venues in the country. A perfect locale for one of the longest-tenured and most renowned rivalries in all of college football.

The Vanderbilt Streak: 1983–2004

General Neyland was hired, in great part, to defeat Tennessee's intrastate rival from Nashville. For modern-day Tennessee fans, that might be hard to process.

Neyland would have been proud of the undefeated streak the Volunteers were able to put together against Vandy from 1983 to 2004 (and though the Commodores won in 2005, they went on to lose against Tennessee the next six straight years). There have been many longer streaks, such as Navy's 43 years of fruitless play against annual opponent Notre Dame (which ended in 2007) and Nebraska's 36-game streak over neighboring Big 8 foe Kansas, but the UT-Vandy series represented more of a true underdog, David vs. Goliath, big-brother-takes-on-little-brother rivalry that is rarely seen.

Vanderbilt University. A private school of approximately 7,000 undergraduate students with an academic reputation at the top of the list of universities in the South. Vanderbilt fielded its first football team in 1890 and found success early in its program. It has finished undefeated twice—in 1921 and 1922. Although unofficial, Vandy claims national championships for these seasons.

However, the Vandy Commodores became an afterthought in the college football world for the last half of the 20th century. From 1955 to 2007, Vandy appeared in just three bowl games and won one—25–13 over Auburn in the 1955 Gator Bowl.

The 1982 squad, coached by George MacIntyre, won eight games, including a regular-season-ending 28–21 besting of Tennessee in Nashville. Senior quarterback Whit Taylor scorched the Volunteers defense with 391 yards passing, finding wide receiver Chuck Scott for 42- and 6-yard scoring strikes. Taylor scampered into the end zone in the game's waning minutes for the winning margin.

And then the wait would begin for the Vandy faithful.

The 1982 Commodores represented a rare exception to the rule of Vanderbilt finding itself the butt of jokes in the college football world. The team included four All-Americans: tight end Allama Matthews, Chuck Scott, punter Jim Arnold, and defensive back Leonard Coleman.

From 1983 through 2004, Vandy sported eight All-Americans. By contrast, the Vols had 24 All-Americans recognized during that same stretch.

The talent level clearly was nestled in the hills of East Tennessee, slanted heavily in favor of the state university clad in orange.

However, the records might as well have been thrown out in late November when Tennessee and Vanderbilt played. While Tennessee played for improved bowl positioning and even SEC and national title consideration, Vanderbilt played for its pride.

If one could describe a one-sided rivalry as a heated and competitive one, UT and Vandy might be its poster children. Tennessee's streak featured a number of landslide results when UT rolled over an outclassed Vanderbilt squad.

But there were plenty of memorable, hard-won battles along the way, too. And it started with the next meeting in 1983 between a 7–3 UT squad and a 2–8 Vandy group.

Tennessee, behind the strength of more than 200 rushing yards on the day by Johnnie Jones, had staked a 20–10 third-quarter lead and were looking to put the game out of reach. But Vanderbilt would not quit, with quarterback Kurt Page, who set a then–school record with 3,034 passing yards, leading the offense. He found wide receiver Phil Roach from 12 yards out on a play-action pass to make it 20–17. Running back Louis Stephenson ended Vandy's next drive with a one-yard touchdown run, and Vanderbilt held an improbable 24–20 lead.

But in the fourth quarter, Jones took a pitch on a counter option from quarterback Alan Cockrell, cut it inside, and burst through the middle and away from the Commodores secondary for a 70-yard touchdown and a 27–24 lead that UT would not relinquish. The Vols triumphed 34–24.

The fans in 1987 saw another close, high-scoring affair in Neyland Stadium. Trailing 38–28 late in the fourth quarter, Vandy quarterback Eric Jones found Carl Parker wide open on a post corner route for a touchdown. The ensuing two-point conversion brought Vandy to within two, at 38–36. However, a third-down offside penalty by Commodores linebacker Chris Gaines allowed No. 16 Tennessee to bleed the clock out and improve to 9–2–1, on their way to a 27–22 Peach Bowl win over Indiana. Vandy ended the season at 4–7.

And who could forget 1995? Tennessee, trailing Vandy for virtually the entire game following a missed extra point, escaped with a 12–7 victory after Jay Graham bulled his way over the goal line and into the end zone with only three minutes remaining. It was one of the closest calls in an otherwise dominant and memorable 11–1 season in Knoxville.

Tennessee did not clinch its first SEC East title easily. After losing 33–20 in Gainesville earlier in the season, a couple of Gators stumbles to LSU and Georgia opened the door for Tennessee to claim the Eastern Division crown...if it could get by its 3–7 intrastate rivals from Nashville, who were winless in the SEC.

That goose egg would not matter on November 29, 1997.

Leading Vandy 10–3 in the third quarter, cornerback Dwayne Goodrich picked off quarterback Damian Allen, which led to a one-yard bootleg touchdown run by Peyton Manning. Manning, playing his final game in Neyland Stadium, completed only 12 of 27 passes for 159 yards and a touchdown against the SEC's No. 1 overall statistical defense. But it was a bruising UT running back who led the team. Freshman running back Jamal Lewis ran for 196 yards to pick up the slack for a struggling Tennessee offense. Tennessee won 17–10.

How about a Houdini-esque escape in 2000 in the teams' first matchup in the Tennessee Titans' Adelphia Coliseum? Trailing 21–6 entering the fourth quarter, a Vanderbilt triumvirate of quarterback Greg Zolman, running back Jared McGrath, and wide receiver M.J. Garrett brought the Commodores storming back. The first play of the quarter was a slant pass from Zolman to McGrath for 22 yards. Zolman's 11-yard strike to Garrett brought Vandy to 21–12. Zolman hit Garrett again with eight minutes and change left to pull within two, at 21–19.

Not to be outdone, Casey Clausen hit Cedrick Wilson on consecutive passes of 16 and 15 yards to push Tennessee's lead to 28–19.

Two runs by McGrath gained 30 yards, and McGrath busted through the Tennessee defense for a one-yard touchdown with less than four minutes to play, making it 28–26.

Travis "the Big Cheese" Henry, who carried the Tennessee offense with 184 rushing yards on 33 carries, salted the game away, moving the chains with runs of 1 and 15 yards, respectively, as the Vols hung on to complete an 8–3 regular season.

Tennessee crushed the Commodores in the 2001–03 meetings without allowing a single point, winning 38–0, 24–0, and 48–0. A 38–33 win in Nashville in 2004 served as the last conquest in two-plus decades of dominance by Tennessee.

The 2005 season finale for Vanderbilt (UT still had Kentucky to play) showcased two prominent NFL players in the Black and Gold—quarterback Jay Cutler and wide receiver Earl Bennett. Although Tennessee freshman tailback Arian Foster filled the familiar role of a UT back against Vanderbilt (he carried 40 times for 223 yards and two touchdowns), the future Chicago Bears teammates on the other side of the field stole the show.

Trailing 21–7 in the second quarter, Tennessee stormed back on the strength of Foster's frenetic ground attack, taking a 24–21 lead with 8:25 to play. With 1:40 left, Vandy took possession at its own 37-yard line. Cutler found Bennett for 15 yards and 31 yards on consecutive plays. Two plays later, Bennett ran a slant and pulled in a ball near the ground for a six-yard touchdown and a 28–24 lead with 1:11 left.

Rick Clausen got the Vols inside the Vandy 20, but his final pass into the end zone was intercepted. The streak was over, after 22 straight wins for UT.

64 Tee Martin Sets NCAA Record for Accuracy vs. Gamecocks in 1998

In the eyes of many, the 1998 season was fueled offensively by a trio of running backs (four, if you count fullback Shawn Bryson) who helped carry Tennessee to a second consecutive SEC crown and the national title. Down went Jamal Lewis with a season-ending knee injury at Auburn, and in stepped Travis Henry and Travis Stephens, who carried the load admirably and took the pressure off Tee Martin and the passing game.

But it was Martin, the walking question mark of the 1998 off-season, who shined throughout the year after stepping into the Shaquille O'Neal–sized shoes left by Peyton Manning.

And there was no greater performance by Martin—or perhaps any UT quarterback ever—than what happened on Halloween 1998 in Columbia, South Carolina.

The No. 3 Tennessee Volunteers entered the matchup red hot, especially defensively. In the previous five contests, the Vols had allowed a total of 54 points.

Conversely, South Carolina, following a season-opening win against Ball State, had fallen on its collective face. A 38–0 home loss to Mississippi State, followed by road losses at Kentucky and Vanderbilt, left the Gamecocks at 1–7 and placed fifth-year head coach Brad Scott firmly in the hot seat.

Martin entered the game having completed just 51.3 percent of his passes on the season. That number would be significantly higher three hours and many completions later.

After recovering a South Carolina fumble near midfield, Tennessee made quick work of the Gamecocks defense on its opening drive. Martin completed his first three passes, the last

Tee Martin steps into the limelight.

going to Jermaine Copeland on a corner pattern for a 21-yard touchdown.

The Tennessee faithful—and the college football world—had no idea what kind of powder keg Martin had just lit.

Three completions were offset by a missed handoff and tackle of Martin, resulting in a punt. But on Tennessee's next possession, Martin completed his eighth pass of the game for 31 yards to Cedrick Wilson. His ninth was a dart to Peerless Price for 25 yards, who was running free on a post pattern.

His 10th pass found pay dirt—a three-yard touchdown pass to Wilson, who was standing all by himself in the end zone on a simple out pattern. Tennessee 14, South Carolina 0. Martin: 10 passes, 10 completions.

After South Carolina missed its second field goal of the half—this one blocked—Tennessee switched gears into a hurry-up offense. Three minutes later, the Volunteers offense was celebrating a 21–0 lead 93 yards downfield, as the boos from the South Carolina fans rang down at their bumbling special teams and overmatched defense. Peerless Price snared a third-and-12 pass on a corner route between a group of South Carolina defenders and knocked over the pylon as he went to the ground for the 14-yard score.

To quote Tennessee play-by-play announcer John Ward: "Peerless Price through a host of defenders! How in the world he came out of there with the oval, I do not know, nor care. Touchdown, Big Orange!"

Where the boos from the Gamecocks fan should have turned to cheers was in appreciation for the rarefied air that Martin and the Tennessee offense was placing itself in: Martin was throwing what would be the equivalent of a perfect game in baseball. No quarterback had ever thrown so many passes and finished a game with 100 percent completion percentage.

The Vols stuck the dagger in the Gamecocks' collective heart early in the third quarter, and it was Martin and Price who delivered the coup de grace. Early, as in second-play-of-the-half early, Martin found Price on a quick hitch, who turned up the sideline and outraced the Gamecocks secondary for a 72-yard touchdown and a 28–0 lead.

What were once boos had turned to silence from the home crowd, mixed with the sounds of "Down the Field" from the Pride of the Southland Marching Band and cheers from the orange patches of the Tennessee faithful throughout Williams-Brice Stadium.

Stan White, quarterback of the 1993 undefeated Auburn squad, held the SEC record for most consecutive completions in a game. Martin's touchdown pass to Price gave White company in the record books. Martin's next completion to Copeland on a busted wide receiver screen pass gave Martin the conference record. Another completion to Copeland stretched the streak to 20 completions, which tied the SEC record held by Mississippi's Ken Austin for most consecutive completions (spanning more than one game). A screen pass to Henry, who weaved through Gamecocks defenders down to the one-foot line, set the new conference mark at 21.

With their foot on the gas pedal, up 35–0 and in South Carolina territory, Martin connected with Copeland on a quick hitch for completion number 22 of the game. And, given that Martin's last pass attempt in the Vols' previous game, a 35–18 win over Alabama, was a completion, Martin had tied the NCAA record for consecutive completions at 23.

Later in the drive, Price took off downfield on third-and-8. After 10 yards, he turned, and the ball was waiting for him. First down Tennessee, and Martin had set the NCAA record. The previous record for two games of 23 consecutive completions was shared by Southern California's Rob Johnson and Maryland's Scott

Milanovich. Martin's 23 consecutive completions broke the NCAA one-game record of 22 by Iowa's Chuck Long in 1984 and the completion percentage of 95.8 (23 of 24) broke the mark of 92.6 (25 of 27) set by UCLA's Rick Neuheisel in 1983.

And it wasn't just a hot hand du jour for Martin. Since halftime of the Vols' 22–3 win at Georgia, Martin had completed 44 of his last 51 passes. Martin was firmly establishing himself as one of the premier quarterbacks in the nation, and the record-setting performance in Columbia was a microcosm of the maturity and improvement Martin showed throughout the season.

The streak ended on the next play, but Martin, who was 23 of 24 for 315 yards and 4 touchdowns, received an ovation from both fan bases for the record-setting performance they had all just witnessed. Tennessee rolled to a 49–14 victory, with Martin watching from the sideline in the fourth quarter.

It wasn't a "perfect game," thanks to one incompletion, but it's the closest equivalent that one will ever see on a football field.

Satisfy a Late-Night Craving at Gus's Good Times Deli

Stop and ask any Tennessee student his or her place of choice to stumble for a late-night feast after drinking on the Strip, and the most likely answer will be Gus's Good Times Deli. Strategically located on the edge of campus within walking distance between the main row of bars, the dorms, and the off-campus student housing, Gus's has been the premier late-night dining spot for UT students since 1981, serving up some of the greasiest and tastiest food you can find any time of day, whether it's 3:00 AM or 3:00 PM.

When you walk inside the place, you'll see maybe two dozen cheap booths and tables in a large open room that serves as a shrine to all things Tennessee football–related. Football schedules from the 1980s, ticket stubs from even older games, autographed photos to Gus (Captain—the original owner who has since sold the place) from former players, framed newspaper articles detailing past UT football conquests, and a giant UT mural cover every square inch of the walls.

"This place is laid-back," said Aaron Hale, a former delivery guy who eventually took over as owner from Captain. "We are definitely different from most places on the Strip. The biggest thing we have on our side is history. We have so much memorabilia from players and other guys who actually ate here. We didn't buy it wholesale on eBay like some places. These guys were here and hung out here just like the kids do today, and some of them still come back here."

The menu has something for everyone who, at least temporarily, has no qualms about his or her caloric intake. The appetizers are outstanding, ranging from fried mushrooms and fried pickle spears to jalapeno poppers and boneless Buffalo wings. The half-pound burgers served with Gus's signature fries—thin, crispy fries covered liberally with seasoned salt—are a safe and tasty bet; if you're feeling the urge, you can also smother your burger and fries with Gus's hearty chili. Basically, the perfect greasy, tasty food to fill your stomach and soak up the draft beers you consumed around the corner for the past few hours.

But what Gus's is best known for is their deli-style sandwiches and gyros. The "steak in a sack"—green peppers, onions, and thinly sliced ribeye steak tucked inside a warm pita with Italian dressing—is a popular sell, and the chicken and steak Philly sandwiches (with provolone cheese, for you Philly connoisseurs) are a hit. The prices are also reasonable, with appetizers ranging from three to seven dollars, burgers around six bucks, and deli sandwiches/gyros up to seven and a quarter.

Despite its school and football-time popularity, Gus's history is not one without problems. The restaurant, as do most establishments on the Strip, faces a drought when the students are home for the summer. Also, the original building burned in 1994, but it was quickly rebuilt by the fall of 1995 with the intention of keeping the original atmosphere alive.

And alive and well it is today. For many Vols fans making the trek from Nashville, Charlotte, or other parts of the Southeast, a trip by Gus's on game day is a checklist activity for the trip. If you haven't added it to your game-day weekend plans, do it. You certainly won't regret it.

Wide Receiver U

Ask a fan of any major football power about the strongest historical positional group of his or her team, and more likely than not, that fan will refer to team *X*'s great group of tackles, defensive backs, linebackers, or quarterbacks.

In reality, many teams claim to be "the original (positional) U" based on that team's historical success at that position. Case in point: USC claims to be Linebacker U, and the stats tend to back up their claim. Only Alabama has had as many linebackers drafted in the first round of the NFL as the Trojans over the past half century.

Miami's incredible run from Jim Kelly, Bernie Kosar, Vinny Testaverde, Steve Walsh, Craig Erickson, and Gino Torretta resulted in each quarterback after Kelly either winning a national

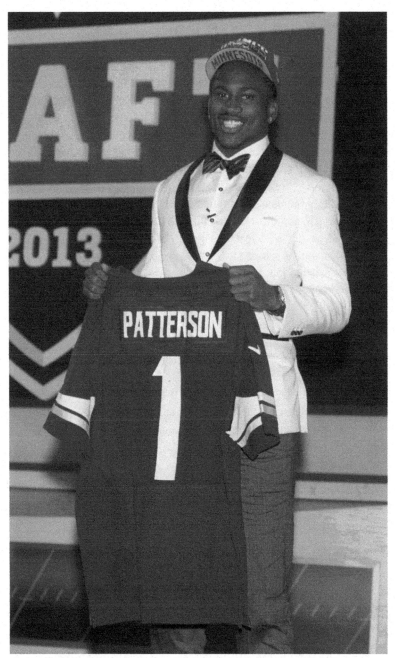

A sharply dressed Cordarrelle Patterson celebrates being selected by the Minnesota Vikings in the 2013 NFL Draft.

Wide Receiver U in the NFL Draft

Going back to 1969, Tennessee wide receivers have a prolific history of being selected by teams in the NFL Draft, which dovetails with the moniker Wide Receiver U, by which the university has been known for decades. The first true Tennessee wide receiver ever drafted was Richmond Flowers, in the second round of the 1969 NFL Draft. Since Flowers, Tennessee has a long and rich history of stocking the NFL with playmakers, with 33 former wide receivers getting their names called on Draft Day. A look at some noteworthy draftees:

- Stanley Morgan—First round of the 1977 NFL Draft by the New England Patriots. Morgan amassed more than 10,000 yards receiving in a 14-year career with the Patriots and the Colts, catching six passes for 51 yards in Super Bowl XX. He was selected to four Pro Bowls and was named NFL All-Pro twice.
- Anthony Hancock—First-round selection of the Kansas City Chiefs in 1982. Played five seasons in Kansas City.
- Willie Gault—First-round pick of the Chicago Bears in 1983. Pulled in a game-high 129 yards in Chicago's 46–10 Super Bowl XX win. Amassed 6,635 receiving yards in 11-year career in Chicago and L.A. (Raiders).
- Tim McGee—First-round pick of the Cincinnati Bengals in 1986. In nine seasons with the Bengals and Redskins, McGee hauled in more than 300 passes for more than 5,000 receiving yards. He helped lead the Bengals to a 12–4 record in 1988 and a Super Bowl appearance.
- Anthony Miller—First-round pick of the San Diego Chargers in 1988. Caught 595 passes for more than 9,000 yards with 63

championship or bringing home the Heisman Trophy. And Kelly played in, you know, four consecutive Super Bowls. Not bad there. So Miami certainly earned the moniker Quarterback U during its run to four national titles in eight years.

As for Tennessee, there is plenty of empirical evidence to support the nickname Wide Receiver U. Although Biletnikoff Awards (given to the nation's top collegiate wide receiver) aren't touchdowns in his career. Selected for five Pro Bowls in his career with San Diego, Denver, and Dallas.

- Alvin Harper—First-round pick of the Dallas Cowboys in 1991. Caught a touchdown pass in the Cowboys' 52–17 destruction of Buffalo in Super Bowl XXVII. Also caught a key pass to set up goal-to-go and Emmitt Smith's game-clinching run in Super Bowl XXVIII. Led the NFL in yards-per-catch average with 24.9 yards per catch in 1994.
- Carl Pickens—Second-round pick of the Cincinnati Bengals in 1992. Selected to two Pro Bowls and received two All-Pro nods.
- Joey Kent—Second-round pick of the Tennessee Oilers in 1997. Appeared for the Titans in Super Bowl XXXIV against the Rams.
- Peerless Price—Second-round pick of the Buffalo Bills in 1999. Pro Bowl alternate in 2002. Caught 403 passes for more than 5,200 yards in his career, with 31 touchdowns.
- Donté Stallworth—First-round pick of the New Orleans Saints in 2002. Compiled more than 4,800 yards receiving in 10-year active career. Was a member of the 18–1 2007 New England Patriots team that lost Super Bowl XLII to the New York Giants.
- Robert Meachem—First-round pick of the New Orleans Saints in 2007. Meachem caught nine touchdown passes from Drew Brees in the Saints' 2009 Super Bowl–championship season.
- Cordarrelle Patterson—First-round pick of the Minnesota Vikings in 2013. Received Pro Bowl and All-Pro selections in 2013. Credited with the longest play in NFL history—a 109-yard kickoff return on October 27, 2013, against the Green Bay Packers.

on display at the Neyland-Thompson Sports Center, Tennessee's history of developing playmakers out wide—many of whom earned All-America honors and were drafted in the NFL—is unmistakable.

In fact, since 1971, 34 Tennessee wide receivers were selected in the NFL Draft. In the past 30 years, Tennessee leads all collegiate programs with 11 first-round wide receiver draft picks. Including recent first-round selection Cordarrelle Patterson by the

Minnesota Vikings in the 2013 NFL Draft, Tennessee's success in placing wide receivers in the first round of the NFL Draft goes back to 1977, when Stanley Morgan was taken with the 25th overall pick by the New England Patriots.

Tennessee has also had four wide receivers recognized as consensus first-team All-Americans since 1982. Robert Meachem in 2006 is the most recent selection. The others are Carl Pickens (1991), Tim McGee (1985), and Willie Gault (1982).

Thus, when it comes down to both quantity of wide receivers drafted in the NFL and the number of nationally recognized players in college, it's hard to argue that Tennessee isn't at the front of the line for schools fighting to call themselves the true Wide Receiver U.

67 1938–40: Unprecedented Dominance in Knoxville

In life, things constantly change and evolve. It's no different in football. Parity and athleticism have led to increased scoring and offensive output. Offensive philosophies have changed as players' abilities and skill sets have changed.

What won't be seen again is the complete dominance and defensive fortitude that General Neyland's 1938–40 football teams showed. Led by a trio of All-Americans in guard Bob Suffridge, defensive end Bowden Wyatt, and running back George Cafego, Tennessee went on an incredible streak of 23 consecutive regular-season games without allowing a team to reach double digits on the scoreboard.

And it all started on September 24, 1938.

The Sewanee Tigers came to Shields-Watkins Field and did what very few teams would do to the Volunteers that season: put points on the stadium scoreboard. Tennessee won 26–3.

The following week, UT handed Clemson its only loss of the year, a 20–7 triumph in Knoxville. Clemson's touchdown and extra point would be the most points Tennessee would allow until Alabama put 12 on the board against Tennessee in 1940 in Birmingham.

Shutouts against Auburn at home—a 7–0 contest that would be the closest of the season—and a 13–0 win at Alabama grabbed the attention of the national media, as Tennessee landed in the AP rankings at No. 8.

LSU came to Knoxville for Tennessee's homecoming game, having outscored its previous four opponents by a tally of 77–6. It would be a battle between two SEC heavyweights, with LSU being paced by SEC Most Valuable Player and future Chicago Bear Ken Kavanaugh, who had also earned the Distinguished Flying Cross as a pilot in World War II. After Tennessee marched 72 yards on the opening kickoff for a 7–0 lead, LSU answered on the soft hands of Kavanaugh, who pulled in a pass from quarterback Ashford Simes. Following an LSU fumble, Cafego scored his first touchdown of the season in the fourth quarter for a 14–6 win.

Having passed arguably its toughest test of the season, the Tennessee defense would not allow another point for the rest of the year, shutting out Chattanooga, Vanderbilt, Kentucky, and Mississippi by an incredible combined score of 152–0.

Ranked No. 2, the Vols were slotted to face No. 4 Oklahoma in the Orange Bowl. Like Tennessee, Oklahoma had ridden an incredible defensive effort into Miami, having shut out five straight opponents and having allowed only six points since its season opener.

It was all Tennessee in the Orange Bowl. In the opening quarter, an Oklahoma penalty and a strong George Cafego punt return gave Tennessee the ball at the Sooners 27. They drove for a touchdown from there, Bowden Wyatt hitting the extra point for a 7–0 lead. An Oklahoma fumble in the second quarter gave the Volunteers the ball at the Sooners 27 again, and from there they drove to a Wyatt field goal and 10–0 halftime lead. In the final quarter Tennessee quickly moved 73 yards for another touchdown against a worn-down Oklahoma defense, finishing the scoring. George Cafego rushed for 114 yards, and the Vols outgained Oklahoma 260 yards–to–94 yards in total offense.

Although TCU, led by its sensational quarterback Davey O'Brien, claimed the No. 1 spot in the final AP poll, Tennessee garnered the top spot in the final Billingsley, Dunkel, Football Research, Houlgate, Litkenhous, Poling, and Sagarin polls. The school claims 1938 as its first national championship.

If Tennessee had done something special in 1938, it one-upped itself the following season. The 1939 Tennessee Volunteers did what no team had ever done before and what no team has done since: pitch a shutout for the entire regular season. Starting with a 13–0 win at North Carolina State, Tennessee would outscore the competition 212–0 on the year, including a 21–0 home win over then–No. 8 Alabama and a victory over No. 18 LSU at Tiger Stadium as the nation's No. 1 team.

Although the season ended with a 14–0 loss to USC in the Rose Bowl, Tennessee would continue the regular-season dominance going into the early part of the 1940 slate. After outscoring Mercer, Duke, and Chattanooga by a combined 115–0 margin, Tennessee allowed its first points in a regular-season game since 1938 in a 27–12 win over Alabama in Birmingham.

Tennessee's defense returned to its dominant form, shutting out Florida, LSU, Southwestern, Kentucky, and Vanderbilt on the way to another 10–0 regular season. Only Virginia could find the end zone, scoring 14 points to Tennessee's 41.

Tennessee lost to Boston College in the Sugar Bowl, but the polls had already come out. Tennessee topped the Williamson and

Dunkel polls for the school's second recognized national championship in three years.

From 1938 through the 1940 season, Tennessee went 31–2, with its sole losses coming in the Rose and Sugar Bowls. Of those 31 wins, 26 came by way of shutout.

68 2001 SEC Championship Game: A Turning Point for the Program

The confetti rained down on the field inside the Georgia Dome. LSU's band boomed the famous "Tiger Rag" as elated purple-and-gold-clad LSU fans high-fived players who streamed to the corner of the Georgia Dome. An LSU player raised the SEC banner in celebration.

Meanwhile, the mostly partisan crowd dressed in orange and white took in the atmosphere in silent disbelief. Those fans that had not departed the dome stood, hands in pockets, watching Casey Clausen, Jason Witten, Kelley Washington, and the rest of the Volunteers players file off the field amidst the celebration.

The 31–20 loss denied the Vols their first SEC title since 1998 and ended all hopes of another Big Orange caravan west to see UT play for the BCS national championship.

For Vols faithful, the loss served as rock bottom in a rollercoaster season that had risen higher than the stratosphere just one week prior.

In their 34–32 victory at Florida on December 1, 2001, Tennessee exorcised a number of demons. It was the first Tennessee team to win in Gainesville in exactly 30 years, when Phillip Fulmer sported a No. 65 jersey as a guard on the last victorious team.

This time, head coach Phillip Fulmer jumped and hugged his players, who streamed onto Florida Field as SEC East champions. While the Gators' championship aspirations were done, fullback Will Bartholomew led the band in playing "Rocky Top," a celebration of a seemingly bright end to the season for Tennessee. The 17½-point Orange and White underdogs had dominated an opponent—the game wasn't as close as the final score indicated—that had consistently had their number for the previous decade.

Thousands arrived at the Knoxville airport that night to greet their Volunteers heroes, who exited the plane with swagger and dreams of the Rose Bowl, site of the national championship game.

With losses by Nebraska and Texas to two-loss Colorado, the door opened for the Vols to make the trip to Pasadena. The Tigers closed that door, and in the process ended an era of dominance by Tennessee.

Losers in Knoxville earlier in the season, LSU relied on a backup quarterback to lead them to victory in Atlanta. Rohan Davey, who had started the Tigers' 26–18 loss in September, succumbed to an internal upper-body injury in the second half.

Enter Matt Mauck. Trailing 17–16, the Tigers sprang to life with Mauck under center.

Although Mauck completed only 5 of 15 passing attempts, it was his ability to escape that left John Henderson, Albert Haynesworth, Jabari Greer, Dominique Stevenson, and the rest of a talented Tennessee defense baffled. Mauck found the end zone twice, once for a 7–0 lead, and later for a 24–17 lead that Tennessee would never recover from.

Tennessee's dismantling of Michigan in the 2002 Citrus Bowl would serve as one of the last high moments in Tennessee football. Casey Clausen, who flourished on the road throughout his career, had a marquee day, completing 26 of 33 passes for 393 yards and three touchdowns.

A disappointing 2002 season saw lopsided home losses to Alabama and Florida before a 30–3 pounding at the hands of Maryland in the Peach Bowl. The Vols' five losses would be the most they suffered in the Fulmer era, and the most in a season since 1988. By contrast, the 1998 senior class suffered five losses in a four-year span.

The Vols bounced back to win 10 games in 2003, winning their second consecutive game in the Swamp, 24–10. However, a three-way tie in the SEC East went to Georgia, who beat the Vols 41–14 in Knoxville for the second straight trip.

Despite finishing with a 10–2 record and as SEC East cochampions, athletic director Mike Hamilton and SEC commissioner Mike Slive could not persuade the Fiesta or Orange Bowls to take the Vols, with the Orange opting for a Miami–Florida State rematch and the Fiesta picking the Buckeyes as an at-large selection over the Vols to face Kansas State. The deflating news led to a deflated effort in a return trip to the Peach Bowl for the Big Orange, this time resulting in a 27–14 punchless loss to the Clemson Tigers that didn't feel as close as the score indicated.

That was the last time that Tennessee was in the conversation for an at-large spot in a major bowl game until the BCS disbanded following the 2013 season in favor of a college football playoff.

Since the start of the 2002 season, the Vols have compiled a record of 92–72 and have lost five or more games in a season nine times. The Big Orange caravan hasn't seen the Vols play in a "major/BCS" bowl since the 2000 Fiesta Bowl against Nebraska.

There have been far more ebbs than flows in the past 14 years for UT fans. Tennessee used to be synonymous with chasing conference and national championships.

No longer, at least not presently. And the change in fortunes can be traced back to one heartbreaking evening in December 2001 in Atlanta.

69 Steve Spurrier vs. Phillip Fulmer

The barbs were unforgettable from the loose lips of Florida head coach Steve Spurrier. Although Spurrier spread his unique form of media wisecracking to other rivals, "You can't spell *Citrus* without *UT*" is a phrase that burrowed under the skin of many Tennessee fans, and became especially painful with each loss to the hated Gators that derailed several potentially promising seasons in Knoxville. Spurrier also hit Tennessee football between the eyes in referring to Peyton Manning's decision to return for his senior season: "I know why Peyton came back for his senior year. He wanted to be a three-time star of the Citrus Bowl."

Just as the Michigan Wolverines were the annual bugaboo to former Ohio State head coach John Cooper—who could never quite get the Buckeyes to the top of the college football mountain—so was Spurrier to Phillip Fulmer and Tennessee fans for much of the 1990s.

The SEC had become, for all intents and purposes, a two-horse race. The Florida-Tennessee matchup on the third Saturday of September had become can't-miss television. It was typically the first game of the season between teams ranked in the Top 10 and was one of the most anticipated games of the year.

And for more than just the play on the field. Of course, the Fun 'n' Gun offense employed by Steve Spurrier lit up scoreboards and revolutionized offensive football for the decade. Shane Matthews and Heisman Trophy winner Danny Wuerffel made cannon fodder out of SEC defenses, finding streaking wideouts in Chris Doering, Harrison Houston, Reidel Anthony, and Ike Hilliard en route to winning conference championships and contending for national titles.

And with Spurrier, it was personal for Tennessee fans. A star quarterback at Science Hill High School in Johnson City, Tennessee, Spurrier won a Heisman Trophy in 1966 as quarterback of the Gators before embarking on a pedestrian NFL career in San Francisco and Tampa Bay. But it was on the sideline in Gainesville where Spurrier became the ultimate villain in his native East Tennessee.

From 1993, Phillip Fulmer's first full season as head coach of the Vols, through 1997, Tennessee was handed a loss by Spurrier that would change the tone of the season and put the Volunteers in catch-up mode in the SEC East, a seemingly futile feat that Tennessee managed to pull off once, in 1997. Florida won a shootout at Florida Field in 1993 41–34. In 1994 Spurrier's Gators shut out the Vols at home in Manning's first action against Florida. Vols fans saw a promising first-half performance in 1995 in the Swamp, where Tennessee led 30–21 at halftime. Florida went on to score 41 straight points to blow out the Vols in their only loss of the 1995 season. The No. 2 Vols allowed a 35-yard fourth-down touchdown pass from Wuerffel to Reidel Anthony in 1996, jump-starting a run by the fourth-ranked Gators to a 35–0 lead. Tennessee rallied but fell short 35–29 to the eventual national champions. In Peyton Manning's final start against Florida, Tennessee's offensive line was manhandled by Jevon Kearse and the Florida defensive front, who harassed Manning all game in a 33–20 UT loss that ultimately crippled Manning's Heisman Trophy chances. Although Tennessee earned a trip to Atlanta and claim its first SEC title since 1989, they remained just outside of the national championship picture, as undefeated Michigan and Nebraska split the title.

It was a difficult pill to swallow in Knoxville. Manning, the All-American, likeable star went 0-for-4 in his career against Florida. Fulmer, a Tennessee, native and former UT lineman who, in storybook fashion, had claimed his dream job as head coach of the Vols, had fallen in five consecutive matchups against Florida.

But the series took a drastic turn in 1998. Tennessee overcame Spurrier and the two-headed quarterback rotation of Jesse Palmer and Doug Johnson, forcing five Florida turnovers and winning 20–17 in overtime. The win was the Vols' first over Florida since 1992, when running back Mose Phillips salted the game away in the fourth quarter with a 65-yard catch-and-run touchdown on a soggy Neyland Stadium turf. It was also Tennessee's first overtime game in school history.

It also represented a change in the rivalry between a seemingly outcoached and outclassed Tennessee team, in that the games from 1998 to 2001 (Spurrier's last season in Gainesville) were intense battles and tight games for four quarters. In their second game of the 1999 season, the defending national champion Volunteers trailed 23–21 in the final minutes of the fourth quarter, holding the ball at the Florida 42 and facing fourth-and-3. Always known for trying to be the more physical team, and showcasing one of the best tailbacks in the country in Jamal Lewis, Fulmer elected to call a toss sweep to the short side of the field. Alex Brown, who had sacked Tee Martin five times in the game, and the Gators defensive front swarmed Lewis well short of the first-down marker to snuff out the Vols' last chance to stretch their winning streak to 15 games.

The 2000 matchup was possibly more painful for UT fans. Leaning on the running game for the lion's share of the day, with new quarterback A.J. Suggs under center, it appeared Fulmer's game plan was going to work. Travis Henry rushed for 175 yards on the day, and the Volunteers offense needed just one short-yardage third-down conversion to move into victory formation.

They never got it. Henry was stuffed, and the Vols punted the ball away on fourth-and-2. Jesse Palmer methodically led the Florida offense 88 yards down to the Tennessee 3-yard line with

17 seconds remaining and no timeouts left. On the ensuing play, Palmer found wide receiver Jabar Gaffney in the end zone for a controversial touchdown. The ball hit Gaffney in the numbers, hesitated in his arms for no more than a fraction of a second, then dropped to the turf after UT defender Willie Miles knocked it free. Linesman Al Matthews, a Vanderbilt graduate, signaled a touchdown, inciting a deafening shower of boos from the partisan Knoxville crowd.

Another close battle had swung Florida's way, and the Gators went on to claim the SEC championship with a win over Auburn in Atlanta.

However, Fulmer would get the last laugh against Spurrier in the latter's final game in Gainesville as Florida's head coach, where, in a perfect story of better-late-than-never, the ol' former lineman's pound-the-rock philosophy paid dividends against an overmatched Gators defense. In a game rescheduled for December due to the events of 9/11, Travis Stephens, one-half of the two-headed Travis monster at running back that spelled an injured Jamal Lewis in UT's 1998 title run, finally got his chance to shine. Stephens gashed the Gators defense time and again, rolling up 226 yards on the ground. Defensive tackle John Henderson, who reportedly threw a hotel chair in anger after seeing the 17½-point line in favor of Florida entering the game, helped anchor a defensive front alongside Albert Haynesworth that harassed quarterback Rex Grossman all game.

Despite the physical mauling that the Tennessee offense put on the Orange and Blue defense, Florida still had a chance to pull even late in the game. Trailing 34–26, Grossman found Carlos Perez for a two-yard touchdown. The game came down to a two-point conversion. Grossman saw Gaffney open and fired. The pass fell incomplete behind him.

A domino effect ensued. Tennessee had displaced the second-ranked Gators from the SEC and national championship pictures with one loss. The next month, Spurrier resigned to take the head coaching job for the Washington Redskins. For Fulmer and UT, it was the school's first win at Florida Field in 30 years, when Fulmer helped pave the road for a UT victory in 1971. It gave UT a second win in four years against Spurrier and the Gators, the school's best run against Florida on Fulmer's watch.

While Spurrier got the better of Fulmer in Gainesville, the face-off between the two legendary coaches continued when Spurrier took over as the head coach at South Carolina on November 23, 2004.

It didn't take long for the familiar disappointment to strike Vols fans, and for a grinning Steve Spurrier to reappear in Neyland Stadium. Josh Brown drilled a 49-yard field goal to give South Carolina a 16–15 win in 2005, the school's first-ever win in Knoxville.

However, Tennessee responded with wins the following two seasons in tightly contested games: 31–24 at South Carolina in 2006 and 27–24 in Knoxville in 2007.

The coup de grace for the rivalry between the coaches came on November 1, 2008. At 3–5, Tennessee stumbled into Columbia as a team that had disappointed as much as any team in the nation. As had been the case against Florida and at Auburn, Tennessee's offense sputtered to six points as South Carolina cruised to a methodical 27–6 win that ultimately sealed Fulmer's fate. Mike Hamilton announced later that week that the 2008 season would be Fulmer's last as head coach.

Fulmer and Spurrier led teams that created the unquestioned marquee matchup of the early college football season in the 1990s. Although the Tennessee–South Carolina game didn't mean as much on a national scale from 2005 to 2008, the desire to beat

Steve Spurrier and see him throw his visor in disgust never subsided for Vols fans.

Spurrier finished with nine wins head-to-head against Fulmer's five.

Holloway's Miraculous Throw Lifts Vols Over Clemson in 1974

Helmets flew in the air, nearly landing by Smokey, who howled loudly next to the dog pile of orange-jerseyed players mobbing in the corner of the end zone.

Not exactly the scene one would expect to see following a midseason matchup between a 3–3 Clemson team visiting a 2–3–1 Tennessee squad that was barely a blip on the college football national radar.

As such, tickets for the contest between the middling, unranked foes were a hard sell for scalpers, despite the warm, sunny weather gracing Neyland Stadium on October 26, 1974. But those who were there witnessed one of the most thrilling and memorable endings in Tennessee football history. The game served as a microcosm for the freakish athleticism and playmaking ability that legendary quarterback Condredge Holloway brought to the position.

Trailing 28–21 late in the fourth quarter, Tennessee drove the ball down to the Clemson 7-yard line with seconds remaining in the game. Head Coach Bill Battle had all but stamped US MAIL on the back of wide receiver / running back Stanley Morgan on the drive, and Morgan would finish the job. Taking the pitch from Holloway, Morgan cut past the kickout block from fullback Paul Careathers and ran through the tackles of two Tigers defensive backs and over the goal line.

As fans celebrated, Battle spoke with his quarterback on the sideline. He sent Holloway back onto the field, foregoing the option of an anticlimactic tie, a mediocre result in the throes of a mediocre season.

Battle went back to the well on a play that the Vols had run successfully earlier in the game, and one that capitalized on Holloway's dual-threat ability. Holloway would roll to his right and look for his target, wide receiver Larry Sievers from nearby Clinton, Tennessee. If he was open, he would throw the ball. If he wasn't, he would tuck the ball and dart for the end zone.

As both lines set and the ball was snapped, one would have thought the Clemson defense had a man on the Tennessee sideline. Holloway rolled right but stopped in his tracks, as four Clemson defenders had him all but boxed in.

Instead of making a panicked throw to the end zone while backpedaling, Holloway cut left and darted back across the field, stepping through the would-be tackle of a defender. With a fraction of a second to look and throw, Holloway lobbed the ball against his body, just before a second defender slammed him to the ground.

The ball floated through the air and fell right into the hands of Sievers in stride, and he had a step on his defender in the end zone.

Tennessee 29, Clemson 28.

On the ensuing play after kickoff, Tennessee linebacker Hank Walter, who played at Webb High School in Knoxville, intercepted a desperation pass, sealing the win.

Although 1974 was a seemingly forgettable season through the first half, the 29–28 win was a turning point and catapulted the Vols forward to a 4–0–1 record for the remainder of the regular season. They defeated Maryland 7–3 in the Liberty Bowl and finished the season at 7–3–2 and ranked No. 15 in the Coaches Poll and No. 20 in the AP poll.

And the winning two-point play served as one of the best of Holloway's many exciting and unforgettable moments in his memorable Tennessee career.

71 The Tennessee-Kentucky "Beer Barrel" Trophy

College football rivalries bring out some of the most passionate moments in sports. While Ohio State–Michigan, Texas-Oklahoma, and Notre Dame–Southern California have proved to be among the biggest national rivalries, there are countless others in which fans of both sides are equally passionate about beating the pants off the other side. Oftentimes those rivalries are manifested in some type of nickname or phrase, such as Georgia and Georgia Tech's "clean, old-fashioned hate." Other times there are trophies and other physical spoils that encapsulate the rivalry. Minnesota and Wisconsin play each year for Paul Bunyan's Axe. Army, Navy, and the Air Force Academy compete for the Commander-in-Chief's Trophy. Arkansas and LSU fight for the Golden Boot. And Iowa and Minnesota play for the Floyd of Rosedale, a trophy of a pig with a scarf draped over it that displays the scores from each year on it.

Trophies come in all shapes and sizes. For Tennessee, their only trophy in modern history was the "beer barrel," an orange-white-and-blue-painted barrel. Although the football series began back in 1893, the barrel wasn't introduced into the rivalry until 1925.

For decades, the barrel became a symbol of the rivalry between two states with a history of distilling quality spirits, both legally and illegally. For that reason, the beer barrel started off with a different name.

"It was originally called the 'bourbon barrel,'" University of Tennessee historian Tom Mattingly told WBIR in Knoxville. "At one time, it had the words ICE WATER on it to satisfy the local temperance unions."

The barrel, well protected in Knoxville for the majority of its existence thanks to the Vols' dominance on the gridiron, was a source of pride for the players. After leading Tennessee to a thrilling 34–31 shootout win at Commonwealth Stadium, Peyton Manning raised the barrel over his head.

The barrel was removed from the rivalry in 1998 when tragedy struck. Shortly before Kentucky made its annual late-season jaunt down I–275 to take on Tennessee, Artie Steinmetz, a Kentucky player, and his friend Scott Brock were killed in a drunk-driving accident. The administrations of both schools agreed that, symbolically, playing for the beer barrel would portray a bad image in light of the tragedy. The trophy was discontinued, and its current whereabouts are unknown.

While some UT fans have, as of 2014, attempted to petition to have the trophy brought back into the rivalry, the barrel has passed on, a relic of a bygone era.

"It was a symbol for a different time and society," Mattingly told the UT newspaper the *Daily Beacon*. "It's a different time, and society is just more sensitive about things like that than they used to be."

72 Remember Tennessee's Great Linebacking Tradition

The terms Quarterback U, Running Back U, and Wide Receiver U are amorphous creatures. They change, depending on the era, and where the teams stand in said era. The University of Miami's run of starting quarterbacks who either left school with a national championship or Heisman Trophy was legendary, stretching from 1983 until 1992. USC churned out one incredible tailback after another in the 1960s and 1970s, including Anthony Davis, Marcus Allen, Charles White, and O.J. Simpson.

Tennessee may claim Wide Receiver U among its historical accolades—and for good reason—but the school's history of producing top-level linebackers, both on the collegiate and pro football levels, is unquestioned. Starting with Frank Emanuel in 1965, Tennessee has had a linebacker earn All-America honors in each decade. When Doug Dickey became head coach in 1964, eliminating the two-way player requirement in the process, Emanuel flourished, spearheading a defense that allowed only 98 points in 1965. It's the lowest point total a Tennessee defense has allowed to date.

Jack Reynolds, Steve Kiner, Jackie Walker, and Jamie Rotella all earned All-America honors between 1968 and 1972. Walker, UT's first African American to be named to the All-America team, helped redefine the position. He swarmed the ball carrier, as evidenced by his 82 tackles in 1970, but he also finished his career with 11 interceptions, most by a non–defensive back during his era. His five interception returns for touchdowns set an NCAA record. Kiner earned SEC Defensive Player of the Year and All-America honors after Tennessee's 41–14 victory over Alabama in 1969. He had five sacks, eleven tackles with five assists, four quarterback hurries, an interception, and a forced fumble. Kiner went on to a nine-year NFL career, and helped to turn around the Houston Oilers franchise in the late 1970s.

It would be 16 years between All-America linebacking selections for Tennessee, with Keith DeLong earning honors through an incredible 1988 season. Keith, son of former UT and San Diego Chargers defensive end Steve DeLong, tallied an incredible 159 tackles, a bright spot in a dismal 5–6 season. Against Alabama, he earned SEC Player of the Week, collecting 19 tackles, 4 assists, a pass deflection, and an interception. He was named a finalist for the Butkus Award, given to the nation's top linebacker.

Tennessee returned to its place among the nation's elite programs in the 1990s, in no small part because of a talented and physical defense laden with future NFL talent. Leonard Little, Al Wilson, and Raynoch Thompson all earned All-America honors in their respective senior seasons—1997, 1998, and 1999. Little, named SEC Co–Defensive Player of the Year, helped Tennessee secure its first SEC title in seven years. Wilson served as the leader of the Tennessee defense that claimed the school's first national championship in the major polls in 47 years. His 12-tackle performance against No. 2 Florida, in which he also forced three fumbles, remains one of the most generally beloved performances by a Tennessee defender in program history.

Vols Edge Wildcats in Four Overtimes to Claim 2007 SEC East Crown

Tennessee, Kentucky's chief rival which it hadn't beaten since 1984, entered Commonwealth Stadium in the team's regular-season finale, needing only to beat the 7–4 Wildcats to clinch the SEC East crown and secure a coveted spot in the SEC Championship Game.

With eight seconds remaining in regulation, Tennessee clung to a 31–28 lead. Kentucky had pushed the Volunteers defense back to its own 1-yard line. With no timeouts remaining, Kentucky coach Rich Brooks called for a rollout run/pass option for dual-threat quarterback Andre' Woodson. Woodson fumbled the shotgun snap, rolled right, and slung a pass over the head of a wide-open intended receiver. The Commonwealth Stadium scoreboard read 0:01.

Lones Seiber, a Knoxville native, lined up and banged the chip-shot field goal through to send the game into overtime.

Tennessee and Kentucky traded quick scores in the first overtime, moving the game to the second. Two plays in, it seemed as though Kentucky had all but sealed the win.

On second-and-6, quarterback Erik Ainge lobbed a passed toward wide receiver Lucas Taylor, who was well covered. The ball was tipped in the air and intercepted by Kentucky linebacker Sam Maxwell.

All the Wildcats needed was a field goal to end a 22-game streak of heartbreak to their neighbors to the south. As strangers high-fived and hugged, Kentucky handed off three times, setting up Seiber for a 35-yard try from the near hash mark. Seiber lined up for the kick. The snap was out. The ball was placed down. The kick was blocked.

As the air was sucked out of the collective gut of the 60,000-plus Kentucky fans in Commonwealth Stadium—a regular feeling for them—Tennessee's Dan Williams, who got a mitt up to block the kick, and his teammates sprinted downfield, looking to end the game with an improbable return. After a streaking Eric Berry was slung down by his face mask, the game went into a third overtime.

Keenan Burton pulled in a third-and-7 pass along the sideline for a 44–38 Kentucky lead. Woodson's pass was intercepted, and Tennessee needed a touchdown and two-point conversion to win the SEC East.

After lobbing a third-down throw off his back foot to Gerald Jones for a first down, Ainge hit Austin Rogers on a wide receiver screen, and Rogers ran 13 yards for the game-tying touchdown.

Suddenly Tennessee was in the driver's seat, only two yards, and just one two-point conversion, away from a division championship. From shotgun formation, Ainge handed off to tailback Arian Foster, who cut left to the short side of the field and was tackled short of the goal line by a host of Kentucky defenders. To make matters worse, Foster was flagged 15 yards for flinging the ball into the air in disgust after the play.

Tennessee 44, Kentucky 44. Start of fourth overtime.

Starting from the 40-yard line, Tennessee got the ball first and this time put the full pressure on Kentucky's offense. On first down, Ainge launched downfield and found a wide-open Quentin Hancock, who caught the ball without a defender around him and sprinted the last 12 yards for a 40-yard touchdown. On the conversion attempt, Ainge hung in the pocket and found Rogers dragging across the goal line for the conversion.

Tennessee 52, Kentucky 44.

As the slugfest between the two heavyweight fighters continued, Kentucky landed one more punch. Three plays into the drive. Derrick Locke bowled over the Tennessee defense for a three-yard touchdown run. Tennessee's defense had bent, and quickly, but coach Phillip Fulmer and defensive coordinator John Chavis dialed up the right call to make sure it wouldn't break. Woodson took the snap out of the shotgun, and with nobody open, he broke right toward the end zone. Flushed away from the pocket, defensive end Antonio Reynolds brought Woodson to the ground short of the goal line.

Final score: Tennessee 52, Kentucky 50. Four overtimes.

Tennessee had claimed the school's first division title since 2007, extended its school-record streak over Kentucky to 23 straight, and had completed an improbable journey to Atlanta that had begun with a nightmarish 59–20 loss in Gainesville and included a frantic, come-from-behind 25–24 win against Vandy, when the Commodores kicker Bryant Hahnfeldt's 49-yard field goal attempt grazed the upright wide with seconds remaining.

Despite losing 21–14 to eventual national champion LSU in the SEC Championship Game, Tennessee rebounded with a 21–17 win against Wisconsin in the Outback Bowl, finishing No. 12 in the AP poll, the school's highest finish through the end of the 2014 season.

74. The Lane Kiffin Experiment

Amidst the chaotic scene on the University of Tennessee campus, he slipped away into the night. Just as quickly as he had arrived in Knoxville to replace a legend, the Lane Kiffin era had ended with an impromptu press conference that lasted only a matter of seconds. The 21st coach in University of Tennessee history had just resigned, in favor of returning to the University of Southern California as its new head coach, where Kiffin had won championships as an assistant under former head coach Pete Carroll.

Kiffin had just led Tennessee to a 7–6 record, including blowout wins over ranked rivals Georgia and South Carolina. His incoming recruiting class was ranked in or near the Top 5 by most major recruiting services. Despite Kiffin's head-scratching barbs—such as the shots he took at Florida head coach Urban Meyer, and letting future South Carolina great Alshon Jeffery know that he'd end up "pumping gas" if he went to South Carolina—most fans were willing to put up with the disrespect in the hopes of an improved future they hoped Kiffin would bring.

Head coach Lane Kiffin goes down against the Gators in 2009.
(USA TODAY Sports)

While Kiffin was accepting his "dream job" as head coach of the Trojans, the scene in Knoxville was a nightmare. As word of Kiffin's imminent resignation spread across campus, students started to gather near the lobby of the Neyland-Thompson Sports Center. Within an hour, the group had turned into an angry mob, looking to keep Kiffin from departing the facility.

Indeed, Kiffin was holed up in the Neyland-Thompson Sports Center that evening as an angry but civil crowd of about a thousand students gathered outside. While the anger was palpable, only a mattress or two, some Kiffin T-shirts, and a couple other small items were set aflame. The Rock was quickly spray-painted HEIL LANE, with an X over Kiffin's face. Then it was repainted with the words IT'S TIME TO QUIT — a parody of UT's slogan during football season.

Social media, while not quite as prominent in early 2010 as it is in 2015, still provided some insight into the level of disdain students felt by the perceived betrayal by Kiffin. Former UT basketball player Renaldo Woolridge Tweeted during the chaos, "THEY JUST TEAR GASSED EVERY1!!!" Kiffin finally departed the facility at 4:00 AM, bound for the airport and Southern California.

Meanwhile, Tennessee scrambled to pick up the pieces. Athletic director Mike Hamilton eventually hired Derek Dooley, a young and seemingly rising coach who had managed to avoid confrontation with opposing conference coaches. Derek Dooley, son of the South and of Georgia coaching legend Vince Dooley, came to Tennessee with a losing record from lowly Louisiana Tech but the pedigree of having worked under Nick Saban at LSU.

Dooley's 4–19 SEC record, including a 2011 streak-snapping loss to Kentucky and its third-string wide-receiver-turned-quarterback, ended with a thud after the 2012 season, leaving Tennessee in a coaching quandary yet again. Tennessee hired Butch Jones to replace Dooley, and Jones led the Vols to a 7–6 season and a win against Iowa in the TaxSlayer Bowl to conclude the 2014 season, the Vols' best record since Kiffin's year in Knoxville. Jones' 2015 recruiting class was ranked in the Top 5 in team rankings by most major recruiting services.

Jones appears to be in it for the long haul for the Volunteer Nation. Meanwhile, Kiffin was fired in the airport following USC's 62–41 loss to Arizona State in Tempe. Kiffin's overall record at his "dream job" was 28–15. Wherever Kiffin has held the job as the head man—Oakland Raiders, Tennessee, and USC—Kiffin's production has resulted in nothing more than a mediocre product on the field. For that, Tennessee fans should be grateful for him leaving sooner than later.

While fans were angry about Kiffin's muted departure and the manner in which he stepped on the proud University of Tennessee program on the way to what was perceived as a higher job, they can take solace in the passion, intensity, and pride that Butch Jones has reinfused into the football program.

75 "Sweet" Comeback: Tennessee 23, Virginia 22, 1/1/91

There have been plenty of important games in the history of Tennessee football. In a program that ranks second in the SEC in wins, conference titles, and national championships, it's only natural that its history would be replete with thrilling and meaningful moments.

While the 1991 Sugar Bowl might not have been the most important game in the history of Tennessee football—or really anywhere close to it—the drama provided in the second half in the Superdome was as tense and unforgettable as almost any game in the previous 100 years of UT football being celebrated at that time.

Virginia entered the game unranked, having lost three out of its last four games after starting 7–0 and rising to No. 1 in the polls. At that time, smitten with what they had seen so far, the Sugar Bowl committee extended an invitation to Virginia, which accounts for the 8–3 Cavaliers playing on New Year's Day in the Big Easy. Tennessee accepted the other bid as recognized champions of the SEC, due to Florida's ineligibility for postseason play due to NCAA sanctions. Tennessee thrashed Florida 45–3 in Knoxville on October 13, 1990, the Gators' only SEC loss of the year.

Things were not where they should have been in the second half, at least not where Las Vegas and the prognosticators would have had it. Leading 16–3 in the third quarter, Virginia had their foot on the collective throat of the 10th-ranked Tennessee Volunteers, inside the Tennessee 20-yard line and ready to deliver the kill shot to the Volunteers.

Virginia completely dominated the first half of play. The Cavaliers, who scored on 71 of 148 possessions over the season, held the ball for 22 of 30 minutes, as running backs Nikki Fisher and Terry Kirby combined for more than 100 rushing yards. All-American quarterback Shawn Moore was also impressive as Virginia took a 16–0 lead into halftime.

The game featured a trio of future NFL wide receivers. Carl Pickens set a school record with 13 catches against Notre Dame earlier in the season. Alvin Harper entered the game second on Tennessee's all-time list in career receiving touchdowns, with 15. Virginia's Herman Moore had a record-setting season, in as many aspects as one could imagine. He set the NCAA record with 10 consecutive games with a touchdown catch. He set an ACC record for receiving yards in a season (1,190) and Virginia records for catches (54), touchdown catches (13), and receiving yards (2,504).

Moore would go on to lead the Detroit Lions in career receptions (670) and was selected to four Pro Bowls. Harper became a mainstay across from Michael Irvin in the Dallas Cowboys' Super

Bowl runs in the early 1990s. Pickens was the NFL Offensive Rookie of the Year in 1992 and set Bengals records for catches (99) and touchdown catches (17) in 1995 in an All-Pro season.

Despite the firepower out wide, it would be running back Tony Thompson and a resolute Tennessee defense that would turn the tide for the Volunteers in the Big Easy. Tennessee's Floyd Miley intercepted Moore's pass at the UT 6-yard line, avoiding disaster and sparking the Vols' second-half comeback.

Head coach Johnny Majors called upon Thompson to carry the freight for the Vols 94 yards from pay dirt. He accounted for 80 of the Vols' 94 yards on the ground, scoring on a seven-yard touchdown run to make it 16–10.

The Cavaliers responded with a field goal, and Tennessee inched closer on its next drive. Starting at its 20-yard line, Tennessee marched 80 yards and found the end zone when quarterback Andy Kelly hit Pickens on a 15-yard strike.

Virginia 19, Tennessee 17.

Again Virginia answered with a field goal, pushing the lead out to 22–17 with 2:31 remaining in the game. Tennessee would have to go 79 yards to claim victory and cap a furious second-half comeback.

On the steady arm of Kelly, who completed seven of nine passes for 64 yards on the drive, Tennessee was suddenly on the doorstep and ready to punch it in. Kelly's final completion was a rollout to Harper along the sideline that set up UT with first-and-goal at the 5-yard line. Two plays later, Thompson capped his 151-yard day on the ground by leaping over the line for the touchdown.

Tennessee 23, Virginia 22, with 31 seconds left.

To make matters worse for Virginia, quarterback Shawn Moore, who was absent in two of the three late-season losses with a thumb injury, was suddenly out of the game with an injured hand, so a comeback seemed all but lost.

And it was. Backup quarterback Matt Blundin was sacked, and his final desperation toss was intercepted by Dale Carter as time expired.

"Rocky Top" blared from the Pride of the Southland Marching Band, as Tennessee players flooded the field in a joyous celebration. Tennessee made 1990 a year to remember for the Volunteers faithful and capped off its 100th year of football in style: as SEC and Sugar Bowl champions.

76 1967: A National Championship Claimed

Doug Dickey had succeeded in bringing some pride back to the University of Tennessee. The former Florida Gators quarterback was hired to replace Jim McDonald, who served as an interim coach for a year after Neyland fired Bowden Wyatt in 1963. To say that Tennessee struggled during Wyatt's tenure would be an understatement, the the Vols had not reached a bowl game since the 1957 season.

Dickey and his T formation offensive system had begun to make headway in Knoxville, both as an accepted system (as opposed to the legendary single-wing formation upon which the Tennessee program had been built under General Neyland) and with the results on the field.

A record of 4–5–1 was understandable for a first-year head coach in 1964, and 8–1–2 and a Bluebonnet Bowl victory was a positive step forward in 1965.

By 1967 Tennessee was coming off back-to-back eight-win seasons and bowl victories, the last an 18–12 win over Syracuse in the 1966 Gator Bowl.

Tennessee had the pieces to win in 1967, although they didn't get much national attention. Senior quarterback Dewey Warren, MVP of the 1966 Gator Bowl, was returning to lead an offense that would average just fewer than 26 points per game. Warren, UT's first-ever quarterback to throw for more than 1,000 yards in a season, would finish his career with 3,357 yards passing and 27 touchdowns, far and away the most in school history at that time. Warren would be drafted by the Cincinnati Bengals in the sixth round of the 1968 NFL/AFL Draft. Center Bob Johnson, who would be drafted with the second overall pick of the 1968 NFL/AFL Draft, anchored the offensive line.

Aside from a veteran quarterback, the Vols defense was spearheaded by some young but very talented linebackers in Jack Reynolds and Steve Kiner. Reynolds would be drafted in the first round by the Los Angeles Rams and would win two Super Bowls with the San Francisco 49ers. Kiner, a member of Tennessee's 100-year team, would embark on a nine-year NFL career in which he helped turn around the struggling Houston Oilers franchise in the late 1970s.

Tennessee stumbled out of the gate, losing 20–16 at UCLA. Tennessee took advantage of early UCLA mistakes to jump out to a 13–3 lead with touchdown runs by Charles Fulton and Richard Pickens. However, trailing 16–13 late in the fourth quarter, UCLA quarterback Gary Beban converted a fourth-and-2, scoring the winning points on a 27-yard touchdown run.

Tennessee would go on a memorable run of nine straight wins to close out the regular season, starting with a four-game run against Auburn, Georgia Tech, Alabama, and LSU. The win snapped a 25-game unbeaten streak for the Tide. Outside of the opener, no team in the regular season would score more than 14 points against Tennessee, who allowed a paltry 11.5 points per game for the season.

At 9–1, Tennessee finished at No. 2 in the AP and Coaches Polls, behind O.J. Simpson and the No. 1 USC Trojans. However, the Litkenhous poll, a recognized poll in determining a national champion, listed Tennessee as No. 1, marking the school's first claimed national championship since 1951.

Tennessee would lose 26–24 to Oklahoma in the Orange Bowl. Down 19–0, Tennessee fought back to within two points in the final two minutes. Warren moved the offense downfield, but Karl Kremser's 43-yard field goal sailed wide right as time expired.

Tennessee, Charter Member of the SEC

After the expansion of the SEC from 12 to 14 schools in 2012, more money, new markets, and unfortunately broken rivalries followed. Although the SEC's reach now extends into the Lone Star State, as well as Missouri and the heartland of America, it's important to remember one thing that many schools and their fans pride themselves on in the South: history.

Looking back at the formation of the SEC in 1933, there were originally 13 members that left the Southern Conference and formed the Southeastern Conference: Alabama, Auburn, Florida, Georgia, Georgia Tech, Kentucky, LSU, Mississippi, Mississippi State, Sewanee, Tennessee, Tulane, and Vanderbilt. The conference remained at 13 teams until 1940, when Sewanee left the conference, placing a reduced emphasis on athletics.

For more than two decades, the conference remained strong with 12 members, until 1964. Georgia Tech pulled out of the conference and became an independent, eventually moving to its current home in the ACC in 1979. The SEC expanded again in

Charter Members of the SEC and their Respective Records

Alabama and Tennessee rank first and second, respectively, among the charter members of the conference in most major categories, including wins, winning percentage, Southeastern conference titles, and claimed national championships. Here's how the rest of the schools compare, ranked based on career winning percentage:

3. LSU. 762–401–47 (.649); 11 SEC titles; 3 claimed national championships
4. Georgia. 778–410–54 (.648); 12 SEC titles; 2 claimed national championships
5. Auburn. 742–421–47 (.633); 8 SEC titles; 2 claimed national championships
6. Florida. 691–400–40 (.629); 8 SEC titles; 3 claimed national championships
7. Mississippi. 645–501–35 (.561); 6 SEC titles; 3 claimed national championships
8. Vanderbilt. 585–591–50 (.498); no titles
9. Kentucky. 588–598–44 (.496); 2 SEC titles; 1 claimed national championship
10. Mississippi State. 532–558–39 (.488); 1 SEC title

1992, adding Arkansas out of the Southwest Conference and independent South Carolina.

While some teams have come and gone from the SEC over the years, the 10 core schools have created, through a history of national championships, a legacy of a superior product on the field and an unbeatable game-day experience off it. Some of the nation's oldest rivalries—a lifeblood of college football—arose from and exist in the SEC. The Iron Bowl remains one of the most popular college football games every season, regardless of record. The Third Saturday in October has experienced ebbs and flows through the peaks and valleys of both Tennessee and Alabama, but it remains one of the most renowned rivalries in college football. Auburn and Georgia claim to be "the Deep South's oldest rivalry."

And where tradition and history have become a staple of Southern football and the SEC, Tennessee's lofty place among the conference record books should raise a great deal of pride in the supporters of the Vol Nation. Neyland Stadium's 102,455 remains the largest-capacity stadium in the SEC. Tennessee's 811 wins rank second in the SEC, as do its .680 winning percentage, 13 SEC championships, and 6 claimed national titles. Only Alabama ranks higher than Tennessee in each category.

While times change, and sometimes conference allegiances and rivalries do too, Tennessee fans can sit back and enjoy their rich and nearly unparalleled level of historical success in one of the most competitive and championed conferences in the country.

78 Learn About the All-Americans

While it may not seem plausible to remember *all* of the All-Americans in Tennessee history—after all, there are 72 first-team All-America players in Volunteers history through 2014—it is worth a UT fan's time to go back and take a closer look at some of the greatest players ever to put on the Orange and White. For those who cheered on Tennessee through the 1995–98 era of dominance, some of its cornerstones need no introduction, such as Peyton Manning, Al Wilson, Leonard Little, Cosey Coleman, and Deon Grant. The splash plays and excitement that Dale Carter and Carl Pickens generated on their respective sides of the ball were unforgettable, and contributed to some of the most memorable moments in the Johnny Majors coaching era, including the 1991 Sugar Bowl comeback. The extra point has become something of a formality in the game today, but Chattanooga native John Becksvoort drilled a perfect 59 of 59 extra points, an SEC record, and 12 of 13 field goals in 1993.

These names, along with Reggie White, Tim McGee, Willie Gault, and more recently Eric Berry remain at the forefront of names that come to mind when you think about greatness exhibited at the University of Tennessee. But the remaining dozens of All-Americans who might not be household names also created moments that helped build the foundation for the strong brand that the University of Tennessee has become.

Larry Sievers, from down the road in Clinton, became the first wide receiver in UT history to break the 800-yard receiving mark, leaving UT as the career leader in receptions (117) and receiving yards (1,924). His catch of Condredge Holloway's two-point conversion pass to beat Clemson in 1974 remains one of the single-most exciting moments in the decade.

Hank Lauricella was one of the most accomplished players during General Neyland's coaching days. His weaving 75-yard run in the 1951 Cotton Bowl set up the game-winning touchdown. The next year, the talented back paced the Tennessee offense, gaining 7.9 yards per attempt in helping the Vols complete a 10–0 regular season and claim a consensus national championship. Like Peyton Manning and Johnny Majors, Lauricella finished second in Heisman Trophy voting in 1951.

George Cafego's bruising running style and hard hits from the safety position epitomized the physicality and toughness of the Tennessee teams that ran over the competition from 1938 to 1940. The native West Virginian rushed for 1,589 yards in his career and was named the SEC Player of the Year in 1938, helping Tennessee complete an 11–0 season.

Ahead of Cafego and fellow running backs Bob Foxx, Leonard Coffman, and Sam Bartholomew, All-American guards Bob Suffridge and Ed Molinski and tackle Abe Shire paved the road.

Molinski, Suffridge, and Cafego would all be inducted into the College Football Hall of Fame.

Among all the great tailbacks in UT history—from Jamal Lewis to Chuck Webb to James Stewart to Johnny Majors—no player has scored more points in a season than UT's first-ever All-American selection in 1929—halfback Gene McEver. McEver also scored five touchdowns in the 1929 season finale against South Carolina, a mark that still stands today as the most touchdowns scored by a single player in one game in UT history.

Take the time to go back and look at the 72 men who were selected as the very best at their respective positions over 80 years. Each man's accomplishments tell a story of excellence that deserves to be remembered and cherished.

79 Reggie White: A Once-in-a-Lifetime Player

If there ever was a more fitting nickname for a player than the Minister of Defense was for Reggie White, it's hard to think of one.

White was raised by his mother and his grandparents in Chattanooga. The family was deeply religious. They attended the local Baptist church regularly, and as a youngster White was inspired by the ministers and teachers he met there. According to his mother, the preteen White had announced that he wanted to be two things: a football player and a minister.

It didn't take him long to accomplish both. At the age of 17, White became an ordained minister. A few years later, he had developed into a dominating football player in Knoxville. In his four years with the Vols, Reggie White set the school record with 32 sacks, making him the most accomplished pass rusher in Tennessee history.

The 1983 team captain collected 100 tackles on the season, 72 of them unassisted, and set the school record with 15 sacks for the year. He had a sack in every game but two and set a school record for sacks in a single game with four against the Citadel.

White was named the SEC's Player of the Year and while earning consensus All-America and All-SEC honors.

Like Herschel Walker and other talented players in the early 1980s, White began his professional football career in the now-defunct United States Football League. Upon his move to the NFL in 1985, White made an immediate impact with the Philadelphia Eagles starting in Week 4 against the New York Giants. He racked up two and a half sacks, and deflected a pass that was intercepted

A young Reggie White, with coach Johnny Majors, in 1983.

and returned for a touchdown. Despite only playing in 13 games, White was a co-leader of the Eagles defense with 13 sacks and was named the NFL's 1985 Defensive Rookie of the Year. In 1986 White terrorized opposing quarterbacks to the tune of 18 sacks to earn his first of his incredible 13 straight Pro Bowl selections.

In 1987 White recorded one of the finest seasons ever posted by a defensive lineman in the history of the game of football. In the Eagles' opener against the Redskins, he sacked quarterback Doug Williams, stripped the ball, and then picked it up and raced 70 yards for the first of his two career touchdowns. In just 12 games (the season was shortened due to a work stoppage), White accumulated 21 sacks to earn his first of two consecutive league sack titles.

In 1993, after recording 124 sacks in 121 games over eight seasons in Philadelphia, White became the first big-name free agent to switch teams. He joined the Green Bay Packers and instantly helped turn the fortunes of the once-proud franchise.

The team steadily improved and, in 1996, returned to glory with White leading the NFL's top-ranked defense to the Super Bowl. In Super Bowl XXXI he set a Super Bowl record with three sacks of New England quarterback Drew Bledsoe, including back-to-back sacks in the third quarter. The Packers beat the Patriots 35–21.

White played two more years in Green Bay. During that period he added 27 more sacks to his staggering total. White returned for a final season with the Carolina Panthers in 2000 after taking one year away from the game in 1999.

White was voted first-team All-Pro 10 times in his 15-year career and retired as the NFL's all-time sacks leader, with 198. He was named to the NFL's All-Decade Teams of the 1980s and 1990s and to the 75th Anniversary All-Time Team.

After his playing days were over, White's passion extended back to his ministries and giving back to his Tennessee community. White was an associate pastor at a local Knoxville church. He also donated $1 million to start up a bank for inner-city residents who had trouble qualifying for loans.

On December 26, 2004, White passed away at his home in Cornelius, North Carolina. An autopsy revealed that White had died from cardiac arrhythmia, an irregular heartbeat caused by complications from sarcoidosis.

White was posthumously inducted into the Pro Football Hall of Fame in 2006.

80 The Stop: Vols Upset Billy Cannon and No. 1 LSU in 1959

"I will go to my grave believing I was over."

Those words were spoken by LSU legend Billy Cannon about his run on LSU's two-point conversion attempt to try to take a one-point lead in Knoxville on a chilly November 7, 1959, afternoon.

Top-ranked LSU entered Knoxville 7–0 and still living on cloud nine just one week after Cannon's legendary Halloween night punt return against Ole Miss that Tigers fans still fondly recall to this day. LSU was ranked No. 1, and Ole Miss was No. 3. With LSU trailing 3–0 in the fourth quarter, Cannon fielded a Rebels punt at his 11-yard line, broke through half a dozen tackles, and burst down the sideline for a game-winning touchdown. LSU had vanquished its border rival, retained the No. 1 ranking, and kept pace with Georgia for top honors in the SEC. The run is still considered one of the most famous plays in LSU history, and it all but locked up the Heisman Trophy for Cannon, the school's only winner of college football's highest honor.

The 1959 Tennessee squad, coached by Bowden Wyatt, was an afterthought in the final SEC standings, losing to Vanderbilt and

Kentucky and finishing the season 5–4–1. But it was a season filled with some unforgettable individual moments. Tennessee started the season by upsetting No. 3 Auburn 3–0 at Shields-Watkins Field. A close loss to No. 3 Georgia Tech and a tie at Alabama were followed by a win at North Carolina.

Ranked No. 13 in the AP poll, the Vols were positioned to shock another top-notch SEC program in Knoxville, this time the nation's top-ranked LSU Tigers.

Cannon followed up on his Heisman campaign early, running for a 26-yard touchdown to give LSU an early 7–0 lead, which held until halftime. LSU hadn't allowed a touchdown in 10 games, and Tennessee's offensive output of 38 yards did very little to make anyone except the most staunch Tennessee backers believe a comeback was possible.

However, it would be LSU's offense and Tennessee's defense that would swing the game in Tennessee's favor. Vols defensive back Jim Cartwright picked off a pass by LSU quarterback Warren Rabb and returned it 59 yards for a touchdown.

LSU 7, Tennessee 7.

On the Tigers' next drive, Tennessee recovered a fumble by LSU fullback Earl Gros. Four plays later, UT fullback Neyle Sollee plowed his way into the end zone as Shields-Watkins Field broke out into bedlam.

Tennessee 14, LSU 7.

Early in the fourth quarter, it was Tennessee's turn to set up LSU in prime position to even the score. Bill Majors fumbled the ball, and LSU fell on it at the Tennessee 2-yard line. LSU snuck in the ball for a 14–13 score.

With 13:44 remaining in the fourth quarter, head coach Paul Dietzel called for a two-point conversion to push LSU out in front. As the two-point conversion was introduced into college football in 1958, Tennessee had not defended one. It's first would arguably be its most memorable, more than 50 years later.

Cannon took the ball on a sweep to the right, with running back Johnny Robinson blocking ahead of him. Through a mass of bodies, defensive lineman Wayne Grubb met Cannon as he hit the line of scrimmage. As Cannon's momentum carried him to the goal line, defensive backs Charlie Severance and Bill Majors stood him up. Whether or not they forced him down short of the line remains debated to this day.

The only person who mattered was the linesman, who waved his arms *no good*. Despite rushing for more than 200 yards on the day, LSU gained only two and a half yards on that play when they needed three. The Stop was born, and the Shields-Watkins Field crowd erupted.

With more than 13 minutes left, LSU had plenty of time to make up one point. They became their own worst enemy over that span, however, turning the ball over in their final three drives of the game. Cannon fumbled inside the Tennessee 20-yard line. Then Cartwright made his second pick of the game on the next drive, with LSU having pushed back into Tennessee territory. With LSU's last gasp near midfield, Cannon, who rushed for 122 yards in the game, was stopped on a fourth-down run, cementing the win for UT.

While Tennessee got the win, LSU dominated statistically. The Tigers tallied 334 yards of total offense to Tennessee's 112. In fact, both Cannon (122) and Robinson (115) rushed for more yards than Tennessee generated.

But with the chips on the line, the Tennessee defense answered time and again, thwarting Cannon and the LSU offense in the fourth quarter. Despite the loss, Cannon went on to win the Heisman Trophy.

LSU finished the regular season 9–1 and No. 3 in the final polls. They went on to lose a rematch with No. 2 Ole Miss in the Sugar Bowl, 21–0. Tennessee dropped three straight to end the season: 37–7 to Ole Miss and shutout losses to Kentucky (20–0) and Vanderbilt (14–0).

81 Heath Shuler

The men who came before and after him did their parts to push Tennessee football from afterthought to national power.

Andy Kelly certainly helped to start the process of bringing Tennessee football back to the forefront of SEC and national relevance, going 24–5–2 as a starter from 1988 to 1991, engineering unforgettable comeback wins at Notre Dame and against Virginia in the Sugar Bowl, and helping the school lay claim to two SEC championships and a Sugar Bowl title. His place in Tennessee lore is secure.

Peyton Manning cemented himself as the greatest quarterback in school history, ultimately beating out Branndon Stewart in 1994 and embarking on a record-setting college career that culminated with an SEC championship and an outside shot at a national championship in the 1998 Orange Bowl. Without question, Manning left Knoxville as the most talented quarterback ever to play the position at UT.

But in between, North Carolina native Heath Shuler served as more than just a bridge from the end of the Johnny Majors era and the start of a prosperous run under Phillip Fulmer. Shuler set the standard for excellence in high school coming out of Swain County High: he completed 190 of 332 passes for 3,626 yards and 42 touchdowns. He also rushed for 850 yards and 15 more TDs, and was named the North Carolina Class 1-A Player of the Year for two consecutive years.

Heath Shuler rolls out during UT's 1993 game against Vanderbilt.
(RVR Photos-USA Today Sports)

Suddenly the starter, with a smattering of 1991 game experience under his belt as Kelly's backup, Shuler served as a springboard for the successful beginning to the Fulmer era, starting in 1992. With Majors on bed rest following an open-heart procedure two weeks before the Vols' season opener against Louisiana-Lafayette, Shuler, Fulmer, Charlie Garner, and the Tennessee Volunteers raced out to an unlikely start to the season.

Much of that success resulted from the rumors that came to fruition about Shuler. Could he run? Boy, could he. Shuler's athleticism was unquestioned by the end of the 1992 season. The 6'3", 208-pound Bryson City, North Carolina, product finished as the Vols' fourth-leading rusher of the season, behind the running back triumvirate of Garner, James Stewart, and Aaron Hayden. Shuler actually finished ahead of RB Mose Phillips in the rushing yardage category, and Shuler's 11 team-high rushing touchdowns were four more than second-place Stewart. Shuler also completed 58 percent of his passes for 1,712 yards with 10 touchdowns to only 4 interceptions.

And Tennessee responded early, led by its new playmaking quarterback and young and inspiring interim head coach Fulmer. Tennessee escaped Athens with a thrilling 34–31 win over No. 14 Georgia, and it was Shuler, who displayed his two-way talents, that helped the Vols come away with a win. In the last 25 minutes, Shuler converted, with his arm or legs, five of eight third-down conversions and two of two fourth-down conversions. His third-down plays included a 44-yard run that set up his six-yard TD on third down for a 27–17 lead. On the final drive, Shuler's fourth-down, 22-yard pass to Davis kept alive the chance for him to score the winning TD on a three-yard keeper with 50 seconds left in the game.

Against Florida, Shuler showed brilliance with his legs and arm. He ran for two TDs and threw a 66-yard touchdown pass to Phillips as the Volunteers upset the Gators 31–14 in a driving rainstorm in Knoxville. The game remains the largest margin of victory over the Gators since, through the 2014 season.

Tennessee followed up a 20–0 win in Baton Rouge, Majors' first game back on the sideline, with a trio of heartbreaking losses. A last-second field goal by Arkansas capped a furious fourth-quarter rally in a 25–24 Arkansas win. Alabama came to town next and, as they did for much of the season, relied on a fierce defense to bottle up Majors' offense in a 17–10 UT loss, Alabama's seventh straight win in the series. Despite the loss, the Vols still had a shot at the first-ever SEC Championship Game in Birmingham if they could beat a 2–5 South Carolina squad in Columbia on Halloween night. Tennessee fell 24–23 when Shuler's pass to Stewart came up short of the goal line. The loss was Tennessee's first to South Carolina in 89 years. Tennessee went on to beat Boston College 38–23 in the Hall of Fame Bowl to cap a 9–3 season that was a handful of plays away from being much, much more. Still, Shuler performed well on the national stage, going 18-for-23 for 245 yards and two touchdowns through the air, and two more on the ground.

Having established himself as not just a leader on the Tennessee team and one of the top quarterbacks in the SEC, Shuler followed up 1992 with a tremendous effort in 1993.

As a junior, he led one of the most prolific offenses in the history of Tennessee football. The Vols began the year as a Top 10 team and finished the regular season 9–1–1. The Vols lost a 41–34 Shuler–Danny Wuerffel shootout to Florida, and tied No. 2 Alabama 17–17 in a game Shuler played with a separated shoulder.

Shuler completed 184 of 285 passes (64.6 percent) for 2,353 yards and 25 touchdowns with 8 interceptions, setting a new school record for touchdown passes in a season. He also was able to get out of the pocket and make plays with his feet. He could roll out, read the defense, and fire a dart to his receiver for a big gain. He could also take off and make a big play happen with his feet. The difference in 1993 was his decision-making ability and maturity, resulting in 28 touchdowns on the ground and through the air to become one of the nation's big playmakers.

Under Shuler, Tennessee averaged 40.3 points per game, second out of 106 Division I-A teams. But as would be the case, Tennessee would come up just short in their eventual house of horrors—Florida Field—by a score of 41–34, putting them in the backseat in the race for the SEC Championship game. UT also tied No. 2 Alabama in a game Shuler played with a separated shoulder. Tennessee finished the season 9–1–1 and No. 6 in the AP poll, earning a bid to the Fiesta Bowl to play No. 13 Penn State. The Nittany Lions rolled over the Vols, 31–13.

The 1993 Heisman Trophy Vote

Heath Shuler pulled the strings of a 1993 offense that set Tennessee records that still stand today. The 1993 Vols scored the most points in school history (471) and averaged the most points per game (42.8), total touchdowns (62), and average yards per play (6.9). Still, Shuler finished a distant second in the Heisman Trophy voting, due in large part to the impressive season Charlie Ward put together in the Seminoles' 1993 national title run. The voting breaks down accordingly among the top five vote getters:

1. Charlie Ward, quarterback, Florida State—2,310 total points. First place (740 votes); second place (39 votes); third place (12 votes)
2. Heath Shuler, quarterback, Tennessee—688 total points. First place (10); second place (274); third place (110)
3. David Palmer, wide receiver, Alabama—292 total points. First place (16); second place (78); third place (88)
4. Marshall Faulk, running back, San Diego State—250 total points. First place (7); second place (74); third place (81)
5. Glenn Foley, quarterback, Boston College—180 total points. First place (5); second place (47); third place (71)

Shuler was invited to the Downtown Athletic Club as a finalist for the Heisman Trophy. Unlike Johnny Majors' screw-job loss to 2–8 Notre Dame captain Paul Hornung in 1956, or Manning's much-criticized loss to Charles Woodson in 1997, Shuler's runner-up status to Charlie Ward was of no surprise to anyone who watched more than 10 minutes of football that year. Ward's spectacular play spearheaded Florida State's first national championship, and what turned out to be one of the biggest runaway Heisman votes in history.

Still, Shuler was believed to be the most NFL-ready quarterback in college football coming into the 1994 draft, for which Shuler declared his eligibility. He was taken with the third overall pick by the Washington Redskins.

As successful as his collegiate career was, his game never translated to the NFL. His rookie season in Washington might have been his best, with 10 touchdowns but 12 interceptions. After eventually losing his job to Gus Frerotte, Shuler was traded to New Orleans, where he had a disastrous 1997 season; he threw 2 touchdowns to 14 interceptions and was sacked 21 times in 9 starts.

He found more success in Congress, where he was a three-time electee to the House of Representatives out of the 11th District of North Carolina. Shuler also went back to UT and got a degree in psychology, after which he formed Heath Shuler Real Estate, LLC.

Regardless of his shortcomings in professional football, Shuler will always be remembered by those who watched him as one of the most exciting, athletic signal callers in Tennessee memory, and he engineered one of the greatest offenses in UT history, in 1993.

82 "On a Hallowed Hill in Tennessee..."

The words to the University of Tennessee alma mater are etched in the heart of the Volunteers faithful who attend home games each fall, when the alma mater is played through the PA system:

On a Hallowed hill in Tennessee,
Like Beacon shining bright,
The stately walls of old UT,
Rise glorious to the sight,
So here's to you old Tennessee,
Our Alma Mater true,
We pledge in love and harmony,
Our loyalty to you!

What most fans don't know is that these words were not thought up and put to paper by a Tennessee graduate. Or even someone closely associated with the University of Tennessee or Knoxville.

No, Mary Fleming Meek was living in Chattanooga at the time that she submitted her words and tune to the University of Tennessee as part of a contest in 1928. Meek won the contest, the school adopted her song as the alma mater, and she earned $50 for her now-famous song.

Meek never was a student at the University of Tennessee, Knoxville. According to her, it was because Tennessee was not a coed school and did not admit women until 1891. Since she was 58 when she passed away in 1929, that would have put her past the typical age of enrollment at the university.

Still, when the Pride of the Southland Marching Band completes its halftime performance and the alma mater begins, take a moment to think about each line of the song and what it means to you as a student, alumnus, or fan of the University of Tennessee. Then think about those words, as they were put on paper and sung by Mary Fleming Meek as she made a gorgeous and memorable offering of song that has remained as strong a tradition as any at the University of Tennessee.

83 Bill Bates, Meet Herschel Walker

On September 6, 1980, Georgia came to Knoxville to take on the Vols. It wasn't exactly a matchup considered worthy of national title considerations, Georgia having gone 6–5 in 1979, but by the time the final whistle blew, most of the country would know who Herschel Walker and Bill Bates were.

Despite being the team without the ranking next to its name, Tennessee had forged ahead to a 15–0 third-quarter lead and had just forced the Bulldogs offense to punt. However, Bates was hit as the ball got there and fumbled, which resulted in a safety for Georgia.

Having seen enough out of his sputtering offense, Georgia coach Vince Dooley put his freshman running back Herschel Walker in the game for his first-ever action. With the Bulldogs settling inside the UT 20-yard line, Walker took the handoff, fought through an arm tackle, and came face-to-face with Bates inside the 10-yard line. Bates was the lower player, but his wide, flat-footed stance proved to be no match for the freight train heading his way.

Walker put his head down, plowed through and over Bates, split two more defenders near the goal line, and trotted into the end zone to make the score 15–9. There was no Twitter or social media at the time, but the hit made national news.

And it served as an energizing moment for the Bulldogs. Georgia escaped with a 16–15 win in Knoxville after Walker scored his second touchdown of the game in the fourth quarter, and Georgia's defense recovered a fumble deep in its own territory to seal the win. The win served as a springboard for the Bulldogs, who won a number of close games en route to an 11–0 season,

Bill Bates and Herschel Walker: In the Pros

Although Bates and Walker remain forever tied to Walker's trucking of Bates in the young running back's first-ever action, the two would come together in Dallas as teammates. After a three-year stint in the USFL, Walker joined the Dallas Cowboys before the 1986 season. Walker would come into his own in 1988 and 1989, rushing for a career-high 1,514 yards and amassing more than 2,000 yards from scrimmage in his 1988 Pro Bowl season. Walker was traded to Minnesota in 1989, which the Cowboys were able to parlay into Emmitt Smith, Russell Maryland, Isaac Holt, Kevin Smith, Darren Woodson, and several others. Walker's production would never be anything close to what he accomplished in Dallas, while the Cowboys had acquired the nucleus to begin its run of Super Bowl championships.

Meanwhile, Bates remained as a constant force on special teams and as a defensive back in nickel packages under head coach Jimmy Johnson. When the Pro Bowl began selecting special teams players to the ballot, Bates was named to the 1984 Pro Bowl squad. He suffered a season-ending knee injury in 1992, playing in only five games, but came back strong in Dallas's 1993 Super Bowl season, earning the Ed Block Courage Award for his comeback and productivity (he led the team in special teams tackles with 25).

Bates' 15 years as a Cowboy are matched only by Ed "Too Tall" Jones and Mark Tuinei. "If we had 11 players on the field who played as hard as Bill Bates and did their homework like he does, we'd be almost impossible to beat," longtime Cowboys head coach Tom Landry told ESPN.com.

including an improbable 26–21 win over Florida in Jacksonville when Georgia quarterback Buck Belue found Lindsay Scott, who pulled down the pass and raced for a 93-yard touchdown in the final seconds to keep Georgia's dream season alive. Georgia toppled No. 7 Notre Dame in the Sugar Bowl to cap a 12–0 season and earn the school's most recent national championship.

Although Walker finished third in the Heisman Trophy voting to winner George Rogers of South Carolina and Pitt's Hugh Green, it was a breakout performance for the young future star in one of the most memorable seasons in Bulldogs football history. And among his 15 rushing touchdowns that season, his first was the most memorable and showcased both him and Bates on highlights for years to come.

Ironically, Bates and Walker came together as teammates on the Dallas Cowboys. Despite Walker's physical talents and ability, it was Bates who made a legendary name for himself on one of the most hallowed professional football franchises ever.

Bates' hustle and special teams play were key components on the 1992, 1993, and 1995 Super Bowl champion squads. When Bates retired following the 1997 season, he tied the club record for service with 15 seasons in Dallas. In that time he had amassed 217 games played (second in team history), more than 700 tackles, and 14 interceptions. Bates joined the Cowboys again as a special teams / defensive assistant coach in 1998 under then–head coach Chan Gailey. He was defensive backs coach in 2000 and defensive nickel package / special teams assistant the following two seasons.

84 Listen to the Story of Perseverance of Inky Johnson

On September 9, 2006, the life of Tennessee defensive back Inquoris "Inky" Johnson changed forever. Tennessee was hosting Air Force Academy, coming off a strong 35–18 home win over the University of California.

Like any other weekend, it was a raucous night inside Neyland Stadium. Having started the season with an impressive win and facing a team it was expected to dominate, the deafening roar of the Orange and White faithful rained down on the field with each snap.

Suddenly, after one play, you could hear a pin drop for what seemed like an eternity.

As the Air Force quarterback lobbed a pass down the sideline, Johnson collided with the receiver at the 32-yard line. The Air Force player made his way to his feet, but Johnson went limp and lay on the sideline, motionless. Air Force trainers immediately dropped down to his attention.

Johnson said:

I hit the guy and my body just went completely limp. I fell to the ground. I blacked out. When I woke up, there was a shock going through my whole body and I couldn't feel anything. They put me on a spinal board and took me to the hospital.

I was in the ER, and I heard the doctor say, "We've got to rush this guy back to surgery because he's about to lose his life." So, my mind-set shifted. Here I am, chasing a dream that I put my heart into. My soul, my spirit. I've been working since a child for this. I've never cheated myself. I've never cheated the game. So you can imagine how this felt to me at this moment.

When this happened to me, they told me that I could go home, take a break, take some time off because it was a traumatic injury. I told them I didn't want to go home. There was nothing for me at home. They didn't know that I had sat on the porch with my grandmother and told her that I was going to graduate from college. Be the first one to graduate in our family no matter what happened.

I said that. So even when this injury came about, I had to switch hands. Learn how to write twenty-page papers with my left hand. It was hard.

According to athletic trainer Jason McVeigh, per UTSports. com:

On Sept. 9, Inquoris Johnson sustained a traumatic injury to the nerves and blood vessels of his right brachial plexus while making a tackle versus Air Force. Initial surgery was performed the morning of Sept. 10 by Dr. David Cassada at UT Medical Center to successfully correct Mr. Johnson's vascular injury.

Since that time, Mr. Johnson has been receiving daily physical therapy by the UT Sports Medicine staff to restore full range of motion to his right shoulder and arm.

Mr. Johnson, his family and representatives from the UT Athletics Department recently were flown to Rochester, Minn., to meet with specialists at the Mayo Clinic and to undergo further diagnostic testing and evaluations. Mr. Johnson is scheduled for reconstructive brachial plexus surgery on his right shoulder and arm at the Mayo Clinic on Dec. 21. The surgery will be performed by Drs. Bishop, Shin and Spinner.

At this time, no decisions have been made regarding Mr. Johnson's playing status on the UT football team.

Shortly after the 2006 season, it was announced that Inky Johnson's football career was over. The damage to his nerves and blood vessels was irreversible to such a degree that he could never hope to play the game he loved again.

"Inky is in school and is doing fine. Got a great attitude. Wants to coach, I think. Inky is just a wonderful young man. If they were all like Inky Johnson it would be a wonderful world," Phillip Fulmer said in February 2007.

Although Johnson's right arm remained significantly weakened due to nerve damage, his determination remained ironclad. Johnson even learned how to write with his left hand and fulfilled his promise to his grandmother: he graduated with a degree in political science with a minor in health studies.

Johnson coauthored the book *Inky*, writing about his faith, football, and what it takes to persevere in life.

Today, Johnson travels across Tennessee telling his story about overcoming adversity and the love and dedication he gave on the football field and how it translates into life. He can be booked for speaking engagements at InkyJohnson.com.

85 Doug Atkins, Pro Football Hall of Famer

Doug Atkins arrived on campus in Knoxville ready to take to his craft and dominate the opposition—on the basketball court.

Originally Atkins entered the University of Tennessee on a basketball scholarship, but once General Neyland saw his combination of size and agility, he convinced him to switch sports and don a football helmet. The transition was smooth for the naturally gifted Atkins, who used his leaping skills and his long frame to dominate the defensive end position. In fact, Atkins ultimately created a trademark move of leaping over—and embarrassing—linemen who dared go low to block him.

Atkins spearheaded a Tennessee defense that pitched five shutouts in ten regular-season games in 1951, on the way to a perfect

Defensive lineman Doug Atkins enjoyed a successful pro career after UT.

10–0 regular-season mark and a consensus national championship. During Atkins' playing time, the Volunteers went 29–3–1.

After Atkins earned All-America honors in 1952, the Cleveland Browns selected him with their first pick in the 1952 NFL Draft.

After two seasons in Cleveland, he was traded to the Chicago Bears, where he became one of the league's best defensive linemen of his era. In addition to his incredible strength, Atkins was—just like in Knoxville—able to continue to use his agility and frame to get into the backfield, including the ability to leap opposing blockers.

An All-NFL choice four times and a participant in eight Pro Bowls, Atkins wrapped up his career with three successful seasons with the New Orleans Saints. His pro career spanned 17 seasons and 205 games, in which Atkins dominated offensive linemen, quarterbacks, running backs, fullbacks, and anyone else who had the misfortune of trying to stop him. There was a common theme amongst former players who faced off against him: don't make Doug mad.

It was common knowledge that tripping Atkins or taking a cheap shot against him would only make him more violent, physical, and even more impossible to handle one-on-one…if such a thing were possible.

Atkins is one of two Tennessee players (Reggie White is the other) to be inducted into both the College Football Hall of Fame (1985) and the Pro Football Hall of Fame (1982).

86 Tennessee Versus Heisman Trophy Winners

Tennessee has always had a love-hate relationship with the Heisman Trophy. Several times the prize has conceivably been within its grasp: Hank Lauricella in 1951, Johnny Majors in 1956, Heath Shuler in 1993, and Peyton Manning in 1997. All of these men led Tennessee to tremendous, memorable seasons. All came in second place in the voting, by varying distances (Charlie Ward's 1993 win over second-place Shuler was one of the biggest landslide victories in the history of the award).

But it's not just the elusiveness of the bronze statue that's been a historical bugaboo for the program; it's also the Volunteers' success, or lack thereof, against eventual winners in the midst of a Heisman Trophy run that has been difficult to swallow.

Against players who were in their Heisman Trophy seasons, the Vols have a 4–6 record in the history of their program, including bowl games. The most beloved and memorable wins of those four probably depend on in which generation you grew up. The most recent, and arguably most memorable, came on January 1, 1996, when Tennessee beat No. 4 Ohio State 20–14 in the Citrus Bowl. In the fourth quarter the Volunteers defense put the clamps down on the Buckeyes offense and Eddie George, who they held to a season-low 89 yards rushing, in completing an 11–1 season.

Older fans may remember No. 1 LSU coming to Knoxville on November 7, 1959, just one week after eventual Heisman winner Billy Cannon's Halloween night punt return for a touchdown that ranks among the most famous plays in LSU history. Tennessee stopped Cannon at the goal line on a two-point-conversion attempt, holding on for a 14–13 win in an otherwise mostly forgettable 5–4–1 season in Knoxville.

Tennessee thrashed No. 1 Auburn 38–20 in Knoxville in 1985, in a game that wasn't even as close as the final score. Eventual Heisman winner Bo Jackson struggled to only 80 yards rushing—one of three games in which he didn't break the century mark—and left the game in the second half due to injury.

Tennessee also clipped Bear Bryant's 1957 Texas A&M Aggies and Heisman winner John David Crow in the 1957 Gator Bowl. On a soggy, sloppy day, the Vols edged the Aggies in the lowest scoring game in Gator Bowl history, 3–0. Vols tailback Bobby Gordon, MVP of the game, collided with Crow on the Vols' march to the winning field goal. Crow appeared to suffer a rib injury, while Gordon held Sammy Burklow's game-winning field goal. It was the Bear's last game at Texas A&M, and the Vols' last bowl game appearance until 1965.

Tennessee's losses include two to the most recent Heisman winners of a chief rival from Gainesville. In 2007 Florida crushed Tennessee 59–20 in a game in which Tim Tebow threw for 299 yards on just 19 passes and accounted for four touchdowns. In 1996 Danny Wuerffel led a 35-point first-half onslaught that Manning and the No. 2 Volunteers never recovered from in a 35–29 loss to No. 4 Florida.

In 2009 UT held Mark Ingram to less than 100 yards rushing and forced his first-ever fumble, while also outgaining the top-ranked Crimson Tide 341–256. But Terrence Cody's block of Daniel Lincoln's last-second field-goal attempt broke hearts in Knoxville as the Tide escaped 12–10 on the way to a national title.

Tennessee was on the tracks of a runaway train in 1981 in the form of USC's Marcus Allen. Allen ran over the Volunteers defense for 211 yards in a 43–7 win. His 2,342 rushing yards still stand as the fourth-most rushing yards in a season in NCAA history.

In 1971 Tennessee led a sloppy Auburn team 9–3 late in the fourth quarter. However, Auburn scored the game's final points with less than three minutes to go after Heisman-winning quarterback Pat Sullivan led the Tigers 86 yards down the field. It was doubly disheartening for UT fans who remember the 1970 Auburn Tigers handing the Volunteers their only loss of the season in Birmingham.

Tennessee's first loss to a Heisman winner came in the season opener in 1967 at UCLA. As if pulled from a Hollywood movie, Bruins quarterback Gary Beban engineered a dramatic comeback in the final minutes, scampering for a serpentine-esque 27-yard touchdown and the game's winning points in a 20–16 Bruins victory—Tennessee's only loss of the regular season. Beban, the school's only Heisman winner, would lead UCLA to a 7–2–1 final record.

87 Take in the View of Campus from Ayres Hall and the Hill

Perhaps you've come back for homecoming, to see the parade and the weekend festivities, culminated by a Volunteers victory in Neyland Stadium on Saturday. Maybe you're just looking to catch up with old friends on the Strip, in the Fort, or on campus to tailgate at an old spot. Throw up an orange-and-white gazebo tent, get the grill fired up, and pull an ice-cold bottle out of a cooler while spinning yarns about yesteryear's good times.

Certainly, there are countless things to do on a game-day weekend. One thing is to take a stroll down memory lane—or in this case, *up* it. Up the steps leading from the student union up to Ayres Hall on the Hill, one of the landmark and signature buildings on campus. Constructed and dedicated in 1921, Ayres Hall was named after the 12th president of the university—Mr.

Brown Ayres—two years following his death. President Ayres, heading an institution of 729 students and 95 faculty (including the medical and dental departments in Nashville), proceeded to make the University of Tennessee a federal land-grant institution and state university.

At last, in 1917, the university received its first million-dollar state appropriation, from which President Ayres and the University trustees began earmarking funds as they made plans for new campus buildings. The construction of a single structure on the summit of the Hill was one of Ayres' dreams.

Today Ayres' vision of the Hill hosts, as the alumni know, various math, science, and engineering classes. Any freshman who had to make the 7:30 AM hike all the way across campus from the dorms in January, through slush or snow, for a Monday morning chemistry lab in Buehler Hall knows that trek far too well.

But go back. Sit on the steps leading down to the rest of campus on a Friday night, as you listen to the faint sounds of live music coming from the nearby Strip. Watch smatterings of people wearing orange moving about, from the gift shop to the parking lot, with Neyland Stadium looming over everything, ready to host 100,000 fans in less than 24 hours. See the sky turn as orange as the sun sets on another glorious evening on campus by the river.

And take a last look around and think about the vision of Brown Ayres before you walk down the steps from the Hill and head into the Knoxville evening in search of entertainment.

88 No. 1 Notre Dame 34, No. 9 Tennessee 29; 11/10/90

Back before the rise of the program under the guidance of Phillip Fulmer, this game was just about as big as they came in Knoxville. It was even bigger when the ranking next to the legendary opponent's name was a 1. Notre Dame came to Knoxville on a sunny, 49-degree afternoon with its golden helmets—and golden legacy—and were only two years removed from a national championship season. The Irish were loaded with talent, with Ricky Watters, Tony Brooks, and Rodney Culver splitting carries in the backfield.

Still, Tennessee had the firepower to keep up, with Carl Pickens, Tony Thompson, Alvin Harper, and quarterback Andy Kelly. Tennessee stood toe to toe with the No. 1 team in the country, holding a lead in the fourth quarter of an incredibly well-played football game.

The problem was that the Irish had the two best players on the field in Ricky Watters and Raghib "Rocket" Ismail, and their performance left no doubt about it. Ricky Watters ran for 174 yards, his bullish style leaving Tennessee defenders in his wake. Watters averaged 10.2 yards per carry, and Notre Dame rolled up 316 rushing yards on the day.

Culver also paid early dividends out of the backfield. After softening the Vols defense with the running game, quarterback Rick Mirer fired downfield to Culver, who broke a tackle inside the 10-yard line and scampered in for a 7–3 lead. Craig Burke's second field goal on the ensuing drive made it 7–6. Craig Hentrich answered with a second-quarter field goal after Ismail's punt return to the UT 10-yard line was called back for an illegal block.

Halftime, Notre Dame 10, Tennessee 6.

Tennessee marched down the field on its opening drive of the second half, in large part due to a long catch and run by Pickens. On third-and-5 from the 10-yard line, Kelly dropped back to pass and handed the ball to Thompson, who broke two tacklers and fell across the goal line for a 13–10 lead.

The lead was short-lived. Two plays later, Watters broke through the middle of the Tennessee defensive line, and as though he was going through the tire drill on the Notre Dame practice field, a host of arm tackles were no match.

In what would mirror two Top 10 heavyweights slugging it out, Andy Kelly delivered a haymaker right back to the Irish defense. Seeing man coverage against Alvin Harper on a post, he lobbed the pass in stride for Harper, who hauled in the ball with a defender draped on his back.

Tennessee 20, Notre Dame 17.

With just less than 10 minutes left in the game, Tennessee held the lead 23–20. Unfortunately for the Vols, Notre Dame's talent eventually won out. The combination of Watters and the Rocket proved to be too much, putting the Irish ahead 27–23 in the second half. The Rocket extended the Irish lead to 34–23 on an end around with 3:31 left.

However, Andy Kelly and the Volunteers, staring possible victory in the face less than four minutes before, fought on. Kelly found a wide-open Alvin Harper in the corner of the end zone to cut the lead to 34–29. The two-point conversion failed, but then Pickens recovered the high-bounding onside kick attempt.

Tennessee had life, and each Kelly pass breathed more life into the collective UT hopes. Completions to Greg Amsler and Pickens put the Vols at the 20-yard line with just more than a minute to play. But Kelly's final pass, intended for Harper, was intercepted by Rod Smith on the 2-yard line, and Notre Dame held on.

The loss, though gut-wrenching, proved just how far Tennessee had continued to rise under Coach Majors. Those same Volunteers went on to claim the SEC championship and raise a Sugar Bowl championship trophy with a 23–22 win over Virginia. The Vols rallied from a 16–0 deficit and prevailed in the final seconds when Thompson leaped the Virginia defensive line for the winning points.

Notre Dame lost its next game 24–21 at home to Penn State, earning a trip to the Orange Bowl to take on Colorado. The Buffaloes defeated the Irish 10–9 to claim a share of the national championship with Georgia Tech.

As for Tennessee and Notre Dame, the Miracle in South Bend the following season would give Tennessee fans the last laugh, and serve as redemption for Kelly. His game-winning pass to Aaron Hayden lifted Tennessee to the 35–34 upset victory.

89 Take an RV Trip to a Rival SEC School

If there is a pilgrimage every Tennessee fan should make at some point, it's to see the Volunteers play on the road. And if you're going to make the trip, and you don't mind close quarters, then traveling by RV or motor coach to a road game is an outstanding way to go. Like Clark Griswold said in the movie *National Lampoon's Vacation*, "Getting there is half the fun."

And it really can be.

Whether you're looking to minimize driving time, or going to see a new part of the country on the way, there is an RV trip for you. The first thing to decide is how far you are going in order to figure out what kind of vehicle you should get. If you have the means, getting a full motor coach that can comfortably sleep six to eight is the way to go. If you have enough buddies willing to put in money, it's absolutely worth it. Most places will require a registered driver who is at least 25 years old, so make sure you have one of those in the group.

The good thing about leaving from Knoxville or the surrounding area is that there really are a number of schools that make for close trips. If you or the members of your group are not comfortable driving a huge vehicle for a long distance, then perhaps picking a road game closer to home, such as at Kentucky, Vanderbilt, Georgia, or South Carolina, would be a good way to start. There's also the alternative of piling into a big vehicle and picking up the RV or motor coach at a city closer to your destination (i.e., this author's friends are greatly pleased at their decision to drive from Knoxville and pick up an RV in Indianapolis for a 2005 trip to Notre Dame, rather than face five hours of additional interstate driving in an unfamiliar vehicle; the serene drive from Indianapolis through the cornfields of northern Indiana made the decision definitely worth it).

Make sure you check the laws of the state(s) you are entering. While it's often as commonplace as peanut butter is with jelly to pile a keg or two on your party bus bound for football and good times, the last thing anyone wants is to get boarded and cited with open containers of alcohol, so be subtle and smart if you choose to go that route.

If you are traveling south, to Gainesville or Baton Rouge, get there at least a couple days in advance. At Tiger Stadium, the RV lot begins filling up during the week, and by Friday, it's a hunt to find any place that's relatively close to the stadium. Given the unique food (pastalaya, alligator sauce picante, and crawfish boils), festivities (try the almost-famous shot-ski near the corner of Skip Bertman and Nicholson Drives), and fellowship among the Tigers faithful, it's worth getting there in plenty of time to get a prime spot to unload your chariot.

Hopefully you'll get a vehicle with slide-outs to give you more space once you arrive. If it's a long trip, you'll be more than thankful for the space. If your coach comes with a rollout canopy, that should suffice to cover the tailgate grill and television that you hopefully brought. In the event your destination's RV lot doesn't open up until game day, Walmart is your friend. Not only can you park there overnight (in most places), but you can also pick up whatever supplies you and your crew need for the next day.

Whether you park near campus in Gainesville; by Tiger Stadium in Baton Rouge; in the large, open fields outside Commonwealth Stadium; or near the Cockaboose Railroad close to Williams-Brice Stadium, chances are, win or lose, you'll be talking about your trip for years to come.

90 Vols in the NFL Draft

Many young men who are fortunate enough to play football at the collegiate level hope to take the next step and play in the National Football League. There are certain programs that have seen more than their fair share of players' names called by the commissioner during the NFL Draft.

Tennessee is one of those programs. With 45 players drafted in the first round of the NFL Draft, Tennessee has a long and proud history of seeing the NFL populated with Volunteers. Through the 2015 NFL Draft, 337 Tennessee Volunteers have been drafted into the NFL (excluding the 15 drafted into the AFL and by the AAFC), which ranks seventh out of all college football programs. The only schools to have placed more players in the NFL are USC, Notre Dame, Ohio State, Oklahoma, Nebraska, and Michigan.

The first Tennessee player drafted into the NFL was defensive end Roy Rose, by the New York Giants in the fourth round in 1936. The first Volunteer taken with the No. 1 overall pick in the NFL Draft was All-American halfback George Cafego, who was selected by the Chicago Cardinals in the 1940 draft.

Tennessee has had seven players selected in the Top 5 of the NFL Draft. Cafego, Bob Johnson (1968, Cincinnati, No. 2 overall), Reggie White (1984 Supplemental Draft, Philadelphia, No. 4 overall), Heath Shuler (1994, Washington, No. 3 overall), Peyton Manning (1998, Indianapolis, No. 1 overall), Jamal Lewis (2000, Baltimore, No. 5 overall), and Eric Berry (2010, Kansas City, No. 5 overall).

Recently, Tennessee had at least one player selected in the first round each year from 2006 through 2010, lean years during which time Tennessee had only one SEC divisional title and only one bowl victory. Still, Jason Allen (2006 Round 1, Pick 16 by Miami), Justin Harrell (2007 Round 1, Pick 16 by Green Bay), Robert Meachem (2007 Round 1, Pick 27 by New Orleans), Jerod Mayo (2008 Round 1, Pick 10 by New England), Robert Ayers (2009 Round 1, Pick 18 by Denver), Eric Berry (2010 Round 1, Pick 5 by Kansas City), and Dan Williams (2010 Round 1, Pick 26 by Arizona) proved that Tennessee is still churning out talented and capable NFL players.

In the past five years, Denarius Moore, Malik Jackson, Mychal Rivera, Justin Hunter, Cordarrelle Patterson, and Ja'Wuan James have all held important roles on their respective teams. Without question, Volunteers pride continues to run strong on the biggest football stage of them all.

91 The Kickin' Colquitts

There have been many family names associated with the University of Tennessee football program over the years that exemplify tradition and legacy within the university. Berry—as in James (captain of the 1981 team), Eric (All-American defensive back, 2009 Jim Thorpe Award winner, and first-round NFL draft pick), and now Evan and Elliot. Majors—Johnny (Heisman Trophy runner-up and 16-year head coach) and Bobby (consensus All-American in 1979).

The Colquitt name might have the deepest bloodline in Tennessee football history—and certainly one that has established itself both on Saturdays and Sundays. It's not many places where a punting legacy springs up, but given the success Craig Colquitt had, it's only natural his sons Dustin and Britton would follow suit.

In the NFL, Craig punted for the Pittsburgh Steelers (1978–84) and Indianapolis Colts (1987). Craig had an average of 41.3 yards per punt and won two Super Bowl rings with the Steelers in the 1978 and 1979 seasons. At Tennessee, things didn't start off so well for him. In his first game, he fumbled the snap, which bounced off his face mask, and he was tackled with the ball. If he could have pulled a Houdini-esque escape at that point, he would have. "I really wanted to run out of the stadium because I figured this was the end for me," he told CBS Denver.

Fortunately, kicking coach George Cafego had some encouraging words and Craig stuck with it. He's glad he did. Craig set the UT record with a 42.5-yard career punting average before moving on to winning Super Bowl rings and raising children.

His record wouldn't last long, and it would be another Colquitt—his nephew Jimmy—who broke it. Jimmy averaged

Britton Colquitt warms up before a game against Air Force in 2006.

43.9 yards per punt from 1981 to 1984, twice earning first-team All-America honors in the process. He averaged an incredible 46.9 yards per punt in 1982, second-best in the nation and best in school history, while also setting a team record for a single-game punting average with 53.0 yards per punt.

Craig's older son, Dustin, also found his name among the All-Americans in the Neyland-Thompson Sports Center at the University of Tennessee. In 2003 Dustin boomed an average of 45.6 yards per punt with a long of 67 yards in garnering first-team All-America honors. He amassed a school record in punts (240), total punting yardage (10,216), and surpassed his father's career punting average by one-tenth of a yard. Dustin currently handles the punting duties for the Kansas City Chiefs.

His younger brother, Britton, finished with a 42.6-yard career punting average, the same as his brother, Dustin. He was named first-team All-SEC in 2006 with a 44.9-yard average. Since 2009, Colquitt has punted for the Denver Broncos. In 2011 Colquitt boomed an incredible 4,783 yards from scrimmage, sixth-most in NFL history, compiling his highest gross punting average at more than 47 yards per kick. Britton punted twice for the Broncos in Super Bowl XLVIII.

Britton and Dustin's ascension to the top of their craft was rewarded when Dustin signed an $18.75 million deal and Britton got an $11.7 million extension.

"People tell me you must be proud," Craig Colquitt told CBS Denver. "I'm glad they have jobs. They just happen to have exceptional jobs."

And the Colquitt name retains an exceptional reputation within the University of Tennessee football program.

Vols Tie Kentucky in 1929; Miss Perfect Season, Rose Bowl

On a day with thoughts of a rose parade and Southern California on the brain, it was a painful déjà vu for General Neyland's undefeated Volunteers in frigid, frozen Lexington, Kentucky, on November 27, 1929.

Just like in 1928, they knifed their way through their primary rivals Alabama and Vanderbilt, the schools General Neyland was hired to beat, by respective scores of 6–0 and 13–0. The goose egg, a common score column item for the general's opposition during his time on the sideline, was the final tally for all but two of UT's opponents in the 1929 season. The season opener against Centre College saw Centre muster six points to the Vols' 40. Ole Miss managed seven against Tennessee's 53 on October 12.

Like a runaway freight train, Tennessee stormed into Lexington a perfect 8–0, riding the legs of the Hack and Mac show in the backfield—running backs Buddy Hackman and All-American Gene McEver—and led by the legendary Bobby Dodd at quarterback. But, like their 1928 matchup that resulted in a scoreless tie, the snowy affair turned into a low-scoring struggle.

"It was a miserable day, as it very often is for the Kentucky game," said former UT tailback Hugh Faust. "We missed going to the Rose Bowl by a couple, maybe three inches. No more. Kentucky scored and missed their extra point. Late in the ballgame, Tennessee got the ball back. Snow covered the field. You couldn't see the lines, the goal line, the 10-yard line, or anything."

On the snow-covered field, Tennessee plowed in late with the apparent game-tying touchdown, in position to win the game on the ensuing extra point.

"We scored, we thought," said Faust. "The official raised his hands up to signal *touchdown*. So Neyland substituted Charlie Kohlase, who was our top extra point man. He was a great drop-kicker. He hadn't missed one all season. Then, after he got on the field, the official scraped the snow back and said it was not a touchdown. So Neyland had to substitute another player for Kohlase. We scored the touchdown. But under the rules of those times, once you went out of the game, you weren't allowed to go back in, in the same half."

Faust continued, "So we tried the [extra point] with a fellow who was rather inept, who wasn't our regular kicker. He kicked the extra point, and it hit the crossbar, went up, and came back down. Two inches higher, and it would have gone over. If we won, we were in the Rose Bowl. But because it was a tie, it went to someone else."

That someone else was the Pittsburgh Panthers, who snuffed out Penn State 20–7 to complete a 9–0 regular season. Their opponent, the 9–2 USC Trojans, thrashed the Panthers—who had traveled to Southern California by train—47–14.

Tennessee completed their 1929 season with a resounding 54–0 shellacking of South Carolina at Shields-Watkins Field to finish with a mark of 9–0–1. The Vols made it to the Rose Bowl, eventually—at the end of their undefeated, unscored-upon 1939 season falling to the Trojans, 14–0.

Bobby Dodd

The name Bobby Dodd has a revered place in the annals of college football history.

Along with Bowden Wyatt and Amos Alonzo Stagg, Dodd is part of a truly remarkable trio: the only men ever to be inducted into the College Football Hall of Fame as both players and coaches.

Given that Dodd played under one of the most successful and revolutionary coaches of his era in General Robert Neyland, it's only natural that Dodd would not only succeed on the field, but also go on to a coaching career himself.

Dodd was recruited to UT out of Dobyns-Bennett High School in Kingsport, Tennessee. At UT, Dodd was a member of the football, basketball, and baseball teams. But it was in football that Dodd was a natural star. Starting in 1928, Dodd flashed his athleticism for Neyland's Volunteers, seeing time at quarterback, running back, and punter. He held a key role, along with the back-field of Buddy Hackman and Gene McEver, in the 15–13 upset of Alabama in Tuscaloosa in 1928. He threw a touchdown pass and pinned Alabama deep at their own 1-yard line late with a "coffin corner" punt.

Perhaps Dodd's finest moment came in his senior season against then–Southern Conference power Vanderbilt. Dodd punted an incredible 14 times for a 42-yard average. He also completed 7 of 12 passes for 159 yards with two touchdowns and rushed for 39 yards on nine carries. He accounted for an incredible 212 of Tennessee's 226 yards of total offense. On the other side of the ball, Dodd also picked off two passes. Tennessee would go on to win 13–0 on the way to a 9–1 season in 1930. Dodd was selected as a first-team All-American.

In 1931 Dodd joined on as an assistant coach for Georgia Tech's football program, where he served and waited patiently for 15 years as an assistant. In 1945 Dodd was named the third head coach of the Yellow Jackets and went on to lead the team to national prominence. During the next 22 years he compiled a record of 165–64–8, the best years in school history. His teams won 9 of 13 bowl games, including six in a row during the early

1950s. Dodd reached the pinnacle of his career in the 1950s, when Georgia Tech was selected as the national champion in the 1952 International News Service poll and finished No. 2 in the AP poll. The Jackets ran the table at 12–0, winning the Southeastern Conference and the Sugar Bowl over Ole Miss, 24–7. Aside from his record, Dodd is also recognized for inventing the "belly series," a play in which the quarterback places the football at the running back's abdomen and, depending on the defense, either gives the ball to the running back or keeps it.

94 The "Hobnail Boot" Game

The 2001 season certainly was an odyssey for Volunteers fans. A roller-coaster season in every metaphorical sense imaginable. Beating LSU 26–18 in Knoxville, only to fall 31–20 to their backup quarterback in the SEC Championship Game and lose a shot at the national championship. Beating Florida in Spurrier's last game in the Swamp as the Gators' head coach in a de facto SEC East title game. Thrashing Michigan in the 2002 Florida Citrus Bowl behind Casey Clausen's 393 passing yards.

And then there was the Georgia game back on October 6, 2001. Mark Richt, in his first season as the Dawgs' head coach, entered the game 2–1, having swept the state of Arkansas (Hogs and Arkansas State) by comfortable margins and lost to South Carolina. Richt brought with him a young but very talented redshirt freshman quarterback in David Greene from Snellville, Georgia, where he had been an All-State selection.

Early on, it seemed Tennessee was well on their way to winning their sixth straight matchup with the Bulldogs in Knoxville.

Clausen hit Kelley Washington and Leonard Scott with first-quarter touchdown passes on the way to a 14–3 lead.

Georgia quickly bounced back. Damien Gary slashed through Tennessee's punt team on the first play of the second quarter for a 72-yard punt-return touchdown to bring the score to 14–10.

Though Tennessee had allowed just 222 yards per game through the air, good for third-best in the country, Greene and the Georgia passing game gave the Tennessee defense fits all game long. Greene found Fred Gibson for a 15-yard touchdown late in the second quarter.

Greene finished 21 of 34 for 303 yards and two touchdowns.

Yet, with Georgia leading 20–17 thanks to a 31-yard Billy Bennett field goal with 5:44 left, No. 6 Tennessee seemed to find a way to escape against the unranked Bulldogs in the final minute. With Travis Stephens having already racked up 176 yards on the ground, Clausen swung a screen pass into the capable hands of the running back, who scampered up the sideline and into the end zone for a 62-yard touchdown and a 24–20 lead. Neyland Stadium nearly shook from the incredible turn of events.

"Well, they're gonna kick off to us, and some stupid miracle could still happen," lamented longtime Georgia radio play-by-play man Larry Munson.

Ask, Larry, and ye shall receive. With only 44 seconds left, Dustin Colquitt's squib kick was fielded and downed by Georgia at the UGA 41-yard line, giving the Bulldogs pristine field position.

Greene found Gary for 12 yards. Two plays later, Greene hit tight end Randy McMichael for 27 yards to the 20-yard line with 20 seconds left. One play later, Georgia was at the 6, after another strike to McMichael.

After the Bulldogs took their last timeout, Richt called up the play nobody on the Tennessee side of the field expected: a play-action pass to the fullback. Greene faked the handoff and lobbed the ball over the linebackers to fullback Verron Haynes, setting off a wild celebration on the sideline—and in the Georgia radio broadcast room in the Neyland Stadium press box.

Munson cried, "Touchdown! My God, a touchdown! We threw it to...we threw it to Haynes...with five seconds left! My God almighty, did you see what he did? David Greene just straightened up, and we snuck the fullback over.... We just stepped on their face with a hobnail boot and broke their nose! We just crushed their face!"

In one of the more heartbreaking endings in Neyland Stadium in recent memory, along with the 2000 Florida–Jabar Gaffney catch-drop, Georgia had exorcised a demon by winning in the most unlikely of fashions in its own personal house of horrors. The win marked a turn in the series, which Tennessee had dominated in the 1990s.

Mark Richt made an early first impression on the Georgia fan base by defeating a rival that Ray Goff and Jim Donnan struggled to beat, and the following years between Phillip Fulmer and Richt became some of the most hotly contested games in the SEC as Georgia rose to SEC and national relevance. By the time Greene left Georgia, he had set the Division I-A record for career wins, with 42.

95 Doug Dickey Revives the UT Program

In 1964 the UT football program was in a state of affairs not dissimilar to the state of the program in 2012.

A proud, dominating football program under General Neyland had seen its fortunes fall under the watch of head coach Bowden Wyatt. Under Wyatt, Tennessee posted records of 6–3–1, 10–1,

8–3, 4–6, 5–4–1, 6–2–2, 6–4, and 4–6 from 1955 through the 1962 season. A change was in the cards.

Enter Doug Dickey. After serving as an assistant coach under Frank Broyles at Arkansas, Dickey accepted the UT head coaching job in 1964. He was inheriting a program that had fallen on hard times, not having made a bowl game appearance since the 1957 season.

Things didn't start easy in 1964, at least as far as garnering results on the field. Dickey opted for the T formation, moving away from the vaunted single-wing formation that had done so well for Tennessee for decades. The Vols squeaked by Chattanooga, Mississippi State, and Boston College and dropped heartbreaking games to Top 10 opponents Auburn and Alabama. However, as perhaps a sign of things to come, Dickey's Vols traveled to LSU on October 24 and, before a nationally televised audience, came away with a 3–3 tie against the seventh-ranked Tigers. The following game against No. 7 Georgia Tech served as a bit of a breakthrough, with UT upsetting the Yellow Jackets 22–14 at Grant Field. Although the Vols then dropped three straight to finish 4–5–1, positive headway had been made.

The next year, Tennessee won eight games for the first time since 1957. At 8–1–2, with only a one-point loss to Ole Miss in a game played in Memphis, Tennessee began to ascend in the SEC pecking order, finishing fourth in the SEC. Both ties were against Auburn, 13–13 at home and 7–7 at Alabama. UT accepted an invitation to the Bluebonnet Bowl, in which they defeated Tulsa 27–6.

Another eight-win season followed in 1966, before UT finally made a run back to national relevance in the fall of 1967. Following a close season-opening loss at UCLA, Tennessee ran the table the rest of the regular season, ascending to No. 2 in the AP poll and accepting a bid to play 9–1 Oklahoma in the Orange Bowl. Even though Oklahoma won 26–24, Tennessee had returned to a place of national relevance where it had previously thrived under General

Neyland. Tennessee was the SEC champion with a 6–0 conference record and was voted No. 1 by the Litkenhous rating system. Dickey coupled his 1967 conference title with another one in 1969, shortly before leaving to become the head coach at the University of Florida, where he had played football in college. Dickey returned to Knoxville in 1985 as the university's athletic director, a position he held until 2002.

Not only did Doug Dickey reestablish an elite football program at UT, he also brought a large helping of tradition that many Vols fans now take for granted.

His teams were the first to run through the band's Power T formation, beginning September 18, 1965, against Army, which has become just as much of a tradition as the game itself.

Dickey also put the Power T on the football helmets during the 1964 season and was the first to order the end zones painted in an orange-and-white checkerboard, beginning on October 10, 1964, against Boston College. The colorful checkerboard is now a UT signature that has extended to several other Vols sports.

The Tennessee Sports Hall of Fame named Dickey Tennessean of the Year in 2000, and in 2001 he was named recipient of the Neyland Trophy.

96 Meet the *Torchbearer*

Every year he serves as the backdrop for countless graduation and football weekend snapshots taken by Volunteers students and visitors. Students at the University of Tennessee pass by the *Torchbearer* every day, sitting like a sentinel on the corner of Volunteer Boulevard and Circle Park Drive. But how much do these students really know about one of the most visible landmarks on their campus?

The actual *Torchbearer* statue was not built until April 19, 1968. But the idea of the *Torchbearer* precedes its placement by decades.

The classes of 1928 to 1932 decided that the university needed an icon that would encapsulate the spirit of service the students of the university have to offer. As such, the school held a sculpture design contest, with the winner to receive an award of $1,000. Theodore Andre Beck, a student at the Yale School of Fine Arts, was announced as the winner on May 12, 1931. Though Beck's design was chosen, many modifications were made before the final statue could be placed in Circle Park.

The university had copyrighted use of the Torchbearer as its official symbol by 1932 and planned to build a statue 26 feet high, including its base, and display it in an amphitheater. However, due to the Great Depression, World War II, the anticipated cost of construction, and other factors, the UT administration used only small replicas of the *Torchbearer* at Torch Night, and for souvenirs and student awards from 1937 to 1968. What ultimately became a nine-foot-tall statue with the sculptor's final design modifications was unveiled in Circle Park on April 19, 1968. The design of the statue was augmented to portray a younger-looking man, which better represented the student body.

As the official symbol of the University of Tennessee, the Torchbearer holds up the torch of enlightenment in his right hand. He wears a sword as a symbol of security and holds in his left hand a globe with the *Winged Victory of Samothrace*, a symbol of success and the individual's ability to make the most of his opportunities despite the world's challenges.

97 Tennessee 41, Arkansas 38, Six Overtimes

From the time Arkansas joined the Southeastern Conference in 1992, the Hogs have provided some of the most exciting and memorable games in Knoxville.

On October 10, 1992, it seemed that Heath Shuler and No. 4 Tennessee, with Johnny Majors back on the sideline, were in good shape to continue their undefeated season, leading 24–16 with less than three minutes to go. Orlando Watters' 71-yard punt return for a touchdown immediately changed that game; however, Todd Kelly's hit on the Arkansas quarterback thwarted the two-point conversion, seemingly sealing the win. Until Arkansas recovered the onside kick and drove to the Tennessee 24-yard line. Todd Wright's field goal set off a wild celebration in the visitors' section and sparked heartbreak throughout the rest of Knoxville.

Tennessee's fortunes would turn in 1998, when Arkansas, this time leading 24–22, turned over the ball with less than two minutes to play when Stoerner tripped over his offensive lineman and fumbled the ball back to Tennessee. Travis Henry almost single-handedly drove back the stunned Arkansas defense and dove over the top for a TD to secure a 28–24 win to keep Tennessee at No. 1.

The Vols wrote a new chapter on October 5, 2002, in Knoxville. No. 10 Tennessee was two weeks removed from a rain-soaked 30–13 loss to Florida in which Casey Clausen fumbled the snap repeatedly to help Florida build a 24–0 halftime lead. Arkansas was coming off a 30–12 home thrashing at the hands of probation-stricken Alabama.

The game started slow, with Tennessee nursing a 10–3 halftime lead that they carried over into the fourth quarter. Cedric Houston was out with a thumb ligament injury, so Jabari Davis was asked to carry the load. Davis answered the bell, rumbling for a 58-yard touchdown early in the fourth quarter to put the Vols ahead 17–3.

Arkansas' four-headed rushing attack—quarterback Matt Jones and running backs Cedric Cobbs, De'Arrius Howard, and Fred Talley—helped the Hogs stage a furious rally in the final six minutes to force overtime. Unable to run out the clock, Tennessee punted back to Arkansas, pinning the Hogs at their own 8-yard line. Trailing 17–10 with 3:30 to go in OT, Jones found wide receiver Richard Smith running free behind the Tennessee secondary. He lobbed the ball over the top, and the Hogs were celebrating the longest scoring play in Arkansas history and a tie game.

The first overtime ended with each team drilling a field goal to keep the score even at 20. Arkansas started the second overtime on offense but could only manage a field goal. The Hogs defense forced Tennessee to settle for a 31-yard field goal to keep the game going into a third overtime. With senior kicker Alex Walls injured, Georgia Tech transfer Philip Newman stepped into the pressure cooker. For a split second, Tennessee fans held their breath as the ball thudded off a leaping Razorbacks defender. The ball wobbled and knuckled toward the crossbar.

The official raised his arms *good*. Jason Witten, on his knees, pumped his arm in joy. A subdued relief swept the stadium, as Tennessee's offense took the field for the third OT. That relief did not last long, as Derrick Tinsley fumbled the ball away. Arkansas needed one Brennan O'Donohoe 38-yard field goal to end the game. But O'Donohoe's kick hooked wide left, and the game moved into the fourth overtime, tied at 23.

Jones' scrambling ability was more than a match for a flat-footed Tennessee defense, as he scooted inside the pylon for a 29–23 lead. The two-point conversion failed, and the Vols needed a touchdown and a conversion to win.

It took just one play to get the first part. Casey Clausen dropped back and lobbed a ball to a wide-open Tony Brown in the checkerboard as Neyland Stadium erupted. On the conversion, Clausen looked to Witten and fired the football, but the pass was broken up by Arkansas cornerback Lawrence Richardson.

Tennessee 29, Arkansas 29. Fifth overtime.

Tennessee started with the ball, and the bullish Davis wasted little time in pushing Tennessee back ahead, cutting a swath through tired Arkansas defenders for a 12-yard touchdown. However, Clausen was stuffed on a quarterback draw, and Arkansas could win with a touchdown and a conversion. Arkansas bulled its way to the end zone on the strong running of Howard. Just like during the previous overtime, a defensive back made a play on the conversion to save the game—this time Tennessee's Julian Battle, who picked off Jones near the corner of the end zone.

Tennessee 35, Arkansas 35. Sixth overtime.

After moving back five yards on their possession, Arkansas coach Houston Nutt sent out a new kicker, David Carlton, to try a 47-yard field goal, cold turkey. The kick sailed through, and Arkansas, up 38–35, still had life.

One play later, it was over. Witten had a free release up the middle, and Clausen slipped a pass right ahead of a defender into his breadbasket. Witten raised a weary arm toward the sky, as his teammates poured onto the field and the 100,000-plus in attendance gave thanks that the longest game in Tennessee history was finally over, and that the outcome was in their favor.

The game was a bright spot and a worthy highlight reel in an otherwise dismal season. Tennessee lost five games—all to ranked teams—including a 30–3 loss to Clemson in the Peach Bowl.

98 Kelsey Finch Runs 99 Yards vs. Florida in 1977

In 1977 Tennessee legend Johnny Majors stepped to the Vols sideline as head coach. While spirits were hopeful, if not high, that Majors could quickly pull a 180 for the program the way Doug Dickey had from 1964 through 1969, it would be a difficult year, with the Vols finishing 4–7. The Vols had started the season losing three of their first five games at Neyland Stadium, including a tough-to-swallow 14–12 loss to Auburn.

In a season of disappointment, sometimes a great performance, or even a great moment, can help take the sting out of a tough season and serve as a moment that fans can look back on with warm feelings.

Kelsey Finch provided that moment at Florida Field in Gainesville on October 27, 1977.

The Vols were backed up to their goal at the south end of Florida Field, third-and-10 at the Vols 1. Florida fans were on their feet and loud, ready for the defense to deliver the coup de grace to the Vols' collective hopes.

The call was an off-tackle run. The reason? Simply to keep Vols punter Craig Colquitt from having to put his heels at the back of the end zone, 10 yards from the line of scrimmage. Tailback Kelsey Finch turned the play into one for the record books, rumbling and weaving 99 yards across the turf of Florida Field for the score.

"We were trying to set it up where we could punt the ball," Finch told the *Knoxville News-Sentinel.* "We had an off-tackle play called. As I hit the hole, there was nobody there. I cut to the sidelines and remember Roland James hollering, 'They're going to catch you.' I remember running for my life. It was an exciting moment."

Florida beat Tennessee 27–17 on that day, but Finch, from Sheffield, Alabama, etched his name into the Tennessee history books and provided fans with one of the most electrifying and exciting plays of the decade. For the junior running back, 1977 was his best season by far during his four years in Knoxville, and one in which he led the Vols in rushing yards (770), touchdowns (8), and total yards from scrimmage (846).

99 Take in a Game Weekend at Calhoun's on the River

Some come for the ribs. Others come for the pulled pork platters. Some come for happy hour gatherings and conversation. Some will show up for the live music outside on the deck, on the Tennessee River, with Neyland Stadium, campus, and downtown Knoxville as the backdrop. Others may come to people-watch, or perhaps to mingle with visiting fans who have invariably been directed to the popular dinner and late-night venue on the bank of the river.

Yes, Knoxville is loaded with a variety of places to go for a cold drink in a number of different settings. The Strip near campus features the Copper Cellar (good if you want to get some red meat at a pretty decent price), Half Barrel (good if you want to pound cheap drinks with college co-eds and visiting college-aged fans), and Cool Beans (a popular spot amongst the Tennessee student body for close to two decades). Slightly off campus, the nearby Market Square offers more varied cuisine, a relaxed atmosphere, and more than a fair share of live music at small bars and restaurants.

Still, Calhoun's on the River on a home-game weekend is about as good as it gets for those looking for more than a few cheap drinks and loud music. The location is intertwined with the Tennessee football program. On Thursday nights, Tennessee head coach Butch Jones and radio play-by-play host Bob Kesling host Vol Calls, fielding calls from fans and discussing the upcoming game live on the Vol Network.

On game days, its massive parking lot fills up with a mixture of tailgaters unloading grills and tents, revelers who want to jump on board with a friend or acquaintance in the Vol Navy, and those who want to get a pregame bite of Southern barbecue, grab a drink on the deck, and watch the boats roll in and tie up to the numerous slips by the dock.

As for the fare, the fall-off-the-bone ribs are as good as advertised, as is the tender pulled pork, but the "Ale" Steak, marinated in Calhoun's own popular microbrew Cherokee Red Ale, is an underrated selection.

As for their microbrews, the Cherokee Red Ale, a balanced, medium-bodied amber ale with a fruity finish, is arguably one of the best microbrews in town. The Mountain Light, a light, American-style lager more closely resembling a common domestic beer, is a very popular choice as well.

Given the location on the water near the stadium, it's little surprise that visiting fans show up in droves, leading to some "interesting" interactions between the Tennessee fan base and any SEC rival in town for the weekend. While things rarely get physical, "Rocky Top" will be sung, game stories will be told, and some new friendships might be formed.

If you're in Knoxville for a home-game weekend, and you haven't been to Calhoun's, do yourself a favor and check it out.

100 Jeff Hall: A History of Clutch

Coach Phillip Fulmer talked so often during his pre- and postgame interviews about the kicking game having so much importance. This is wholly unsurprising, given Fulmer's staunch belief in, and recital of, the game-day maxims of General Neyland. Maxim No. 6: "Press the kicking game. Here's where the breaks are made."

History has proven that when teams are near equal, the kicking game indeed will decide the outcome. Florida State's kicking follies against Miami cost the Seminoles national championship opportunities. Former Gator Collins Cooper's sweeping miss against Tennessee continued the wild ride of the 1998 season for UT fans and put Florida on the outside looking in all season long. Even Vanderbilt's Bryant Hahnfeldt's 49-yard try clanging off the upright in UT's 25–24 win in 2007 opened the door for an SEC East crown for Tennessee.

After months and months of off-season workouts, fall practice, two-a-days, and bloody practice jerseys, a key game often ultimately comes down to the nerves of a young man charged with kicking a football through the uprights in front of 100,000 people. In that moment, fair or not, the weight of an entire fan base falls on that kicker's back.

Tennessee has had a number of terrific kickers, including Fuad Reveiz, John Becksvoort, Daniel Lincoln, and the barefooted Ricky Townsend.

There might be no kicker in the history of Tennessee football with stronger nerves and more focus than Jeff Hall.

Hall's first test came in a game few thought would require a Tennessee field goal at the gun to win it. After all, between Georgia and Tennessee, it was the Volunteers who had the lopsided edge at quarterback, with sophomore Peyton Manning leading a talented Volunteers team featuring Joey Kent, Leonard Little, Jay Graham, Bill Hines, and Scott Galyon, to name a few. The Vols were ranked eighth, while the Bulldogs, with new starting quarterback Mike Bobo under center, came into Neyland Stadium unranked and with little perceived chance of derailing the home team.

It was a fight from the get-go, and one that each team had a chance to finish in the final two minutes. Georgia had the first shot.

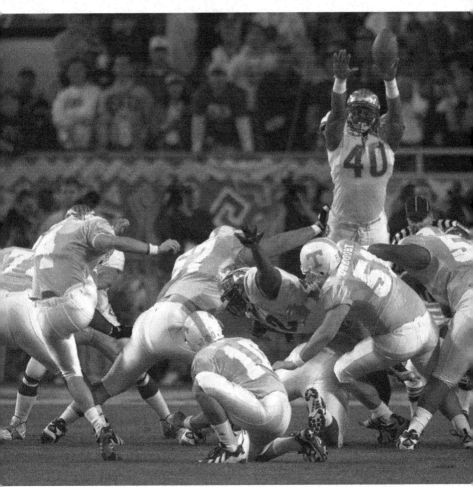

John Hall attempts a field goal against Florida State in the 1999 Fiesta Bowl.

After Bobo's pass to a wide-open Brice Hunter was dropped, the Bulldogs had to settle for a 53-yard field goal attempt from Dax Langley, attempting only his second career kick. Langley reportedly had hit a 60-yarder in high school, and though he had enough leg on the 53-yard try, it sailed wide right.

After Jay Graham caught a Manning swing pass and dodged Randall Godfrey for a 28-yard gain, Coach Fulmer made things easy for his freshman kicker. Manning to Kent for seven yards and out of bounds. Graham rumbled down to the 15-yard line. Manning kneeled in the center of the field.

The stage was set for Hall, who calmly lined up. Snap. Kick. Among the fireworks exploding over the river outside the stadium, the scoreboard operator made the change: TENNESSEE 30, GEORGIA 27. Tennessee survived the last 10 seconds to escape with a memorable win over its border rival.

Flash forward to 1998. After Donovan McNabb and the No. 14 Syracuse Orange had stormed in front of the 10th-ranked Big Orange 33–31 on a Nate Trout chip-shot field goal with 2:38 to play, Hall—then a team captain—was again called upon to keep the Vols' early-season hopes alive. Before a jumping and screaming crowd that color commentator Bill Curry likened to "Baton Rouge on a Saturday night," Hall lined up for a 27-yard attempt from a sharp angle, with only four seconds left. His kick sailed so high into the netting that it took a moment for the camera to locate it. Final score: Tennessee 34, Syracuse 33.

After an off week, the fourth-ranked Vols hosted No. 2 Florida before a record crowd of 107,653. Looking to break a five-game losing streak against the Gators before a nationally televised audience, Tennessee forced five Florida turnovers in pushing the game into overtime tied at 17. Hall had earlier converted a Florida fumble into points with a 39-yard field goal.

Then, after Tee Martin's scramble to the 24-yard line on third down on Tennessee's overtime possession, Hall trotted onto the field. With the eyes of the nation watching, he stood over holder Benson Scott and stepped back for the kick from the near hash mark. The ball sailed off his foot, rose over the line, and split the uprights dead center near the top.

The pressure then flipped onto Hall's counterpart, Collins Cooper, thanks to relentless pressure on Jesse Palmer from Al Wilson and the Tennessee defense. Cooper swung his leg from the far hash mark and the ball boomeranged wide of the left upright.

General Neyland would have been proud. In two of Tennessee's three closest ballgames (Arkansas being the other), Hall's foot determined the outcome in favor of Tennessee. Hall made 19 of 24 kicks, and was 12 of 13 on attempts from inside 40 yards. He led the team in scoring with 104 points and finished with 371 for his career.

After a brief career in the NFL with the Washington Redskins and St. Louis Rams, Hall returned to Knoxville, where he is a certified financial advisor.

Bibliography

Books

Browning, Al. *Third Saturday in October*. Nashville, TN: Cumberland House Publishing, 2001.

Commercial Appeal. *Greatest Moments in Tennessee Vols Football History*. Champaign, IL: Sports Publishing, 1998.

Moore, Randy. *Stadium Stories: Tennessee Volunteers*. Guilford, CT: Globe Pequot, 2004.

Scott, Richard. *SEC Football*. Minneapolis, MN: Voyageur Press, 2008.

Travis, Clay. *On Rocky Top*. New York, NY: HarperCollins Publishers, 2009.

West, Marvin. *Legends of the Tennessee Vols*. Champaign, IL: Sports Publishing, 2005.

———. *Tales of the Tennessee Vols*. Champaign, IL: Sports Publishing, 2002.

Online Resources

20 Years Ago in Big Orange Country. http://www.rockytoptalk. com/2012/8/1/3207753/20-years-ago-in-big-orange-country-the-season-when-one-legend

52nd Annual Sugar Bowl Classic: January 1, 1986. http://www.allstatesugarbowl.org/site106. php

"99 Yards, Kelsey Finch!" http://knoxblogs.com/ volhistorian/2013/08/01/99-yards-kelsey-finch/

1931 College Football National Championship. http://tiptop25.com/champ1931.html

1938. https://generalneyland.wordpress.com/1938-2/

1938 College Football National Championship. http://tiptop25.com/champ1938.html

1956 Heisman Trophy Voting. http://www.sports-reference.com/cfb/awards/heisman-1956. html

1982 UT Football Program – UT vs. Washington State (Oct 2, 1982). http://diglib.lib.utk. edu/fbpro/main.php?bid=226&pg=51&catid=49&s=bates

1985 Heisman Trophy: Bo Jackson. http://grfx.cstv.com/photos/schools/aub/sports/m-footbl/ auto_pdf/jackson-heisman.pdf

1986 Football Program. http://diglib.lib.utk.edu/fbpro/main.php?catid=35

1991 Tennessee 23, Virginia 22. http://espn.go.com/abcsports/bcs/sugar/s/1991.html

1996 Florida Citrus Bowl. http://www.utsports.com/genrel/121401aab.html

40,000 See Vols Triumph Over Crimson Tide, 21 to 0. https://news.google.com/newspapers?i d=Dk1BAAAAIBAJ&sjid=lLcMAAAAIBAJ&pg=6382,4828738&hl=en

Al Wilson's 'Big Heart' Still Inspires a Crowd. http://www.knoxnews.com/govolsxtra/ other-sports/al-wilsons-big-heart-still-inspires-a-crowd_72132734

Alabama vs. Tennessee. http://www.rollbamaroll.com/2010/10/20/1595268/ alabama-vs-tennessee-a-historical-retrospective

286

All-Time Numerical Roster. http://www.utsports.com/sports/m-footbl/fball-history/fb-history-alltime-roster.html

All-Time SEC Championships. http://www.utsports.com/fans/sec-championships.html

A Backup with Bluster Will Lead the Seminoles. http://www.nytimes.com/1999/01/02/sports/college-football-fiesta-bowl-a-backup-with-bluster-will-lead-the-seminoles.html

Beer Barrel Trophy Tradition Sidelined for More Than a Decade. http://www.wbir.com/story/sports/2014/11/14/beer-barrel-trophy-tradition-sidelined-for-more-than-a-decade/19049587/

Calling Kentucky-Tennessee Football a "Rivalry" Really a Stretch Now. http://www.kentucky.com/2014/11/13/3537130_mark-story-calling-kentucky-tennessee.html?rh=1

Casey Clausen Bio. http://www.utsports.com/sports/m-footbl/mtt/casey_clausen_45052.html

Catching Up: Dale Jones. http://www.utsports.com/sports/m-footbl/spec-rel/102111aab.html

Chuck Webb. http://www.sports-reference.com/cfb/players/chuck-webb-2.html

College Football Hall of Fame Inductees. http://www.utsports.com/sports/m-footbl/archive/020604aaa.html

Colleges with Most Draft Picks. http://drafthistory.com/n_college/college_n.html

Colquitts Are NFL's First Family of Punting. http://denver.cbslocal.com/2013/09/28/colquitts-are-nfls-first-family-of-punting/

Condredge Holloway. http://www.utsports.com/sports/m-footbl/mtt/condredge_holloway_713003.html

Epic-Tested Arkansas Beaten in Sixth Overtime. http://scores.espn.go.com/ncf/recap?gameId=222782633

Flashback: The Greatest Games – Alabama 1995. http://gate21.net/2008/05/30/flashback-the-great-games-alabama-1995/

Great Games & Moments in the Tennessee Georgia Series. http://www.utsports.com/sports/m-footbl/spec-rel/100903aaa.html

Hall of Famers: Doug Atkins. http://www.profootballhof.com/hof/member.aspx?PLAYER_ID=17

Holloway Appreciates Bryant's Honesty That Alabama "Wasn't Ready" for Black Quarterback. http://www.al.com/sports/index.ssf/2011/02/holloway_always_appreciated_be.html

Homegrown: Smokey X. http://www.wbir.com/story/entertainment/people/homegrown/2013/11/05/smokey-bluetick-hound-tennessee-mascot-volunteer/3449531/

Homegrown: Tennessee Legend John Ward. http://www.wbir.com/story/entertainment/people/homegrown/2013/09/10/homegrown-tennessee-legend-john-ward-talks-about-growing-up-in-knoxville/2795129/

Home Sweet Home: Lake City Changes Its Name to Rocky Top. http://www.wbir.com/story/news/local/2014/06/26/lake-city-changes-its-name-to-rocky-top/11428281/

Injured Vol Johnson Scheduled for Dec. 21 Surgery. http://www.utsports.com/sports/m-footbl/spec-rel/102006aae.html

James Stewart. http://www.sports-reference.com/cfb/players/james-stewart-3.html

John T. Majors. http://www.tn.gov/tsla/exhibits/majors/exhibit_majors.htm

Leslie County: Rocky Top Has a Different Meaning Here. http://www.kentucky.com/2010/09/12/1430519_fan-fare-rocky-top-has-different.html?rh=1

Little Man's Toughness Catalyst for His Success. https://tennessee.rivals.com/content.
asp?CID=1677566

The Majors Family. http://tshf.net/halloffame/majors-family/

Marching Band History. http://www.utbands.com/marching-band/athletic-bands/

Martin Savors What Manning Missed. https://news.google.com/newspapers?nid=1356&dat=19
990105&id=u6VAAAAAIBAJ&sjid=NQgEAAAAIBAJ&pg=6625,3275682&hl=en

The Memorable Tennessee-Georgia Game 40 Years Ago. http://www.chattanoogan.
com/2008/9/16/135061/The-Memorable-Tennessee-Georgia-Game.aspx

Michigan 31, Ohio State 23. http://library.osu.edu/projects/OSUvsMichigan/news/1995.htm

Namesake: Shields-Watkins Field at Neyland Stadium. http://archive.wbir.com/news/regional/
homegrown/article/190043/228/Namesake-Shields-Watkins-Field-in-Neyland-Stadium

No. 4 Florida 27, No. 9 Tennessee 23. http://espn.go.com/abcsports/bcs/s/2000/0916/748751.
html

No. 5 Tennessee 12, Vanderbilt 7. http://www.apnewsarchive.com/1995/
No-5-Tennessee-12-Vanderbilt-7/id-4f27e57f039ac2fa9909fd8b523f888f

No. 25 Tennessee 28, Vanderbilt 26. http://espn.go.com/abcsports/bcs/s/recap/
tennesseevanderbilt.html

Ole Miss QB Brent Schaeffer Could Finish His Ole Miss Career with One Last Start. http://
usatoday30.usatoday.com/sports/college/football/2007-11-21-1557476199_x.htm

Our Traditions. http://www.utk.edu/aboutut/traditions/

The Pendulum Swing of Heath Shuler. http://www.rockytoptalk.com/2009/4/23/849715/
the-pendulum-swing-of-heath-shuler

Peyton Manning Mulled Michigan, Which May Have Changed Trajectory of Tom Brady's
Career. http://blog.masslive.com/patriots/2014/10/peyton_manning_tom_brady_rival.
html

Peyton Manning's Heisman Snub Was Not Chris Fowler's Fault, and He Can
Prove It. http://sports.yahoo.com/ncaa/football/blog/dr_saturday/post/
Excerpt-Chris-Fowler-can-prove-Peyton-Manning-?urn=ncaaf-wp1803

Phillip Fulmer Talks Butch Jones, Playoffs, ETSU. http://www.
tennessean.com/story/sports/college/vols/2014/12/10/
phillip-fulmer-butch-jones-college-football-playoff-etsu/20224847/

Reflections on a Game-Changing Fall Day in 1968. http://alumnus.tennessee.edu/2012/08/
moving-the-chains/

Remembering Tennessee-Florida 2001 Clash 10 Years After 9/11. http://www.si.com/
more-sports/2011/09/14/florida-tennessee-9-11

Retired Football Jerseys. http://www.utsports.com/sports/m-footbl/fball-history/fb-history-
retirement.html

A Rock-Solid Tradition. http://www.utsports.com/sports/m-footbl/spec-rel/092212aab.html

Rocky Top. http://www.wbir.com/story/life/music/2014/08/26/rocky-top-house-of-bryant-
songwriting-university-of-tennessee-gatlinburg-inn-marketing/14647827/

Rocky Top's Picasso Paints His Masterpiece on Neyland End Zones. http://sports.espn.
go.com/ncf/news/story?page=sec/tennessee

SEC Championship Game History. http://assets.espn.go.com/SEC/football/2015/14sec_championship.pdf

Tee Martin Makes History. http://www.nytimes.com/1998/11/01/sports/college-football-roundup-texas-ends-nebraska-s-home-winning-streak-at-47.html

The Ten Greatest Volunteers Games of All Time. http://bleacherreport.com/articles/31068-tennessee-football-the-all-time-top-10-volunteers-games

Tennessee 31, Penn State 11. http://digitalnewspapers.libraries.psu.edu/Repository/DCG/1971/12/06/036-DCG-1971-12-06-001-SINGLE.PDF

Tennessee 38, Auburn 20. https://news.google.com/newspapers?nid=892&dat=19850929&id=vYtaAAAAIBAJ&sjid=TU8DAAAAIBAJ&pg=4663,5597939&hl=en

Tennessee Beats Florida to End Long Waiting Game. http://www.nytimes.com/1998/09/20/sports/college-football-tennessee-beats-florida-to-end-long-waiting-game.html

Tennessee Football 2012 Record Book. http://www.utsports.com/sports/m-footbl/guides/2012/honors.pdf

Tennessee Football History: All-Americans. http://www.utsports.com/sports/m-footbl/fball-history/fb-history-allam.html

Tennessee Football's 10 Most Heartbreaking Losses, 1989–2007. http://bleacherreport.com/articles/46818-tennessee-footballs-10-most-heartbreaking-losses-1989-2007

Tennessee Football Uniform History. http://tnjn.org/2010/may/10/tennessee-football-uniform-his/

Tennessee Keeps Pace with Best; Beats LSU, 14–6. http://archives.chicagotribune.com/1938/10/30/page/35/article/tennessee-keeps-pace-with-best-beats-l-s-u-14-6

Tennessee Legends: Andy Kozar and Hank Lauricella. http://www.knoxnews.com/story-hold/tennessee-legends-andy-kozar-and-hank-lauricella

Tennessee Rallies to Stun the Irish. http://www.nytimes.com/1991/11/10/sports/college-football-tennessee-rallies-to-stun-the-irish.html

Tennessee Remembers Bobby Denton. http://www.utsports.com/sports/m-footbl/spec-rel/040914aak.html

Tennessee Tops Alabama in 5 Overtimes. http://www.nytimes.com/2003/10/26/sports/college-football-tennessee-tops-alabama-in-5-overtimes.html

Tennessee Traditions. http://www.utsports.com/fans/traditions.html

Tennessee Upsets No. 1-Ranked Auburn: Bo Jackson Is Held to 80 Yards Rushing in Volunteers' 38-20 Victory. http://articles.latimes.com/1985-09-29/sports/sp-18869_1_coach-pat-dye

Tennessee vs. Vanderbilt (Nov. 25, 2000). http://www.utsports.com/sports/m-footbl/spec-rel/ut11.html

The Third Saturday in October. http://espn.go.com/classic/s/beano_tenmia.html

The Third Saturday in October. http://onlineathens.com/stories/102106/football_20061021016.shtml#.VX1zEaPbKYM

Top 10 Pass Rushers in NFL History. http://www.nfl.com/nflnetwork/story/09000d5d8088a0ec/article/top-10-pass-rushers-in-nfl-history

Top 10 Tennessee Comebacks Since 1990. http://www.rockytoptalk.com/2011/7/20/2283872/top-10-tennessee-comebacks-since-1990

UCLA's Comeback Kids Are at It Again, 26-26. http://articles.latimes.com/1985-09-15/sports/sp-23235_1_bruins

UT Knoxville Traditions. http://licensing.tennessee.edu/utk/utktraditions.html

Vols Jersey Countdown #32. http://www.utsports.com/sports/m-footbl/spec-rel/073013aac.html

Vols Jersey Countdown #85. http://www.utsports.com/sports/m-footbl/spec-rel/060712aac.html

Vols Erase 21-Point Deficit to Top Tigers in OT in LSU Home Opener. http://sports.espn.go.com/ncf/recap?gameId=252690099

Vols Hold Off UK in 4 OTs to Clinch Spot in SEC Title Game. http://sports.espn.go.com/ncf/recap?gameId=273280096

The Vols in Orange Pants. http://knoxblogs.com/volhistorian/2007/09/25/the_vols_in_orange_pants/

Vols in the NFL Draft. http://www.utsports.com/sports/m-footbl/fball-history/fb-history-nfldraft.html

Vols Take 1951 Cotton Bowl Victory with Fourth Quarter Rally. http://www.utsports.com/sports/m-footbl/spec-rel/121404aac.html

Volunteers Work Hard for First SEC East Title. http://articles.latimes.com/1997/nov/30/sports/sp-59295

The Vol Walk Celebrates an Anniversary. http://www.utsports.com/sports/m-footbl/spec-rel/102012aad.html

WBIR Vault: 1994 Peyton Manning vs. Branndon Stewart. http://www.wbir.com/story/news/local/2014/11/19/1994-manning-stewart-qb-controversy/18891023/

Which College Football Program Is the Real [Position] U? http://www.sbnation.com/college-football/2013/6/18/4441366/linebacker-u-wide-receiver-u-various-other-us

White Dies Sunday Morning. http://espn.go.com/classic/obit/s/2004/1226/1953400.html

Writer of UT Alma Mater Was Chattanoogan. http://www.chattanoogan.com/2014/11/10/288171/Writer-Of-UT-Alma-Mater-Was-Chattanoogan.aspx

Videos

1928 Tennessee Beats Bama. YouTube video, 1:40; posted by Classic Vol Video, April 28, 2014, https://www.youtube.com/watch?v=XhYIoOefbis

General Robert Neyland: "The Man and the Legend." YouTube video, 50:01; posted by Classic Vol Video, December 12, 2010, https://www.youtube.com/watch?v=cBWJgoBZTeM

Is It a Tennessee Vols Myth? Condredge Holloway – The Artful Dodger. YouTube video, 1:07; posted by ESPN, April 7, 2011, https://www.youtube.com/watch?v=D8vSZm1XXd8

Memorable Moments in #Vols Football History. YouTube video, 4:21; posted by UT SportsFootball, August 30, 2013, https://www.youtube.com/watch?v=wxVK-ZQOsbs

Tennessee – John Ward Tribute 1998. YouTube video, 8:39; posted by Classic Vol Video, November 11, 2009, https://www.youtube.com/watch?v=rMvrlTgrTJo